Politics and Budgeting
in the
World Health Organization

International Development Research Center
William J. Siffin, Director
Studies in Development No. 11

Politics and Budgeting in the World Health Organization

by
Francis W. Hoole

Indiana University Press
Bloomington and London
1976

Published in Canada by Fitzhenry & Whiteside Limited, Don Mills, Ontario

Manufactured in the United States of America

Library of Congress Cataloging in Publication Data

Hoole, Francis W.
Politics and budgeting in the World Health Organization.

(Studies in development; no. 11)
Bibliography
1. World Health Organization—Finance. I. Title. II. Series: Studies in development (Bloomington); no. 11.
RA8.H65 1976   341.7'65   76-19
ISBN 0-253-39611-5   1 2 3 4 5 80 79 78 77 76

To Leanne

CONTENTS

LIST OF ILLUSTRATIONS

LIST OF CHARTS

LIST OF TABLES

FOREWORD

This work is one of a very few efforts to portray in detail the budgetary processes of an international organization. Imposing a sophisticated method of analysis upon the working of a fundamental organizational process, it adds significantly to an understanding of the workings of international organizations. Students of budgeting will find this work useful, as will scholars interested in organizational theory and the behavior of public institutions.

This study offers important insights into the impact of political facets of an organization upon its budgetary processes. It makes novel use of statistical and econometric techniques and provides a suggestive simulation of the future WHO budgets. The attractiveness of the simulation lies in its contribution to our ability to explore the potential ramifications of salient factors affecting budgetary decision-making.

Finally, this is a coherent book, devoid of padding and loose ends. In an era of articles published as books, there is a touch of special appeal in a statement that matches germaneness with parsimony.

William J. Siffin
Director
International
Development
Research Center

ACKNOWLEDGMENTS

The origins of this book can be traced to the 1968-69 school year which I spent in Geneva, Switzerland doing research for the Ph.D. dissertation. That endeavor was financed by the Intersocietal Council at Northwestern University. Support for data analysis during the following year came from the University of Florida. A summer faculty fellowship from Indiana University for 1971 and a summer grant for 1972 from the International Development Research Center at Indiana University allowed me to continue work on the project. Funding from the Wrubel Computing Center at Indiana University supported use of the CDC 6600 computer from 1970 through 1974.

The following individuals provided guidance, suggestions, encouragement, and assistance on the project: Chadwick Alger, Edward Buehrig, Ib Christensen, Fred Cummings, Edwin Fedder, John Gillespie, Jeff Green, Harold Guetzkow, Kenneth Janda, Brian Job, Bernice Newton, Charles Ostrom, Tong Park, Robert Pendley, Marianne Platt, Feliciano C. Sicat, Milton Siegel, William J. Siffin, J. David Singer, Jean Siotis, Harvey Starr, George Stolnitz, John Sullivan, Grafton Trout, Harvey Tucker, Ron Weber, Aaron Wildavsky, and Dina Zinnes. Members of the WHO secretariat provided valuable aid during my stay in Geneva, and participants in my graduate seminar on policy-making at Indiana University during the 1973 fall semester served as critics on an early draft. Final preparation of the manuscript was greatly aided by Karen McGrath, Marie Mitchell, and Kriss Ostrom. My wife, Leanne, and daughter, Tanya, assisted and tolerated me in every way.

I gratefully acknowledge this support. Without it, the book would not have been possible. Naturally, the final product, and any errors contained therein, are the sole responsibility of the author.

1

Introduction

The study of politics is concerned with understanding how authoritative decisions are made and executed. . . .

—*David Easton*

The formulation of the budget in one specific international governmental organization—the World Health Organization (WHO)—is systematically explored in this study. The story of budget-making in WHO involves both conflict and cooperation between nations; it relates how nations successfully engage in collective action while faced with significant difficulties. This volume should, therefore, be of general interest. Furthermore, beyond its substantive content, the study conceptualizes the WHO budget process in policy-making terms and should contribute to the formulation of a general theory of policy-making.

A variety of legitimate research approaches to the study of policy-making exist: the historical, emphasizing reconstruction of particular events; the legalistic, focusing on constitutional provisions, laws, treaties, regulations, and legal bases for action; the ideological, with analyses oriented around sets of beliefs; and the quantitative, or behavioral science, emphasizing behavior, theory, assignment of numerical values to empirical evidence, and statistical analyses. Because of the availability of good data, past traditions in policy-making and budgetary research, and the complexity of the problem, the strategy adopted in this study is the quantitative, or behavioral science, approach.

There is no perfect way to tackle research problems. The behavioral science orientation, like any research approach, has its limitations. For example, adequately measuring most concepts involved in social science theory creates problems. The complex patterns of behavior inherent in social phenomena also impede the formulation of theory, and developing meaningful generalizations about social behavior involves considerable patience and time. In addition, concern for the manner of collecting and analyzing data often demands a rigorous effort to develop techniques which minimize bias. Thus, behavioral science is often slow-moving, full of methodological jargon, and expensive. It is difficult to determine whether the effort and cost which go into such a research approach justify the marginal gain realized from explicit efforts at stating generalizations and using empirical evidence. Hopefully, the results of this study will demonstrate the wisdom of exerting the additional effort.

This study is indebted to (and hopefully will contribute to) five distinct research traditions in the social sciences: quantitative international politics, policy-making in international politics, behavioral budgetary theory, organization theory, and international organizations. The balance of this chapter is devoted to a consideration of these traditions—especially the recent literature—and concludes with a brief outline of the remainder of the book.

Quantitative International Politics

During the past few years, there has been a noticeable shift toward the use of quantification in the study of international politics. A growing body of journal literature plus the existence of a special organization (the Interpolimetrics Section of the International Studies Association) dedicated to problems of the development of empirical theory in international politics reflect this new emphasis.[1] There are a variety of interpretations of this approach: the study of behavior as well as formal institutions and structures; the use of empirical data; the scientific study of phenomena; and the primarily quantitative analysis of events.[2] It is possible to put together a picture capturing the essence of quantitative international politics by examining what seem to be the basic assumptions of the movement. Although the inclusion of each point is debatable, hopefully a generalization will emerge which will prove useful for understanding the field.

One major assumption is that there are discoverable uniformities in the behavior of units under analysis that can be expressed as generalizations or theories with explanatory and predictive value. A theory is "a systematically related set of statements, including some lawlike generalizations, that is empirically testable."[3] Most scholars in the field of quantitative international politics would agree that the eventual goal of their research is the development of empirical theory. They would further agree on the necessity for a comparative empirical approach, since it would then be possible to estimate the extent to which behavior is specific to a given case by examining it in relation to behavior exhibited by other members of the species. In this manner, a range of variation can be determined, and generalizations can be stated which are valid within that range.[4]

A second assumption is that relevant and meaningful measurement is advantageous because it gives specific meaning to phenomena. Measurement is, of course, the "assignment of numerals (or numbers) to objects or events according to rules."[5] Most scholars feel that if one resorts to evidence from the empirical world to examine a generalization, then the means by which evidence is gathered and assigned a value is critical. Thus, problems of reliability and validity are tremendously important, and considerable effort has been devoted to such systematic and rigorous data collection techniques as content analysis, participant and nonparticipant observation, elite and mass interviewing, and coding of secondary data. Likewise, considerable effort has been expended on the application of various scaling techniques, index construction, and other miscellaneous indicator problems.

The recognition of the utility of statistical techniques in the examination of data constitutes the third commonly shared assumption. These techniques most frequently serve three functions: to describe individual variables, to describe relationships between variables, and to estimate the probability of obtaining the reported results. The application of these analytic techniques to empirical data is significant, and scholars concerned with quantitative international politics have allotted it considerable attention.

This book falls within the tradition of quantitative international politics. It attempts to discover empirically testable behavioral generalizations about policy-making regarding international political phenomena. It works over time with empirical data within one organization. The need to expand the examination to other organizations at a future date is acknowledged. One contribution of the study lies in the fact that a new political phenomenon, budgeting activity in international governmental organizations, is subjected to rigorous quantitative analysis for the first time. Thus, the study opens up a new substantive focus within the field of quantitative international politics. More importantly, the book contributes by providing an example of the application of a combination of heretofore infrequently used statistical and econometric techniques to a familiar research problem—the study of policy-making in international politics.

Policy-Making in International Politics

During the past two decades, emphasis on understanding policy-making has greatly increased in the area of international politics. The literature, which has primarily focused on foreign and strategic policy, is not easily nor briefly summarized.[6] Nevertheless, this type of inquiry does seem to have evolved, through incremental contributions by various scholars, into a state where there is a general consensus regarding the nature of the enterprise.

One of the most widely discussed contributions is that of Snyder. The framework for analysis—originally suggested in 1954 by Snyder, Bruck, and Sapin—may be viewed as the beginning of the current era in the study of policy-making in international politics. Snyder and his colleagues legitimized the study of policy-making and focused the enterprise on an explanation of actions of policy-makers. They utilized the concept of a system to give order to their framework and to provide a way of integrating a multitude of interrelated variables. The policy-makers and their characteristics were to be examined in light of constraints imposed by external and internal policy-making environments, as well as by the policy-making process. One of the most important requirements of the framework was that analysis should be carried out through the eyes of policy-makers.[7] Although Snyder has apparently held to this last requirement, other scholars, such as Joseph Frankel, have not felt it to be a necessary one and have discarded it while retaining the remainder of the orientation.[8]

As the use of the system concept became more widespread in political science, a practice greatly influenced by the work of Easton,[9] more and more scholars of policy-making in international politics began using it as an organizing device. The most fully developed and influential work to appear was by Deutsch (*The Nerves of Government*) who suggested that cybernetic theory could be used to study how foreign policy decisions are made.[10] His work was concerned with the communication of information, and he viewed the policy-making process in terms of inputs, throughputs, outputs, and feedback. He further stressed the role of memory, selective perception, and atrophy in the same sense emphasized in cybernetic systems.

The focus on group conflict, incrementalism, and the determination of who governs was sharpened as a result of influential work by Hilsman.[11] He saw foreign policy-making as a group activity involving the full range of political factors and observed that there is a tendency to "decide as little as possible." Furthermore, Hilsman argued that policy-makers are organized into "concentric rings of decision-making" ranging from an innermost circle involving the executive head and his personal advisers to an outermost circle involving interest groups and "attentive publics."[12]

In a series of publications beginning in the mid-1960s, Rosenau surveyed the literature on foreign policy-making and concluded that all relevant variables could be grouped into five clusters: role, societal, governmental, systemic, and idiosyncratic. Moreover, Rosenau significantly argued that policy-making behavior probably varies from issue-area to issue-area and urged scholars to be sensitive to this problem when engaged in research. Rosenau viewed his approach as a pre-theory and suggested that scholars begin by comparatively exploring the interrelationships between variable clusters in specific empirical situations. He argued that in this way it would be possible to develop a policy-making theory in foreign affairs.[13] Rosenau's ideas have been widely embraced, and a new subfield involving the comparative study of foreign policy appears to have emerged from his work.[14]

The latest series of widely influential publications are those written by Allison. He argued that there have been three different models employed to study foreign policy-making. The "rational actor" model emphasizes rational calculations by policy-makers and is apparently used by game theorists such as Schelling and political analysts such as Morgenthau. The "organizational process" model is concerned with organizational factors and incremental calculations and is based largely on organization theory. The "bureaucratic politics" model emphasizes group struggle and views foreign policy action as the result of a series of compromises. As with Hilsman, Allison stresses the nature of the political process and correctly points out that the answers supplied regarding foreign policy-making depend on the questions asked.[15]

This book falls within, and is built upon, the tradition of the study of policy-making in international politics. It examines international political actions from a policy-making perspective and focuses upon previously expressed scholarly concerns regarding the actions of policy-makers, policy-making systems, issue-areas, who governs, policy-making rules, and environmental and process constraints upon policy-makers. The framework for analysis integrates these traditional concerns in a new way and raises questions for further study. By changing a few details, the framework would be relevant for the study of policy-making in settings other than that of the international governmental organization.

The book is relevant for the study of policy-making in the international politics field because of the framework and the manner in which it is utilized to empirically examine policy-making: (1) verbally; (2) econometrically; and (3) in developing a computer simulation model of the policy-making process. This research approach could easily be used to study other policy-making settings in the field of international politics.

Behavioral Budgetary Theory

The scholarly literature on budgeting is both vast and varied. One major segment has centered on how budgetary decisions are made in the public sector. Here, the concern has been with discovering the nature of the political process by which decisions are made, and then explicitly stating and empirically testing the rules which describe the behavior of policy-makers. These rules, usually stated in mathematical form, view budgetary actions as specific functions of some set of variables.

The attempt to develop behavioral policy-making rules is directly related to traditional concerns of students of policy-making in international politics. Indeed, this type of reasoning provides a means of linking the Snyder-Rosenau with the Hilsman-Allison approach. The Snyder-Rosenau tradition has emphasized variables to be considered, yet has been hazy regarding the political process by which they are related (variables are usually correlated in some fashion). The Hilsman-Allison tradition has emphasized the political process by which factors are related but has been unclear about the specific factors involved. Behavioral budgetary theory has explicitly focused on both concerns.

While there have been numerous studies of budget-making, the work of Wildavsky and Crecine has the greatest relevance here. In fact, the beginning of contemporary behavioral budgetary theory in the public sector can be said to have started with the publication of Wildavsky's *The Politics of the Budgetary Process* in 1964. Wildavsky presented a verbal report on the United States Federal Government's budgetary process, the result of interviewing participants in the budget process and a study of documents, hearings, and debates covering the years 1946 to 1960.[16]

Building on that earlier work, Davis, Dempster, and Wildavsky have produced four significant papers in the past decade. In the first three, they developed and tested a series of incremental equations describing alternative budgetary strategies used by the executive and legislative branches. The basic idea of incrementalism which they presented was that any action is determined by making a marginal change from a prior action. The general form of the incremental rule is: $Y = bX + e$, where Y is an action; X is a prior action; b is a fixed parameter, with $b - 1.0$ being the incremental change; and e is a stochastic variate which takes into account circumstances not contained in the remainder of the equation. The various rules in the first three papers were used to generate budget figures for fifty-six governmental agencies for each of sixteen years. The results were then compared with actual data to determine which rules best describe behavior.[17]

In their latest paper, Davis, Dempster, and Wildavsky have added a number of refinements to the earlier work. Most significantly, they became concerned with determining the relative importance of organizational and external factors in calculating the budget total. It should be noted that this is a variation of a concern raised by Snyder and Rosenau—namely, what is the relative importance of different types of input factors? Davis, Dempster, and Wildavsky assumed that their basic incremental rules represented organizational factors and introduced a series of dummy variables to represent external factors previously assumed to be included in the error term.[18]

Crecine has done budgetary work in both the municipal government and defense areas. Generally, his orientation complements Wildavsky's, but his work in the municipal arena is sufficiently different in certain respects to warrant attention. Crecine studied documents, interviewed relevant governmental personnel, and built a computer simulation of the budget process for Detroit, Cleveland, and Pittsburgh. He discovered that the municipal government's requirement of a balanced budget was a major factor which differentiated the process from that observed by Wildavsky. After reasonable calculations by department heads, using incremental rules similar to those described by Wildavsky, it became necessary to bring the budget into balance with revenues by selectively adding or subtracting amounts according to a preference schedule determined by key policy-makers. Crecine also observed that pressures from outside the organizational setting entered into the policy-making process primarily in regard to tax and total revenue considerations.[19]

The work of Wildavsky and Crecine has provided the basic statement of behavioral budgetary theory, and recent developments in the field can be seen as refinements and extensions of the orientation they provided. Gerwin, for example, has extended the analysis to include school districts, while Stromberg and Kanter have examined the defense budget, and Anton and Sharkansky have studied state budgets.[20] Meanwhile, Stromberg, Kanter, and Natchez and Bupp have examined different levels of aggregation of the budget.[21] Williamson, Jackson, and Natchez and Bupp have seriously challenged certain aspects of the basic conceptual orientation.[22] Finally, Wanat has questioned certain statistical interpretations and offered an alternative analysis.[23]

This book falls within the tradition of behavioral budgeting theory in both substantive focus and methodological approach. It posits behavioral generalizations as explicit rules linking certain specific factors to budgetary actions. It utilizes the behavioral budgetary theory's concerns for steps in the budget process, specification of relevant input factors, incrementalism, and building econometric and simulation models of the budget process. The book can be viewed as an attempt to examine behavioral budgetary theory in a new political arena—the international governmental organization. In this sense it expands the scope of the theory to include international organizational phenomena. The book also contributes to the literature on budgeting by expanding the number of steps in the budget process which are included in a single model and provides a new way of viewing various inputs into the policy-making process. Finally, this volume demonstrates how behavioral budgetary theory can be used to examine the practical ramifications of certain plausible alternative futures for a specific political organization.

Organization Theory

The last quarter century has witnessed the development of an interdisciplinary approach to the study of organizations. Scholars from traditional disciplines, such as economics, political science, psychology, business administration, and sociology, have contributed to a body of literature commonly known as organization theory.[24] While the general concern has been with a wide variety of behavioral and legal aspects of all types of organizations, organizational decision-making is of greatest relevance here.[25]

One of the most influential policy-making approaches in the social sciences has grown up in the organization theory field around Simon's ideas of "bounded-rationality." This approach rejects the typical economic decision model which assumes that a policy-maker has complete information, considers all possible alternatives, and decides on the basis of rationality which course of action to follow. Simon insists that it is improbable that a policy-maker will have complete information and consider all possibilities because of limitations on time, resources, and information-processing abilities. In Simon's view, a policy-maker decomposes the problem into smaller, more manageable ones and then searches until he finds a satisfactory alternative. Thus, he "satisfices." The policy-making school built on these ideas has tended to focus on the process by which decisions are made and utilizes computer simulation models of the policy-making process as the medium for the expression of behavioral generalizations.[26]

In the field of organization theory, it is generally recognized that the policy-maker's personality is a potential determinant of behavior. For example, Katz and Kahn have discussed psychological aspects of the thought process and orientation of personality as factors in policy-making, and Cyert and March have studied the influence of risk and uncertainty.[27] However, it is also widely recognized that the individual policy-maker does not operate in a vacuum, but interacts with numerous other factors which stimulate and constrain the effect of inner predispositions. Considerable attention has, therefore, been devoted to the study of organizational constraints on the policy-making process. Such factors as role expectations, established goals of organizations, program repertoires, operating procedures, historical precedents, memory, administrative feasibility, and task environment have been identified as salient policy-making influences.

One of the most important works on organization policy-making is Cyert and March's *A Behavioral Theory of the Firm*. After surveying and summarizing organization theory, they demonstrated empirically how organizational factors influence organizational goals, expectations, and choices. The concepts of quasi-resolution of conflict, uncertainty avoidance, problemistic search, and organizational learning were used to justify the linking of a variety of variables to actions on organizational goals and choice. They also developed a number of process models in the computer simulation mode.[28]

This study shares many of these same theoretical and methodological concerns. It constructs a computer simulation model of the policy-making process which decomposes complex phenomena into a series of manageable problems to which satisfactory solutions can be found. Thus, the orientation of organization theorists toward policy-making is extended to an examination of behavior in international governmental organizations. As will be explained later, only Alker and his associates have undertaken such a task, but their approach was quite different from the one reported here.

International Organizations

The scholarly study of international organizations had its beginnings with the birth of the League of Nations in 1919. Prior to the outbreak of World War II, interest was mainly directed toward the legal and organizational structures of the League. During World War II, attention was turned to an appraisal of the League's failure to contain international conflict and to suggestions for bringing about world order through world government. During the 1950s, scholars began to turn increasingly to nongovernmental organizations and political factors involved in international organizations. During the past few years, additional attention has been directed to regional associations, integration at the international level, and transnational politics.[29]

Thus far there has been limited emphasis on the quantitative approach to the study of international organizations. Alger systematically examined journals and readers published in the United States between 1960 and 1969 and reported that approximately 10 percent of all articles on international organizations during that period were concerned with quantification. He also observed that out of fifty-three quantitative, article-length publications, nineteen were concerned with voting behavior, thirteen with attitudes and beliefs of delegates and secretariat members, six with membership patterns in IGOs, and the remainder with a wide variety of additional topics.[30] Furthermore, Riggs and his associates reviewed professional journals published in America between 1950 and 1969 and noted that 10 percent of the articles concerning the United Nations were in this same research tradition. They also observed that the trend was toward more research of this type, citing the fact that only 2 percent of all articles between 1950 and 1954 were of this character, whereas 19 percent of those between 1965 and 1969 qualified under their criteria.[31]

There is general agreement in the field concerning the importance of understanding how policy is made in international governmental organizations. Studies concerned with policy-making fall into three categories. First, research on multilateral diplomacy contains work on the behavior of representatives of national governments as they engage in policy-making in a multilateral setting. These studies have typically examined negotiating tactics or voting behavior of national delegates in international meetings. It is characteristic that the variable to be explained is some action taken by national representatives; the unit of analysis is the nation-state.[32]

Research on international integration, the second category, is also directed to certain aspects of policy-making in international governmental organizations. These studies usually consider the scope and level of joint policy-making as an indicator of the degree of integration among members of the organization. The dependent variable is the extent of cooperative policy-making by representatives of governments of nation-states with the nation-state as the unit of analysis.[33]

The third category, research on organizational policy-making, contains studies which utilize organizational action as the variable to be explained. This research is generally addressed to legal and formal aspects of organizational policy-making, abilities of specific leaders, and unique influences which condition specific decisions. The international governmental organization is the unit of analysis for studies in this category.[34]

Research reported in this book falls into the third general category and uses the international governmental organization as the unit of analysis. The book investigates the formulation of organizational policy in international governmental organizations and seeks to explain the variable of organizational action. The only prior framework known to the author for the study of organizational policy in IGOs is that advanced by Cox and Jacobson. Beginning with the idea of a system, they were sensitive to issue-area concerns, environmental impacts, different roles of actors, and modes of policy-maker interaction. The framework was employed by a group of scholars, in an empirical but nonquantitative manner, to the study of eight different agencies in the United Nations system.[35] This project is a major contribution to the study of policy-making in international governmental organizations.

Some prior effort has also gone into the examination of budgetary practices in international organizations. The most comprehensive presentation is Colliard's survey of budgetary procedures in over one hundred international governmental organizations.[36] The work of Stoessinger and associates provided an overview of current financial concerns in the United Nations family, while an article by Mangone and Srivastava presented the argument for program budgeting in the United Nations system.[37] Both Higgins and Claude have examined the politics involved in recent United Nations financial crises.[38] Kohlhase has completed a detailed study of the role of permanent missions in the budgetary process of the European Community, the Organization for Economic Cooperation and Development, and the International Labour Organisation.[39] The most comprehensive and detailed budgeting study is Singer's analysis of the budget process in the United Nations during the 1940s and 1950s, *Financing International Organizations*. Of particular relevance here is Singer's delineation of various steps in the budget process.

Only two projects have attempted to systematically apply organization theory to the study of international organizations. Miles was the first to point out the potential utility of organization theory. He presented a list of more than one hundred propositions from organization theory which are of relevance to the study of international organizations. Eleven of the propositions were related to organizational decision-making.[40] The other use of organization theory can be found in the work of Alker and his associates. They began with four basic assumptions (quasi-resolution of conflict, uncertainty avoidance, problemistic search, and organizational learning) contained in Cyert and March, *A Behavioral Theory of the Firm*, and developed a computer simulation model of United Nations decision-making on peace-keeping involvement. After using data to examine the fit of the model, the authors simulated alternative pasts and futures.[41]

This book falls within the tradition of research on

international organizations. It utilizes orientations found in literature on quantitative international politics, policy-making in international politics, behavioral budgetary theory, and organization theory to orient a study of traditional questions about policy-making in international organizations. It demonstrates the relevance of these research traditions, and makes a beginning in the development of a theory of policy-making.

Overview of Book

Some kind of theoretical orientation, whether implicit or explicit, is involved in all research efforts. This study begins in Chapter 2 with a framework designed for the study of policy-making in international governmental organizations. This framework sets out major conceptual concerns and is utilized throughout to empirically examine policy-making behavior.

The empirical analysis focuses on policy-making activity in regard to the regular budget total in WHO. An attempt is made to develop and refine a model of policy-making, based on the WHO experience, in international governmental organizations. Therefore, some perspective on the empirical base being used should prove helpful. An attempt is made in Chapter 3 to locate the position of WHO in the IGO universe and to determine the location of activity on the regular budget within WHO. This chapter should be of primary interest to scholars in the field of international organizations.

The WHO budget process is examined in detail in Chapter 4. Classificatory schemes developed for steps in the policy-making process, inputs, and policy-makers are used to describe policy-making activity. This chapter uses the framework for analysis to consider the WHO budget process and provides the basis for subsequent work of a more theoretical nature. Students of budgetary and organization theory and international organizations should find this chapter most interesting.

Policy-making behavior in the WHO budget process through 1969 is examined in Chapter 5. Plausible alternative policy-making rules for each step in the process are formally presented, and the collection and analysis of data are reported. A set of policy-making rules which best describe actual behavior in WHO for 1951-69 is identified. This, and the next two chapters should be of general interest.

A computer model is especially appropriate for modeling routinized, recurrent, sequential actions which consist of a series of individual behaviors that become complex when added together. Therefore, a computer simulation of the policy-making process on the WHO budget total is developed in Chapter 6. Data from WHO for 1951-69 are used to estimate parameters for policy-making rules contained in the model. The validity of the model is examined by reference to its ability to predict actual budgetary figures for 1970-74.

Execution of the model on the computer produces a statement of what will happen under circumstances specified in the model. Sensitivity analysis involves alteration of variable values, or specification of their relationship, and rerunning the model on the computer. The output from the altered model is a representation of what would occur given the changed assumptions. In Chapter 7, counterfactual analyses are reported for 1951-69, and the impact of factors mentioned in the framework for analysis is evaluated.

Sensitivity analysis, reported in Chapter 8, is then used to examine twelve different plausible alternative futures for the 1970-80 time period. It should be clear that the computer cannot determine which alternative is going to occur in the future. It does, however, give a reasonable estimate of the ramifications of the set of assumptions contained in each scenario. Scholars of quantitative international politics, policy-making in international politics, behavioral budgetary theory, and international organizations should be interested in this chapter.

This study was initiated because of an interest in the formulation of policy in international governmental organizations. By the conclusion, the framework for analysis will have been utilized in the empirical examination of one type of policy-making in one international governmental organization, a computer model will have been developed, and a series of sensitivity analyses will have been examined. The last chapter is devoted to summarizing theoretical contributions and policy ramifications which result from the study and makes suggestions for further research.

2

The Framework for Analysis

---

*First of all [the creation of a frame of reference] is an ordering
enterprise. It consists of specifying a way or ways of segregating
phenomena for description and explanation, normally by means
of definition, classification, categorization, and assignment of
properties to what is to be observed. . . .*

—*Richard C. Snyder,
H.W. Bruck, and
Burton Sapin*

The analysis of policy-making in international governmental
organizations requires a framework. The one presented here
begins with the idea of the policy-making process and proceeds
to develop major conceptual concerns for analysis. An
explication of each of the important aspects of the framework
will be provided. An attempt will then be made to assemble the
entire framework in a coherent fashion. As noted earlier, the
framework is utilized throughout the remainder of the book to
guide empirical examination of policy-making behavior and
to create a model of policy-making in one international
governmental organization. To emphasize the potential utility
of the framework for the examination of other IGOs, the
consideration of basic elements of the framework will include
illustrations from a variety of agencies.

The Policy-Making Process

   A policy-making process consists of the series of activities
involved in making and executing decisions. A decision is a
choice among alternative courses of action. A policy is defined
as a course or line of action. An action is a deed or behavior.

   In IGOs, the policy-making process is both highly
structured and complex and can best be viewed as a system. The
concept of system presents a useful point of view, relying on a
few concepts to provide a pattern for the organization of

complex phenomena. Diagram 1 presents the system orientation in its most elementary form.

DIAGRAM 1   A SIMPLE SYSTEM

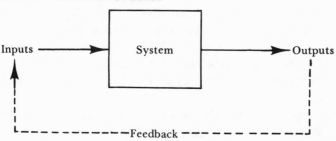

Inputs are those elements which enter the policy-making process and are transformed by it. Outputs are the system's products, called actions. The system is the mechanism, called a policy-making process, which transforms inputs into outputs. Feedback consists of information regarding results of actions and is fed back into the system as a subsequent input.

Five different aspects of the policy-making process will be treated in this book: actions, inputs, policy-makers, behavioral policy-making rules, and steps in policy-making. Accordingly, the framework for analysis addresses itself to these five basic aspects of policy-making. In doing so, it presents a conceptual frame of reference for viewing policy-making in international governmental organizations.

Actions

The phenomenon to be explained is action by international governmental organizations. From the policy-making perspective, IGO actions are conceived to be the result of the policy-making process. Accordingly, the framework for analysis equates actions with outputs from the policy-making process. While only one type of action will be focused upon in this study, it is, nevertheless, obvious that IGOs can take a variety of actions. In order to provide perspective for this and other studies of policy-making in IGOs, the framework for analysis contains a classificatory scheme for these actions.

A number of scholars have specified types of action, or issue-areas, involved in policy-making in international governmental organizations. For example, Lindberg and Scheingold discuss twenty-two types of decisions or actions which may be taken by IGOs; while Cox and Jacobson and Nye list seven types of action; and both Coplin and Alger suggest there are five types of decisions made by international governmental organizations.[1] Furthermore, scholars like Alker and Russett, and Rummel and Pratt have been concerned with using factor analysis to empirically determine issue dimensions in roll call votes in the United Nations General Assembly.[2]

The classificatory scheme of actions will be used only to provide a broader perspective on the empirical phenomena being examined, and any of the aforementioned typologies would probably be useful in this chore. The Alger scheme was arbitrarily selected for use because of its simple straightforward clarity. It identifies five mutually exclusive categories into which all actions by international governmental organizations fall.[3]

Administrative actions. Actions concerned with the secretariat of the organization are considered to be administrative in nature. Any actions regarding staff rules, office accommodations, and awards are in this category. An example of an administrative action occurred in May 1951 when the Fourth World Health Assembly of the World Health Organization adopted a set of staff regulations for WHO.[4]

Election-appointment actions. This category includes all appointments and elections which come before the formal bodies of the organizations. Actions such as the selection of the executive head of the agency and the president of a policy-making body are included. The appointment in September 1957, by the United Nations General Assembly, of Dag Hammarskjold to a second term as Secretary-General of the United Nations is an example of an election-appointment action.[5]

Procedural actions. All actions relating to procedures of the body taking the action are classified as procedural actions. Agenda item actions, judgments on whether to vote or postpone items, and designation of the committee to which an item will be sent are included in this category. The action by the United Nations General Assembly in December 1962 which convened the Fourth Special Session of the General Assembly to discuss UN financial problems is an example of a procedural action.[6]

Program actions. Program actions are directly concerned with the program carried out by the organization. These include actions regarding expert committee reports as well as actions on legal conventions. The approval, in May 1950, of a "Proposed General Program of Work Covering the Specific Period 1952-1955," by the Third World Health Assembly of the World Health Organization, is an example of a program action.[7]

Budget-finance actions. All actions relevant to the budget and financing of an organization are included in this category. Actions regarding appropriation resolutions, assessments, voluntary contributions, other sources of income, transfer of funds between appropriation sections, and actions on details of the budget are all considered to be budget-finance actions. The adoption of an appropriation resolution regarding the 1967 budget for the International Labour Organisation (ILO) by the ILO Governing Body at its 164th Session in March 1966 is an example of a budget-finance action.[8]

Inputs

An input is information which enters a policy-making process. The action, or output, is the reaction of the policy-making process to inputs. In this study, one of the primary efforts regarding the relative impact of different types of inputs upon the policy-making process involves building on prior concerns expressed in the literature of policy-making in international politics, behavioral budgetary theory, and international organizations.

Several political scientists (including Easton, Deutsch, Rosenau, Lindberg and Scheingold, Nye and Schmitter) have provided schemes appropriate for classifying inputs.[9] Because of its clarity and generality, the Rosenau typology appears to offer the best opportunity for the development of cumulative knowledge regarding the relative impact of different types of inputs. It will, therefore, be used in this study as the basis for classification of inputs. This decision is an arbitrary one. Certainly, the use of other classificatory schemes would provide different questions and answers also of considerable interest.

The Rosenau typology was created to analyze foreign policy-making; consequently, it must be modified slightly for use in this study.[10] The net result involves dropping two of Rosenau's original categories and retaining three salient potential clusters of input factors. It should be noted that the division of inputs is based on those types of factors which provoked the input and provides categories into which all inputs in a policy-making process can be coded.

Organizational inputs. Inputs from sources within the institution which are based on normal organizational factors are considered to be organizational inputs. Organizational factors appear to be especially important in international governmental organizations. For example, organizational history and precedents help form an incremental basis for policy-making, while organizational goals, program repertoires, and availability of information all condition organizational responses to a situation. The amount of the budget total approved for 1966 for the ILO by the International Labour Conference is an example of an organizational input into the proposal development step in the 1967 ILO budgetary process.[11]

External inputs. Information originating from sources outside the organization is considered an external input. These include specific communications from other IGOs, sudden demands by governments for assistance in crisis situations, and relevant new scientific and technological information. An example of an external input occurred when the United Nations General Assembly recommended a UN system pay increase in 1969. This input caused WHO to make a decision on whether or not to award WHO civil servants a pay raise.[12]

Leadership inputs. Inputs based on special innovations,

instead of by appeal to organizational or external factors, are considered leadership inputs.[13] In most international governmental organizations, there are individuals who offer leadership and direction in the handling of problems and usually initiate leadership inputs. In 1962, the proposal, sponsored by the Director-General and the representative from the United States government, that WHO greatly expand its regularly budgeted activities by adding a malaria eradication program, is an example of a leadership input into the WHO budgetary process.[14]

Each organizational action is probably affected by a slightly different set of inputs into the policy-making process. A primary concern in this study will be to determine the manner in which inputs affect actions and to evaluate the relative importance of various types of inputs. Since the participants in the policy-making process evaluate inputs and decide on organizational actions, let us now consider the policy-makers in international governmental organizations.

Policy-Makers

The literature being built upon in this study has focused upon two major questions regarding policy-makers: who governs, and what behavioral rules are used by policy-makers.[15] To assist in addressing these questions all policy-makers in international governmental organizations will be classified into seven categories.[16]

Governmental diplomats. All policy-makers who are members of their country's diplomatic corps and participate in the policy-making process of an international governmental organization as governmental representatives are included in this category. These diplomats become involved in policy-making in IGOs as members of permanent missions, as aides to delegates, or as delegates to conferences.[17] For example, in 1968, Ambassador R.W. Tubby served as a delegate from the United States to the Twenty-First World Health Assembly of the World Health Organization. In this instance, Ambassador Tubby was considered a governmental diplomat.[18]

Governmental technical representatives. This category includes all participants in the policy-making process who serve as representatives of their governments but who are not members of the diplomatic corps. Technical expertise dictates their presence, and they frequently come from a governmental agency involved in activities similar to the IGO. These specialists assist in detailed planning and implementation of programs, projects, and treaties; frequently serve on a country's delegation to a conference; and advise the nation's other policy-makers on technical aspects of an IGO's activities. In 1968, for example, Dr. W.H. Stewart, the Surgeon General of the United States, served as chief delegate of the United States delegation to the Twenty-First World Health Assembly of the World Health Organization.[19] In this instance, Dr. Stewart was considered a governmental technical representative.

Executive head. The executive head is the chief IGO administrative officer.[20] He is involved in most agency activities, preparing proposals for consideration, presenting and defending them, and bearing responsibility for their implementation. His continuity in office, expertise, and ability to structure a discussion provide him with initiative in numerous areas of organizational concern. From 1948 until 1970, David Morse served as Director-General of the International Labour Organisation and participated in policy-making activities of that agency as the executive head.[21]

Members of secretariat. All of the international civil servants employed on a full-time basis in an IGO are considered members of the secretariat.[22] However, in this category we will only include those members of the secretariat not included in the cadre of close advisers to the executive head. Everyone at or above the Assistant Director-General level will be arbitrarily placed in the executive head category because he or she is considered to be part of the Director-General's personal team. Individuals in the category, "members of the secretariat," handle details of planning, coordination, and implementation of activities of the organization. Although they usually do not attend meetings of the policy-making bodies and have little opportunity to exert leadership, members of the secretariat handle individual items which make up the total program of the organization. For example, a United Nations Resident Representative is intimately involved in the planning and execution of UNDP field projects, although he may not attend meetings of the Governing Council of the United Nations Development Program.[23]

Representatives of international governmental organizations. International organizations with members that are national governments are called international governmental organizations (IGOs). There are almost three hundred such organizations in existence today.[24] Representatives of these agencies become involved in the planning and implementation of joint projects and activities, as well as lobbying and speaking at meetings of policy-making bodies of other international governmental organizations.[25] The attendance of Rafik Asha as a representative of the United Nations Development Program at the Fourteenth Session of the Conference of the Food and Agriculture Organization in 1967 is an example of an IGO representative becoming involved in the policy-making process of another international governmental organization.[26]

Representatives of nongovernmental organizations. Organizations whose members are not national governments are called nongovernmental organizations.[27] Representatives of these organizations become involved in the planning and implementation of joint activities and attend and participate, formally and informally, in meetings of IGO policy-making bodies. The attendance of Louis Carreri as a representative of the International Chamber of Commerce at the Fourteenth Session of the Conference of the Food and Agriculture Organization in 1967 is an instance of a representative of a nongovernmental organization becoming involved in the policy-making process of an international governmental organization.[28]

Experts. Individuals with technological expertise who participate in an IGO's activities in their personal capacity, rather than as representatives of their countries, are called experts. They are usually prominent in their fields and often serve on committees which generate advice on specific technical subjects. They are consulted on an individual basis (both in person and by mail) by members of the secretariat and come together in expert group meetings. For example, in October-November 1968, eight experts met at WHO headquarters in Geneva on the topic of "Community Water Supply."[29] This group recommended guidelines for the development of programs of action.

Even though each type of policy-maker has the potential of becoming equally involved in the process, it is likely that some types of policy-makers are more important than others and have more overall influence, a point examined in the empirical part of this study. Furthermore, policy-makers bargain and negotiate over proposed actions, evaluate various inputs into the system, and produce an output called an organizational action. In the process of this political activity, they develop patterns of behavior. Discovery of these behavioral patterns—policy-making rules—is a major concern in this study.

Policy-Making Rules

A policy-making rule is the calculus by which information coming into a policy-making process is transformed into organizational action. Such a rule expresses outputs as specific functions of particular input variables and can be viewed as a formal statement of the behavior of policy-makers on a specific issue. The politics of policy-making are contained in policy-making rules.

For example, Davis, Dempster, and Wildavsky have suggested that the United States Congress uses the following policy-making rule in regard to the federal budget: $Y_t = a_o X_t + n_t$, where Y_t is the budget appropriation passed by Congress for a given agency for the year t; X_t is the appropriation requested by the agency for the year t; n_t is a stochastic error term which takes into account circumstances in period t not contained in the remainder of the equation; and $a_o - 1.0$ is the percentage of marginal change involved in the action. The a_o is viewed as the result of collective deliberations which take into account a variety of factors.[30]

In similar fashion, Oliver E. Williamson argues that the following rule describes Presidential action regarding the federal budget: $X_{it} = B_i^n X_{it-n}$, where X_{it} is the President's budgetary action for expenditure class i in period t; X_{it-n} is the President's budgetary action for expenditure class i in a prior period; B_i^n is a rationally calculated multiplier for expenditure class i for a certain period, and B_i^n - 1.0 is the percentage of marginal change involved in the action.[31]

Considerable attention has been devoted in the literature to the general nature of policy-making rules. For example, discussion has concerned the elite and pluralistic, incremental and comprehensive, rational and bounded rational, executive and legislative, and individual and collective nature of policy-making.[32] In the development of a system of policy-making rules, we will proceed by explicitly specifying rules and then empirically examining their correspondence to actual behavior. Thus, policy-making rules will be fully specified, operationally defined, and empirically examined for goodness of fit.

In the specification of variables, an attempt will be made to provide a statement of the construct involved, an operational definition, clarification of any subscripts, and an indication as to whether the variable is endogenous or exogenous.[33] The dependent variable(s) in the policy-making rule will always be an organizational action. The selection of independent variables is, of course, at the heart of the research endeavor. If the incremental assumption is made, then one of the independent variables will be a prior action in the policy-making process. Regardless of the nature and number of independent variables, a stochastic variate will be included as one of the independent variables. This variate stands for factors not otherwise included in the policy-making rule and requires specification of assumptions about the probability distribution of the variable.[34]

In specifying the relationship between variables, an effort will be made to identify and justify the form of the relationship (linear-curvilinear, additive-interactive, etc.) and any parameters used in the policy-making rule. For parameters, an attempt will be made to provide a clear statement of the concept represented (e.g., Williamson's treatment of the B_i^n as a rationally calculated multiplier which takes into account a variety of factors for expenditure class i for a certain period[35]), and a statement of how parameters will be estimated.

Finally, it should be noted that in the event two or more alternative policy-making rules provide plausible explanations for a given action, the rule providing the most accurate prediction to actual behavior will be tentatively accepted.

Steps in the Policy-Making Process

The idea of the policy-making process as a system involving actions, inputs, policy-makers, and behavioral policy-making rules is summarized in Diagram 2. However, a number of political scientists (including Davis, Wildavsky, Crecine, Frankel, Lindberg, and Singer) have observed that a policy-making process involves a number of analytically distinct steps.[36] Each step takes place at a different point in time, and each involves distinct actions. Furthermore, each step involves a slightly altered situation with potential differences existing in inputs, activities of policy-makers, and policy-making rules. In order to be sensitive to these varying influences and activities, it will be necessary to decompose the policy-making system and treat the steps in the policy-making process as subsystems. It has been arbitrarily decided to examine five different steps, or subsystems, in the policy-making process.

Proposal development step. The first step in the policy-making process involves preparing a specific proposal for action. This may entail drafting a preliminary resolution in a national capital, informal consultation and negotiation with other governments over the resolution's substance, development of a group of sponsors and a parliamentary strategy, and the submission of a formal proposal for consideration by the IGO's policy-making bodies. This step may also consist of such activity as the identification of a problem by the agency's executive head, detailed development of a solution by members of the secretariat, informal consultation with representatives of member-states and other

DIAGRAM 2   PRELIMINARY VIEW OF POLICY-MAKING PROCESS

Policy-Making Process

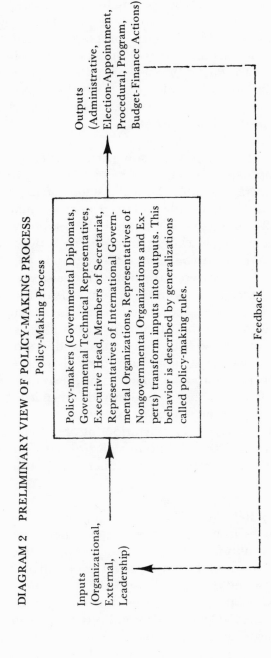

Inputs
(Organizational,
External,
Leadership)

Policy-makers (Governmental Diplomats,
Governmental Technical Representatives,
Executive Head, Members of Secretariat,
Representatives of International Governmental Organizations, Representatives of
Nongovernmental Organizations and Experts) transform inputs into outputs. This
behavior is described by generalizations
called policy-making rules.

Outputs
(Administrative,
Election-Appointment,
Procedural, Program,
Budget-Finance Actions)

Feedback

international organizations, and the submission of a formal proposal for approval by the organization's policy-making bodies. Regardless of details, the chief characteristic of this step is the generation of a specific proposal for action by the agency's policy-making bodies. An example of this activity took place in the fall of 1965 when the Director-General of the United Nations Educational, Scientific, and Cultural Organization (UNESCO) developed for that agency a formal budgetary proposal for 1967-68.[37]

Executive body step. Once submitted, it is customary for a formal proposal to be reviewed by an executive body of the agency's general assembly. Most IGOs have an executive body consisting of certain members of the general assembly (e.g., the Executive Board of UNESCO)[38] or, in the case of organizations with few members and a large parliamentary body consisting of numerous representatives from each state, an executive body consisting of a representative from the government of each member-state (e.g., the Council of Ministers of the European Common Market).[39] The function of the executive body usually is to oversee the administration of the agency, make decisions in its own area of competence, and screen proposals going to the larger parliamentary body. Formal debate and informal negotiation take place in the executive body. A proposal for action may be approved, amended, tabled, or rejected. If appropriate, a proposal then advances to the next step in the process. Consideration of the 1967-68 budget proposal by the UNESCO Executive Board at its 71st Session in the fall of 1965 is an example of the functioning of the executive body step.[40]

Assembly step. Most IGOs have an assembly composed of representatives from all member-states. The United Nations General Assembly is an example of such a body.[41] The assembly usually sets policy at the most general level, and in many IGOs it is the supreme policy-making body. The third step in the policy-making process involves the consideration of the proposal by the IGO's general assembly or parliamentary body. Formal debate and negotiation occur at this step, and a proposal for action may be approved, amended, tabled, or rejected. Approval of the 1967-68 UNESCO budget by the Fourteenth UNESCO General Conference in November 1966 is an example of action taken at the assembly step in the policy-making process.[42]

Supplementary change step. After a proposal has been approved at the assembly step, a number of formal changes may still be made in the adopted resolution. This activity comprises the supplementary change step in the policy-making process. Changes may involve formal amendment of the approved resolution or adjustments within specified limits by the administrator. When the change requires a formal amendment to the adopted resolution, a proposal must be developed, and the executive body and assembly will usually consider the amendment. Debate and negotiation then occur; and an amendment may be approved, amended, tabled, or rejected. The addition of $560,600 to the formally approved WHO expenditure level for 1967 is an example of a supplementary change to an appropriation resolution.[43]

Implementation step. The last step in the policy-making process involves carrying out the approved resolution. This includes hiring a staff, purchasing materials, and executing in detail the program of action. As the members of the secretariat interpret and implement the approved resolution, changes often result. However, unlike the situation in the supplementary change step, changes in the resolution are not formalized and considered by the agency's policy-making bodies until after completion of the implementation. As in the proposal development step, activity during the implementation step takes place primarily outside the organization's policy-making bodies. Administration of the approved ILO budget for 1965 by the secretariat of that agency is an example of the functioning of the implementation step in the policy-making process.[44]

Each of these steps will be viewed as a subsystem with its own inputs, outputs, feedback, and process characteristics. The decomposition into steps makes possible a more accurate portrayal of the actual policy-making process and a more

DIAGRAM 3   INTEGRATED FRAMEWORK FOR ANALYSIS OF POLICY-MAKING PROCESS IN IGOs

Feedback to Subsequent Activities

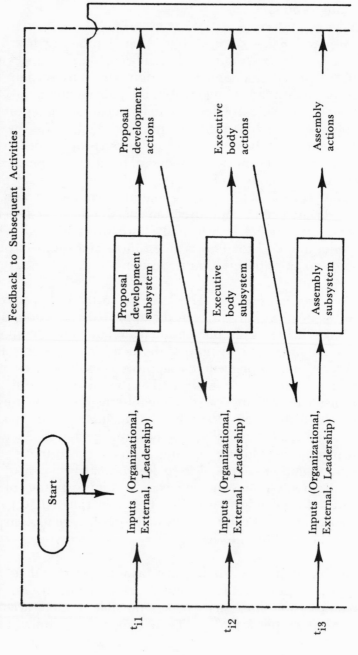

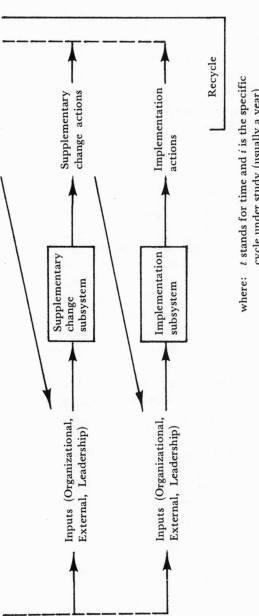

where: t stands for time and i is the specific cycle under study (usually a year)

NOTE: There are five basic types of actions which may be taken in each subsystem: administrative, election-appointment, procedural, program, and budget-finance.

There are seven basic types of policy-makers who may become involved in each subsystem: governmental diplomats, governmental technical representatives, executive head, members of secretariat, representatives of international governmental organizations, representatives of nongovernmental organizations, and experts.

The policy-making rules form a block recursive system, with a block for each subsystem.

sensitive analysis of the factors in the framework. For example, it should be noted that each subsystem in the policy-making process has a different set of potential inputs since each step takes place at a different point in time. Furthermore, even though each type of policy-maker has the potential for becoming involved at each step in the process, it is likely that some types of policy-makers are more important at some steps than at others. Finally, division of the policy-making process into five subsystems, or steps, means that there will be five sets of policy-making rules. Indeed, the timing of steps in the process means the system of policy-making rules will be recursive in form.[45]

Integrated Framework

An integrated view of the policy-making system in international governmental organizations can be obtained by bringing together the basic elements of the policy-making process (see Diagram 3). As a specific proposal for action proceeds through the policy-making process, it elicits responses at the subsystems. Through policy-makers' use of specific rules at each subsystem to determine organizational responses, inputs are transformed into outputs (actions). Feedback to subsequent actions constantly occurs throughout the system.

This integrated framework provides a set of factors to be taken into account when studying policy-making in international governmental organizations. In the application of the framework, an empirical examination of one type of action in one international governmental organization will be undertaken. In the next chapter, an attempt will be made to place in perspective the empirical base used in this study. In the following chapters, the framework is used to guide the empirical analysis of the WHO budget process.

3

The World Health Organization and Its Budget

The objective of the World Health Organization . . . shall be the attainment by all peoples of the highest possible level of health.

—WHO Constitution

The empirical focus of this study is on policy-making activity in regard to the budget total in the World Health Organization.[1] In order to place that particular empirical base into perspective, this chapter will present a description of WHO and its position in the IGO universe.[2] Consideration will also be given to policy-making activity surrounding the budget total and a determination of this activity's place in the larger WHO policy-making enterprise.

The World Health Organization

Historical precedents for WHO go back over 130 years. Efforts in the field of international public health began in 1838 when the Ottoman Empire founded the *Conseil superieur de Sante de Constantinople*.[3] This was followed in 1840 by the establishment of the *Conseil sanitaire de Tanger* by the Emperor of Morocco, and the creation in 1843 of the *Conseil sanitaire maritime et quarantenaire d'Egypt* in Alexandria. A fourth regional council, the *Conseil Sanitaire de Teheran*, was established in 1867. As with its predecessors, it was lacking a secretariat. The International Sanitary Bureau, the first international health bureau with a secretariat, was founded in the Western hemisphere in 1902. In 1923, it became the Pan American Sanitary Bureau and, like all of these organizations, was created to deal primarily with regional quarantine problems. Following World War II, it was reorganized and its name was changed to the Pan American Health Organization.

It is the only one of these regional health organizations which still exists today.

Worldwide efforts in international public health began in 1851 when the International Sanitary Conference was convened in Paris. Representatives from twelve countries attended the meeting which was called because of cholera epidemics of the preceding twenty years. Between 1851 and 1897, nine additional international sanitary conferences were held, and the number of nations represented grew. The Eleventh International Sanitary Conference in 1903 initiated studies which led to the establishment of the *Office International d'Hygiene Publique* (OIHP) in 1907. A permanent committee was established to give direction to this office, a budget was established, and a staff was organized to carry on research and disseminate health information. The office was located in Paris and was quite active until the outbreak of World War I. Following the war, an attempt was made to establish a health organization within the League of Nations which would expand international health work and assume the duties of OIHP. However, United States participation in OIHP and its nonparticipation in League activities precluded the merger of the two health organizations under the League. Both agencies continued to exist separately and cooperate closely until after World War II.

The origin of WHO can be traced to the San Francisco conference which produced the United Nations Charter.[4] Participants adopted a resolution calling for a general conference to be convened for the purpose of establishing an international health organization within the United Nations system. When the Economic and Social Council came into existence in early 1946, it responded to the San Francisco resolution by establishing a Technical Preparatory Committee and requested that the Secretary-General of the United Nations call a meeting for the purpose of establishing a new health agency.

The International Health Conference, convened in New York on June 19, 1946, produced the WHO constitution; established an Interim Commission to prepare for a World Health Assembly; and provided for absorption of the duties and functions of the League of Nations Health Organization,

Office International d'Hygiene Publique, and the United Nations Relief and Rehabilitation Administration. The WHO constitution was signed on July 22, 1946. The organization legally came into existence as a specialized agency on April 7, 1948, with formal ratification of the constitution by the required number of member-states.

The constitution enumerated twenty-two different functions for the organization. Among these were the responsibilities "to act as the directing and co-ordinating authority on international health work; . . . to assist Governments, upon request, in strengthening health services"; and "to furnish appropriate technical assistance and, in emergencies, necessary aid upon request . . . of Governments."[5] A World Health Assembly, Executive Board, and Secretariat were created to carry out the work of the new agency. The constitution also provided for regional organizations within WHO and for relations with other agencies. Membership was declared open to the governments of all nation-states, and each member was given one vote in the World Health Assembly.[6]

The First World Health Assembly met during June-July, 1948. Representatives of fifty-three member-states attended the meeting, along with observers from nine non-member states, eight international governmental organizations, and five allied control authorities. The Assembly passed 143 resolutions, selected Geneva as the site for WHO headquarters, established relationships with other IGOs, approved regulations for relations with nongovernmental organizations and rules for financial and staff matters, and created priorities for program activities. The Assembly provided for decentralization by establishing regional organizations in the Eastern Mediterranean, Western Pacific, Southeast Asia, Europe, Africa, and America. It also approved a budget for August-December, 1948, and the organization's first annual budget for 1949.[7]

Early in the history of the organization, existing sanitary regulations were updated and codified into two different international sanitary regulations. These have been monitored and enforced throughout the years and remain the only examples of formal regulations established by WHO. While these international health regulations are important, since the beginning there has been an emphasis on technical research and assistance rather than establishment of formal international laws.[8]

WHO's primary work can be divided into two general categories: technical programs and advisory programs. The former have been concerned with subjects such as statistical nomenclature and definitions, standards for drugs, collection of worldwide health statistics, medical research on specific health problems, dissemination of technical information in the field of public health, and the convening of committees and panels of international experts to advise on specific public health problems. The technical programs are research oriented and usually result in recommendations for action by WHO or its member-states. Advisory programs are concerned with direct advice and assistance to member-states. These programs involve approximately 80 percent of the organization's manpower and resources. The major focus of advisory programs has been on malaria, tuberculosis, health services and medical care, maternal and child care, and smallpox. In these programs WHO provides technical advisers and fellowships, but little in the way of equipment and supplies.

WHO and the Universe of IGOs

At the end of 1966, there were 199 international governmental organizations. Of that total, 174 agencies existed outside the United Nations family and twenty-five organizations inside it.[9] Within the United Nations family, there were fourteen semi-autonomous organizations in the economic and social field which were known as specialized agencies.[10] WHO, specializing in the world's health problems, was one of those agencies.

There is no typical or normal organization in the group of specialized agencies. In fact, great variation exists in agency practices and characteristics. In order to gain some perspective on where WHO fits in this group, data were collected for 1966 on eleven organizational characteristics for each of the fourteen specialized agencies and the United Nations Organization itself (data summarized in Table 1).

As can be seen from the size of the standard deviations, dispersion about the mean is relatively large in most instances.

TABLE 1   SUMMARY OF 1966 ORGANIZATIONAL DATA

Organizational Characteristic	Mean	s	Kurtosis Coefficient	Skewness Coefficient	WHO Value
Age of Agency	29	29	1.65	1.77	18
Number of Members	110	19	.39	-1.05	127
Total Secretariat	1,911	2,716	4.19	2.16	3,174
Total Expenditures ($000)	37,052	45,556	.49	1.27	74,064
Percent Regular Budget	69	24	-1.38	.29	58
Percent Secretariat on Technical Assistance	17	16	-1.79	-.08	33
Percent Assessment Largest Contributor	25	10	.31	-1.31	31
Years Between Assembly Meetings	2	2	-.25	1.16	1
Percent Members on Executive Board	21	4	-.04	-.65	19
Number Regional Offices	2	3	-.93	.88	6
NGOs with Official Relations	63	106	2.96	2.05	68

SOURCE: *Yearbook of the United Nations, 1966* (New York: United Nations, 1968), pp. 508, 956-7, 973, 975-7, 980-2, 984, 987-90, 993-5, 999-1002, 1006, 1009-14, 1017-21, 1025-9, 1033-8, 1041-3, 1045-8, 1051-3, 1055-60, 1069-70, 1091, 1124-5; *Everyman's United Nations* 8th ed. (New York: United Nations, 1968), pp. 9, 15, 489-90, 493, 498, 503, 509-10, 514, 518, 520, 524-5, 530, 532-4, 537-8; United Nations Economic and Social Council, *Expenditures of the United Nations System in Relation to Programmes* Document E.4351 (New York: United Nations Economic and Social Council, 1967), pp. 8-18; *Yearbook of International Organizations*, 12th ed. (Brussels: Union of International Associations), pp. 34, 618, 690, 742-3, 776-8, 1043.

Furthermore, coefficients measuring kurtosis and skewness indicate that for most variables the deviation from a normal distribution is considerable. The findings are a reflection of diversity among organizations on these particular variables.

The data indicate that WHO is one of the largest of the specialized agencies (see Table 1). It is among the leaders in size of membership and secretariat, total expenditures, number of regional offices, and number of nongovernmental organizations with official relations. In fact, among the specialized agencies, more money is spent through the regular budget of WHO than through the regular budget of any other organization. Furthermore, WHO spends the largest percentage of the regular budget on program activities.

In order to obtain a more parsimonious description of the dimensions along which these characteristics fall, and to obtain a refined picture of the place of WHO in the group of agencies, a factor analysis was performed. The R factor analysis was carried out using the product moment correlation coefficient, a principle components solution, unities in the diagonal, a cutoff of an eigenvalue of 1.0, and Varimax rotation. The unrotated and rotated factor matrices are presented in Table 2.[11] Three factors emerged which account for 81 percent of the total variance in the correlation matrix. By looking at the final communalities, it can be seen that most of the variance in each of the variables is contained in the extracted factors.

The unrotated first factor accounts for 39 percent of the total variance. As indicated by the factor loadings, it is characterized by strong relationships with the following variables: number of members, total secretariat, total expenditures, percent regular budget, percent secretariat on technical assistance, percent members on executive board, number regional offices, and nongovernmental organizations (NGOs) with official relations. These variables are all characteristic of organizations with large staffs and programs of action, and this first dimension will be labeled the resources factor. The unrotated second factor accounts for 30 percent of the total variance in the correlation matrix. This factor is characterized by strong relationships with the following variables: age of agency, number of members, percent assessment largest contributor,

TABLE 2   FACTOR MATRICES FOR 1966 ORGANIZATIONAL DATA

	Unrotated Factors			Final Communality	Rotated Factors		
Organizational Characteristic	Factor I	Factor II	Factor III		Factor I	Factor II	Factor III
Age of Agency	.03	-.86	-.41	.91	-.01	.95	.05
Number of Members	.70	-.56	-.10	.81	.40	.53	.61
Total Secretariat	.83	.35	-.28	.90	.89	-.18	.26
Total Expenditures ($000)	.58	.43	-.43	.70	.82	-.18	-.03
Percent Regular Budget	-.80	.44	-.32	.95	-.25	-.24	-.91
Percent Secretariat on Technical Assistance	.64	-.38	.55	.85	.02	.07	.92
Percent Assessment Largest Contributor	.28	.79	.40	.86	.21	-.88	.18
Years Between Assembly Meetings	.08	-.93	.00	.88	-.24	.82	.38
Percent Members on Executive Board	-.70	-.13	.39	.66	-.79	-.06	-.18
Number Regional Offices	.76	.06	.41	.75	.33	-.25	.76
NGOs with Official Relations	.74	.25	-.27	.68	.78	-.09	.24
Percent Total Variance	39	30	12		28	26	27
Cumulative Percent Total Variance	39	69	81				
Percent Common Variance	48	37	15		35	32	33

and years between assembly meetings. It appears to be measuring differences between agencies established before World War II and newer agencies. It will be labeled the age factor. The unrotated third factor accounts for 12 percent of the total variance and is characterized by a strong relationship with only one variable: percent secretariat on technical assistance. It will be labeled the technical assistance factor.

To clarify the interpretation of the factors, an orthogonal rotation was performed. To obtain an indication of the relationship among the sample agencies, the factor scores for the first two rotated factors have been plotted (see Diagram 4).

DIAGRAM 4   PLOT OF FACTOR SCORES FOR 1966 ORGANIZA-
TIONAL DATA

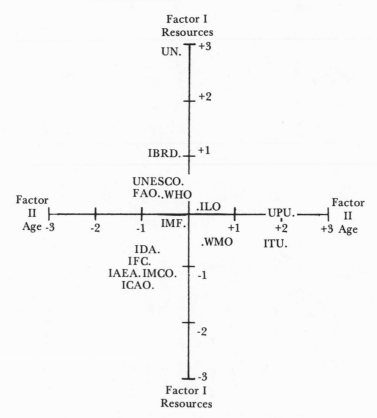

As can be seen, the United Nations (UN); Food and Agriculture Organization (FAO); World Health Organization (WHO);

United Nations Educational, Scientific and Cultural Organization (UNESCO); and the World Bank (IBRD) all fall into the upper left-hand quadrant. The International Labour Organisation (ILO) and International Monetary Fund (IMF) are located nearby. It is interesting to note how the International Development Association (IDA), International Atomic Energy Agency (IAEA), International Finance Corporation (IFC), Intergovernmental Maritime Consultative Organization (IMCO), International Civil Aviation Organization (ICAO), and World Meteorological Organization (WMO) are clustered together. Appropriately, the Universal Postal Union (UPU) and International Telecommunication Union (ITU) are located near each other and at some distance from the other agencies.

The Budget Total in WHO

A perspective on the place of the budget in WHO can be obtained by noting the frequency of occurrence of various types of actions. Resolutions adopted by each of the first twenty-two World Health Assemblies were coded according to the typology of actions presented as part of the framework for analysis. Results of the coding exercise are presented in Table 3.[12] The percentage of administrative, election-appointment, and procedural actions settled into a general pattern. Throughout the years, the combination of these three types of actions averaged just over one-third of the total, with each individual type accounting for about one-ninth of the total. Program resolutions accounted for approximately 50 percent of all resolutions adopted during the early years; but after the Fifth World Health Assembly, they settled into a pattern which varied from 31 to 52 percent of the total. The pattern of budget-finance actions varied somewhat, with the percentage of the total ranging from 16 to 33 percent. The average throughout the years for this type of action was 24 percent.

Policy-making in the budget-finance issue-area was selected as the focus for this study for a number of reasons. First, since most activities require money, the budget represents the overall concerns of an organization. This is especially true in WHO where there is emphasis on the technical assistance program. In WHO, the budget can be viewed as the translation of the

TABLE 3   RESOLUTIONS ADOPTED BY THE WORLD HEALTH ASSEMBLY

Year	Total	Percentage Administrative	Percentage Appointment	Percentage Procedural	Percentage Program	Percentage Budget-Finance
1948	142					
1949	117	14	7	10	53	16
1950	131	11	6	9	55	19
1951	100	7	8	12	54	19
1952	85	10	8	13	47	22
1953	68	9	12	14	43	22
1954	64	9	11	14	33	33
1955	54	9	13	18	41	19
1956	71	9	11	21	38	21
1957	60	22	13	15	32	18
1958	63	12	13	16	38	21
1959	63	21	11	11	33	24
1960	76	9	10	24	33	24
1961	68	13	10	16	31	30
1962	67	12	10	15	40	23
1963	51	10	18	10	37	25

1964	58	5	14	14	34	33
1965	56	7	12	9	43	29
1966	61	10	13	8	43	26
1967	63	10	11	11	43	25
1968	61	15	15	5	39	26
1969	67	8	12	6	52	22
Yearly Average	75	11	11	13	41	24
s	25	4	3	5	8	5

SOURCE: WHO, *Handbook of Resolutions and Decisions of the World Health Assembly and the Executive Board, 1948-72*, vol. 1 (Geneva: WHO, 1973), p. 607; WHO, *Official Records of the World Health Organization*, nos. 21, pp. 15-57; 28, pp. 15-75; 35, pp. 17-59; 42, pp. 17-47; 48, pp. 17-42; 55, pp. 17-45; 63, pp. 17-46; 71, pp. 17-43; 79, pp. 19-47; 87, pp. 19-44; 95, pp. 19-50; 102, pp. 1-32; 110, pp. 1-27; 118, pp. 1-32; 127, pp. 1-24; 135, pp. 1-25; 143, pp. 1-37; 151, pp. 1-28; 160, pp. 1-34; 168, pp. 1-28; 176, pp. 1-33.

annual program activities into dollars. Second, budgetary decisions are among the most important and contested actions taken by any organization. This is certainly true in WHO where the budget process involves collection and allocation of the agency's resources.[13] The importance of its budgetary actions is reflected in the provision which requires that the budget be approved by a two-thirds vote of the World Health Assembly.[14] In the author's judgment, the most significant actions taken each year in WHO relate to the budget. Third, the budget process is one of the few major policy-making processes which is carried on each year or two in each IGO. Thus, the findings of this study can easily be examined in a comparative manner in other IGOs. Fourth, outputs from the budget process are stated in terms of dollars and thus are easily and directly analyzable without excessive measurement or data collection problems. Fifth, the budget process was selected because the communality of activities in the budget cycle means the large body of literature on budgetary policy-making in other environments can be utilized in this study.

The money expended by WHO falls into two general categories: direct and indirect expenditures. The direct expenditures are of three types: regular budget funds, United Nations Development Program funds, and miscellaneous other funds. WHO is also indirectly involved in the expenditure of money from agencies such as the Pan American Health Organization and United Nations Children's Fund.[15] All of the expenditures, both direct and indirect, are a part of the total WHO program. However, money directly expended by the agency really comprises its program. It is, therefore, the pattern of direct expenditures which will be used to provide perspective on the place of the regular budget within WHO.

The regular budget is that portion of the program completely controlled and financed by the organization itself. The formal WHO policy-making bodies decide the total amount of expenditure; allocation of the total among various activities; and regulations by which the regular budget will be developed, evaluated, and expended. The regular budget is funded by assessments on member-states and supplemented by use of casual income and overhead cost reimbursements from the United Nations Development Program (UNDP).

The second category of direct expenditures, UNDP funds, involves money turned over by the UNDP for expenditure by WHO. Under this program, proposals in the health field are developed by representatives of nations with the aid of the WHO staff. The proposals are then submitted to UNDP. The projects, if approved, are subsequently administered by WHO. The total amount of funds, allocations within the total, and regulations governing the program are determined by UNDP. In addition, revenue is raised by the UNDP.

Miscellaneous other funds directly expended by WHO involve money voluntarily turned over to WHO. This category includes funds of the International Agency for Research on Cancer, a subsidiary agency which conducts research on all types of cancer; money given in trust by a state for the initiation of specific projects; funds for reimbursable transactions for member-states, such as the purchase of specific medical equipment for countries without fully developed purchasing departments; and voluntary contributions to an account which allows for implementation of proposed projects to the extent that money is available. In addition, a Special Fund for Servicing Costs is credited with miscellaneous amounts for services provided for other international organizations. None of the expenditures from miscellaneous funds require major decisions by formal bodies of WHO, although governing regulations are enacted and annual reviews conducted by policy-making bodies of WHO.

Where does the regular budget fit in the larger picture of direct expenditures? The amount of total direct expenditures for the 1949-69 period and the percentages in each of the three major categories are provided in Table 4. According to the data, total direct expenditures increased from just under $5 million in 1949 to over $82 million in 1969. Regular budget expenditures ranged from 54-94 percent of the total, averaging 70 percent of all direct expenditures. UNDP funds varied from 0-31 percent of the total, averaging 19 percent. Miscellaneous funds from other sources ranged from 0-28 percent during the period, averaging 11 percent. It is interesting to note that the standard deviations of the expenditures ranged from 8-10 percent, indicating a rather large fluctuation about the mean.

Policy-making on the regular budget in WHO is oriented

TABLE 4   MAJOR CATEGORIES OF EXPENDITURES IN WHO

Year	Total Direct Expenditures ($000)	Percentage Regular Budget	Percentage UNDP	Percentage Other
1949	4,684	91	0	9
1950	6,476	94	0	6
1951	8,328	79	12	9
1952	12,733	67	30	3
1953	12,799	69	28	3
1954	12,537	69	26	5
1955	14,327	69	24	7
1956	15,547	68	31	1
1957	17,682	72	28	0
1958	23,017	61	23	16
1959	23,994	61	20	19
1960	27,328	61	18	21
1961	32,223	60	17	23
1962	44,156	54	18	28
1963	46,117	65	16	19
1964	48,064	70	19	11
1965	55,413	69	14	17
1966	61,156	71	17	12
1967	67,618	76	13	11
1968	76,476	73	17	10
1969	82,234	75	16	9
Yearly Average		70	19	11
s		10	8	8

SOURCE: WHO, *The First Ten Years of the World Health Organization* (Geneva: WHO, 1958), pp. 522-3; WHO, *The Second Ten Years of the World Health Organization* (Geneva: WHO, 1968), pp. 400-1; Private Communications from WHO Secretariat members; and WHO, *Official Records of the World Health Organization*, nos. 27, p. 16; 34, pp. 10-11, 42; 41, pp. 8-9, 43; 47, pp. 8-9, 41; 54, pp. 8-9, 36; 62, pp. 10-11, 13; 70, pp. 10-11, 13; 78, pp. 12-13, 28-30; 85, pp. 12-13, 30-2; 93, pp. 12-13, 30-2; 101, pp. 12-13, 32-3; 109, pp. 12-13, 32-3; 117, pp. 12-13, 32-7; 126, pp. 12-13, 38-44; 134, pp. 12-13, 38-44; 142, pp. 12-13, 40-7; 150, pp. 12-13, 46-52; 159, pp. 12-13, 46-52; 167, pp. 10-11, 40-4; 175, pp. 10-11, 42-6; 183, pp. 12-13, 48-52.

around an appropriation resolution. The resolution spells out the budget total, the amount designated for expenditure in each appropriation section, and the amount of income from each source of revenue. There are three major sets of actions involved in the approval of an appropriation resolution: allocation of resources, raising of revenue, and determination of budget total.[16]

The expenditure side of the budget has usually contained a limited number of general appropriation sections. Once the appropriation resolution has been approved by the World Health Assembly, the Director-General has the power to approve expenditure transfers within appropriation sections, and the Executive Board has power to approve expenditure transfers between appropriation sections.[17] In actual fact, this has meant that power to determine the allocation of resources has rested with the Director-General, since most of the budget has usually been contained in one appropriation section. For example, in the 1968 appropriation resolution there were ten appropriation sections. Four of the sections dealt with regular meetings in WHO, three were related to special funds of a noncontroversial nature, and two dealt with relatively fixed office expenses. The other appropriation section, related to program activities, contained approximately 82 percent of the budget total and fell under the authority of the Director-General for allocation.[18]

Income for the regular budget is derived from three sources: assessments on member-states, administrative overhead cost reimbursements from the UNDP, and casual income. The amount of cost reimbursement from UNDP is a fixed percentage of total UNDP funds administered by WHO. Casual income consists of revenue derived from unbudgeted assessments on new members; cash available from unspent budgetary appropriations; and miscellaneous income from items such as interest from investments, exchange differences, refunds, and revenue from the sale of equipment and supplies. After income from the UNDP and available casual income have been subtracted from the budget total, the residual amount is financed by assessments on member-states. The decision on the actual scale of assessments is a relatively minor one, since the United Nations Scale of Assessments, as adjusted for membership differences, is automatically utilized.[19] The controversy within WHO over the revenue side of the budget may be considered a minor one.

The major conflict in WHO has taken place over the amount of the regular budget total and has, consequently, been of primary concern to policy-makers. In the tradition of Davis, Dempster, and Wildavsky, it shall become the primary focus in the following chapters.

Summary and Conclusions

An attempt has been made in this chapter to provide some perspective on the WHO budget. The chapter began with a brief history of WHO; it was noted that WHO is one of the larger of the United Nations specialized agencies, with more money being spent through the WHO regular budget than through that of any other specialized agency. Having provided background on WHO and its place as an international governmental organization, attention turned to providing perspective on budget activities within WHO. The empirical focus of this book—the set of actions relating to the total for the regular budget—involves the most salient actions taken annually within WHO.

4

The Budget Process in the World Health Organization

Serving diverse purposes, a budget can be many things, a political act, a plan of work, a prediction, a source of enlightenment, a means of obfuscation, a mechanism of control, an escape from restrictions, a means of action, a brake on progress, even a prayer that the powers that be will deal gently with the best aspirations of fallible men.

—Aaron Wildavsky

The making and implementing of budgetary decisions in international governmental organizations are essentially political processes where a number of policy-makers become involved in a struggle over organizational actions regarding the budget. The analysis of this struggle in WHO will begin in this chapter with a description of the WHO budget process.[1] Activity involved in each step will be discussed, followed by an examination of inputs into the budget process. Finally, the role of various types of policy-makers will be considered.

Steps in the Policy-Making Process

The cycle of events involved in planning, approving, executing, and evaluating the WHO regular budget for any year extends over a period of nearly four years. It begins approximately twenty-eight months before the start of the fiscal year in question and ends about five months after the close of the fiscal period.

The WHO constitution states that "The Director General shall prepare and submit to the [Executive] Board the annual budget estimates of the Organization."[2] Activity surrounding development of the Director-General's budget proposal occurs during the first eighteen months of the budget cycle and makes up the proposal development step in the WHO budget process.[3] This step is initiated when the Director-General sends planning instructions to the chief administrative officers of the organization. Approximately five months later, immediately after the winter meeting of the WHO Executive Board, he discusses the budget situation with these individuals at a staff meeting. Following that meeting, the Director-General sends a second letter to each senior administrative officer, giving him a specific budget allocation for the year in question.

At this point, the Director-General is guided in his actions by the World Health Assembly's "General Programme of Work Covering a Specific Period," the Executive Board's principles governing allocation of resources between regions, general resolutions and discussions of WHO's policy-making bodies, reports from expert committees, the percentage of increase recommended for the prior year by the latest Executive Board meeting, the amount needed to cover cost-of-living (including inflation) expenses, and any major additions to the program which have been specifically recommended by policy-making bodies of WHO or other agencies in the United Nations system.[4] Without question, the Director-General also takes into consideration a variety of political factors relating to the amount of budgetary increase he feels will be approved by WHO policy-making bodies.

Following receipt of the Director-General's specific budget allocation in the seventh month of the budget cycle, senior administrative officers direct members of the secretariat to begin concentrating on development of specific budget items. At WHO headquarters, this usually involves consideration of ongoing research and service activities. Away from headquarters the emphasis is on technical assistance projects. Discussion and consultation with representatives of national governments, technical units at headquarters, and other international agencies are initiated by members of the regional secretariat.

Governmental representatives become involved in the policy-making process at this point. In order to obtain technical assistance from WHO, a member-state must submit a formal request. The state's responsibility includes developing a proposal for assistance, defining objectives in operational terms, and analyzing the feasibility of the project. Once a country submits a formal request for technical assistance, a decision is made on whether or not to include it in the Regional Director's budget. The Regional Director's decision is guided by the Director-General's instructions, the preferences of the regional committee, prior decisions of the Executive Board and World Health Assembly, programs of other international and national agencies, cost, and whether the activity is a continuing one.

An important factor in the Regional Director's evaluation is whether the proposal is in line with established WHO policy on assistance to developing countries. The primary purposes of WHO programs are: "(1) the surveying of health situations; (2) the establishing or strengthening of health services; [and] (3) the education and training of health personnel."[5] Assistance may take the form of advisory staff, fellowships, or, in some cases, equipment and supplies. The following guidelines have been established for evaluation of requests for technical assistance:

(1) the probability of achieving successful, useful, and permanent results;

(2) the relative importance of the problem in the whole health programme of the requesting country;

(3) the ability of the country to provide the services required as measured by the availability of trained personnel and of means for training personnel;

(4) the financial and administrative ability of the country to absorb the requested assistance, taking into account all the health projects planned and in operation as well as in other forms (including bilateral assistance) which might overload the country's operating capacity;

(5) reasonable assurance of government co-operation throughout the programme;

(6) reasonable assurance that the project will be continued, and particularly that the government will provide adequate personnel and financial support for its continuation.[6]

In the eleventh month of the budget cycle, immediately following the World Health Assembly meeting which approves the budget for the prior year, the Director-General holds a policy meeting with the Assistant Directors-General and Regional Directors. The program and budget for the year in question are discussed in light of the assembly meeting. In the following month, both headquarters and regional budgets are then completed. After publication, the Regional Director's program and budget proposal are sent to the Director-General as well as to governmental representatives who will be attending regional committee meetings. Budgets of Assistant Directors-General are not published at this time but are submitted to the Director-General.

Regional committees exist to oversee the program and activities of WHO in various regions. They also supervise the activities of regional offices. Governmental representatives to a regional committee are persons technically qualified in the field of public health. They have from one to three months to study the program and budget proposal of the Regional Director. At the regional committee meetings, the Regional Director's budget is examined in great detail by an ad hoc committee and then considered in a more general sense by the entire body. Recommendations by the committee are forwarded to WHO headquarters for consideration by the Director-General as he makes the final decision on his consolidated program and budget for the year.

The Director-General decides what will be included in his program and budget proposal during October of the second year preceding the fiscal year in question. Those proposals are then produced in a lengthy program and budget document which includes a proposed appropriation resolution, scale of assessments, summary of increases over the prior year, overview of the proposed program, and a detailed breakdown of the costs. The document is mailed to member-states, international organizations, members of the Executive Board, and made public on the first day of the sixteenth month of the budget cycle.[7] Additional items may be added to these proposals prior to the Executive Board meeting at the beginning of the eighteenth month of the cycle.

The WHO constitution states: "The [Executive] Board shall consider and submit to the [World] Health Assembly [the Director-General's] . . . budget estimates, together with any recommendations the Board may deem advisable."[8] This activity, which takes place during the sixteenth, seventeenth, and eighteenth months of the budget cycle, comprises the executive body step in the budget process.

The Executive Board, consisting of twenty-four members, acts as the executive organ of the World Health Assembly and is primarily responsible for giving " . . . effect to the decisions and policies of the World Health Assembly."[9] It meets twice annually, for three weeks during the winter, and for two days immediately following the World Health Assembly meetings in the spring. Each member has one vote and is elected for a three-year term, with eight members being elected each year. The constitution provides that:

The Health Assembly, taking into account an equitable geographical distribution, shall elect the Member Countries entitled to designate a person to serve on the Board. Each of these Member Countries shall appoint to the Board a person technically qualified in the field of health, who may be accompanied by alternates and advisers.[10]

This clause has always been interpreted to mean that the "persons" on the Executive Board serve in their individual capacity as public health experts.

Members of the Executive Board do not act on behalf of their governments; indeed, some have even acted contrary to their government's ultimate position. One participant was moved to explain his apparently inconsistent behavior in the following manner:

Some surprise might have been caused by the fact that, as a member of the Executive Board, he has supported the budget submitted by the Director-General whereas, as a member . . . of his country's delegation to the World Health Assembly, he was one of the sponsors of the proposed reduction; the reason for that change of position lay in the fact that, as a member of the Executive Board, he did not represent any country whereas, as a delegate to the Health Assembly, he was under instructions from his Government not to vote for the acceptance of any budget . . . which would entail an increase over the budget for . . . the prior year.[11]

Nevertheless, most Executive Board members are employed by their governments and act in accordance with the countries' official positions.

A detailed examination of the Director-General's proposed budget is probably the most important enterprise the Executive Board engages in during its annual winter meeting. A Standing Committee of Administration and Finance, consisting of approximately one-third of the members of the Executive Board, meets for a week to consider the budget proposal. The Executive Board also devotes approximately one-half of its two-week session to budget considerations.

One of the most important functions performed by the Executive Board is the preparation of a report on the proposed budget. Whereas the Director-General's budget document is essentially a mass of detailed cost estimates, the Executive Board report is a readable summary of the budget proposal. It appears to be closely read and is the primary document structuring the general consideration of the budget in the Health Assembly. Any changes in the Director-General's budget recommended by the Executive Board are reported in this document which is mailed to all member-states, and other international organizations, at the end of the eighteenth month of the budget cycle.

The World Health Assembly has been charged by the WHO constitution with responsibility to "review and approve the budget."[12] This activity, called the assembly step in the WHO budgetary process, begins when the Director-General's budget document is made available at the beginning of the sixteenth month and is completed during the meeting of the Health Assembly in the twenty-first month of the budget cycle.

The World Health Assembly, the supreme policy-making body in WHO, meets for a three-week session each spring to set general policy. Each member-state sends a delegation to the meeting, usually headed by the leading public health officer of each country. Each member-state is entitled to one vote in the Health Assembly.

The budgetary process is probably at its most political stage during these meetings. Delegates often arrive with specific, written instructions from their national capitals to make speeches, initiate proposals, lobby, and bargain on the budget. The environment is typical of a large legislative meeting; informal negotiation occurs both during and between sessions. The Assembly has created two main committees consisting of all member-states: the Committee on Programme and Budget and the Committee on Administration, Finance, and Legal Matters. Each committee considers a portion of the budget to be approved by the plenary session of the Assembly. A two-thirds vote of the Assembly passes the appropriation resolution for the year.

A number of supplementary changes to the budget take place between the time of the Health Assembly's approval of the appropriation (in the twenty-first month of the cycle) and the close of the fiscal year (at the end of the fortieth month).

These changes arise for a number of reasons and take the form of transfers between budget sections, transfers within budget sections, and additions to the budget. Changes within appropriation sections occur with the approval of the Director-General. Transfers between appropriation sections are proposed by the Director-General and approved by the Executive Board. Supplementary additions to the budget are proposed by the Director-General, considered by the Executive Board, and approved by the Assembly.[13]

The need for supplementary changes becomes apparent almost immediately after the original appropriation is approved. Within weeks, during the twenty-fourth month of the budget cycle, revised budget estimates are completed by the secretariat in conjunction with preparation of the budget for the following year. The Director-General reviews these proposed revisions, together with the budget proposal for the following year. If approved by the Director-General, the changes are included in the budget document for the subsequent year. If necessary, these items are submitted in a separate document to the Executive Board.

During the Executive Board winter meetings, in the thirtieth month of the budget cycle, transfers between appropriation sections are considered by the Standing Committee on Administration and Finance and the Executive Board. All member countries are notified of any proposed changes by means of the Executive Board report.

Subsequent requests for transfers between appropriation sections, or for supplementary additions, are formalized just prior to the Health Assembly meetings held during the thirty-third month of the budget cycle. New requests are first considered by an ad hoc committee of the Executive Board. The Health Assembly then considers all proposals for supplementary additions. Immediately following the Assembly meetings, the Executive Board holds a session and considers any proposed transfers between appropriation sections.

Following the Assembly meetings, the Director-General decides on the budget proposal for the second succeeding year. He may also decide to request approval of additional transfers between appropriation sections. This can be accomplished by mail ballots to Executive Board members. At any time until the end of the fiscal year, on December 31, the Director-General may authorize transfer of funds within appropriation sections.

Implementation of the budget begins immediately after the Assembly approves the appropriation resolution in the twenty-first month of the budget cycle, and ends with Assembly approval of the final year-end reports in the forty-fifth month. The implementation step involves expenditure of budget funds and collection of assessments on member-states.

The first business undertaken during the implementation step is negotiation of a specific plan of operation among parties participating in a field project. The plan of operation constitutes a formal agreement concerning details for execution of the project. It is a legal document signed by representatives of WHO, the respective member-states, and any other participating agencies.[14] Once the plan of operation has been completed, the recruitment of staff may begin.

Implementation of the budget is controlled through various techniques by the organization's financial management staff.[15] At the beginning of the fiscal year, allotments for each activity to be implemented are issued to the organization's chief administrative officers. The allotment constitutes the authority to incur obligations and states the purpose and amount for the project. Significant changes in allotments must be personally approved by the Director-General. All obligations are incurred against allotments and periodic internal financial reports are produced and used to evaluate the implementation of allotments. Other management controls involve an internal auditing procedure and a constant review of projects by unit chiefs. Recently, systematic evaluation routines, such as critical path programming and network analysis, have been used on larger field projects.

Control of the implementation phase by WHO's governing bodies is exercised in a number of ways: first, through establishment of operating rules, such as financial and staff regulations;[16] second, through the establishment of audit principles and the hiring of an external auditor;[17] and third, through consideration of both an annual report on organization activities and an annual financial report.[18] These reports are sent to all member-states just prior to the Assembly meetings in the forty-fifth month of the budget cycle. The last activity in the budget cycle is a review of these annual reports by an ad hoc committee of the Executive Board and the World Health Assembly.

Inputs

As indicated earlier, inputs to each step in the policy-making process fall into three general categories. Explicit organizational factors which affect the WHO budget total are quite important.[19] Each year's budget is approached in light of the prior year's budget. The prior year's budget level and the organizationally accepted range for the percentage of increase (including inflation) are major factors determining the budget total.[20] These organizational factors have the result of constraining, but not eliminating, the potential area of influence of other factors. In essence, they define most of the incremental change which becomes the focus of real conflict. Other important organizational factors are specific actions recommended by WHO policy-making bodies in earlier years, prior steps in the budgetary process, and the amount of available casual income.

External factors can generally be viewed as imposing a set of constraints on the actions of WHO. These factors can either be absorbed within the budget total dictated by other factors, or they can directly affect the budget total. In the first case, they appear to be subservient to other factors and are handled by organizational slack. In the second case, they directly affect the budget total. In either case, Crecine's phrase, "organizational adaptation to environmental constraints," seems appropriate.[21]

Specific external influences which have had an effect on the budget total can be grouped into three general categories. The first, inputs from other IGOs, primarily contains demands from agencies within the United Nations system. These inputs have been related to salary and administrative concerns, requests to initiate or assume responsibility for specific programs, and matters related to joint projects. Inputs in the second category, special emergencies, have been related to special health crises of epidemic proportion and special demands resulting from the outbreak of wars. The third category, special budgetary adjustments related to changes in WHO membership, contains demands related to socialist countries quitting and rejoining WHO and to the influx of new nations.

Leadership factors result in shifts within, or additions to, a budget already organized on the basis of organizational or external factors. In WHO, leadership has come primarily from two sources: the executive head and representatives of the United States. In fact, successful inclusion of special additions to the budget total resulting from leadership factors appears to require the support of both these parties. Both supported inclusion of a malaria eradication program, smallpox eradication program, special aid to new nations, and a number of other additions that actually became a part of the budget. However, when the Director-General proposed inclusion of items such as the United Nations Relief and Rehabilitation Administration program (as an addition to the 1950 budget) or an extraordinary increase in the 1955 budget without approval of the United States, he was defeated. Similarly, when the U.S. and U.S.S.R. proposed an international health year as an addition to the 1959 budget, without strong support from the Director-General, the proposal was defeated.

Policy-Makers

The action taken at each step in the policy-making process is the net result of the activities of a variety of policy-makers. In order to gain an overall perspective on the number of those involved, yearly data were collected on the number of members, size of secretariat, number of expert advisory panels, number of IGOs attending the annual Assembly meeting, and number of NGOs with official status with WHO (see Table 5). As can be seen, the number of active member-states nearly doubled during the period covered in the study. In the same period, the total number of members of the WHO secretariat increased sevenfold. The number of representatives of IGOs attending Assembly meetings fluctuated, but the figure always remained under twenty. The number of NGO representatives with official status increased from eighteen in 1949 to eighty-two in 1969. The number of Expert Advisory Panels, averaging just

TABLE 5   INFORMATION ON THE MAJOR POLICY-MAKERS IN WHO

Year	Number Active Members	Number Secretariat	Number Expert Panels	Number IGOs at Assembly	Number NGOs Official Status
1949	68	516	0	8	18
1950	64	720	0	10	22
1951	68	980	29	8	27
1952	69	1197	30	15	27
1953	72	1277	30	15	27
1954	72	1289	33	16	30
1955	72	1400	33	9	35
1956	75	1397	34	18	40
1957	81	1475	36	13	43
1958	82	1697	37	11	46
1959	84	1854	38	17	51
1960	89	1944	38	14	54
1961	105	2117	39	12	56
1962	111	2342	40	15	57
1963	115	2630	43	16	61
1964	116	2675	44	18	65
1965	120	2770	44	18	66
1966	122	2996	44	17	68
1967	124	3118	43	15	71
1968	128	3277	43	19	75
1969	130	3564	43	11	82

SOURCE: WHO, *Official Records of the World Health Organization*, nos. 21, pp. 9-10; 24, pp. 73, 80, 82, 84-7; 28, pp. 9-10; 30, pp. 73, 141, 143-8, 160-1; 35, pp. 11-12; 38, pp. 62, 155, 157-62, 169-70; 42, pp. 11-12; 45, pp. 167, 169-74, 185, 197; 48, pp. 11-13; 51, pp. 155, 157-62, 174, 184; 55, pp. 11-14; 59, pp. 193, 195-8, 200-1, 204; 63, pp. 12-14; 67, pp. 231, 233-7, 240; 71, pp. 9-12; 75, pp. 221, 223-6, 228-9, 232; 79, pp. 12-14; 82, pp. 169, 171-5, 177, 181; 87, pp. 12-14; 90, pp. 237, 239-45, 247-8, 251; 95, p. 13; 98, pp. 267, 269-73, 276, 280, 103, pp. 12-13; 105, pp. 209, 211-14, 217, 221; 111, pp. 12-13; 114, pp. 173-4, 177-84, 187-8, 191; 119, pp. 13-14; 123, pp. 167, 169-74, 177-8, 181; 128, pp. 14-15; 131, pp. 147, 149-52, 154-5, 158; 136, pp. 15-16; 139, pp. 211, 213-20, 226, 230; 144, pp. 17-18; 147, pp. 221, 224-8, 230, 234; 152, pp. 17-18; 156, pp. 237, 240-6, 249; 161, pp. 17-18; 164, pp. 171, 174-9, 182; 169, p. 17; 172, pp. 227, 230-5, 240; 177, p. 15; 180, pp. 253, 256-9, 276, 279.

under twenty persons per panel, was twenty-nine during 1951 and forty-three during 1969.

Diplomats from member-states become involved in the WHO budget process in four ways: as back-up persons to those serving on the Executive Board and Regional Committees; as delegates to the World Health Assembly; as representatives of their countries' permanent missions in Geneva; and as members of the home office in the nation's capital. In the latter capacity, they are involved in developing positions on budget issues and frequently prepare papers and speeches for use in WHO policy-making bodies. However, governmental diplomats are in a position to become deeply involved in only the assembly step of the WHO budget cycle.[22]

The role of diplomats assigned to permanent missions in Geneva is both interesting and significant. These individuals frequently serve as liaison officers with the WHO headquarters secretariat on financial and budgetary matters, handle certain aspects of the preparation of position papers for conferences, file reports following meetings, and participate in WHO meetings where the budget is discussed. Their primary function at these meetings is to follow detailed "position papers" and assist delegates in carrying out instructions contained therein. Diplomats from some permanent missions meet periodically in Geneva, and the WHO budget is quite often the topic of discussion. Diplomats from permanent missions have been known to call upon WHO's chief administrative officers in order to make their countries' positions on budgetary matters clear to the Director-General.

Governmental technical representatives are the most important governmental participants in the WHO budget process and become deeply involved in each step in the policy-making process. In most countries, the WHO secretariat communicates directly with them rather than through a bureau of foreign affairs. As representatives of their own public health departments, these technicians are responsible for requesting assistance from WHO, for supervising counterpart funding, and for cooperating in the execution and evaluation of various WHO projects.

By far, the most important individual in the budget process is the Director-General.[23] As the executive head of WHO, he is responsible for preparation of the budget proposal, its defense before various policy-making bodies, and its implementation. His continuity in office, expertise, near monopoly of information, and ability to structure discussion provide him with the initiative in the budget process. He is intimately involved in every step in the budget process.

Members of the WHO secretariat—numbering 3,600 individuals at the end of 1969—are doctors, public health administrators, medical technicians, medical writers and librarians, biologists, sociologists, and psychiatrists. These international civil servants handle details of planning, coordination, and implementation of WHO programs. Although not directly involved in organization-wide decisions, they do, nevertheless, handle individual items which comprise the total WHO program.

Traditionally, about one-third of the secretariat members have been located at WHO headquarters in Geneva, one-third in WHO regional offices, and another third in various countries on field projects. About three-quarters have been supported by regular budget funds, and almost 60 percent have been classified as professional workers. Members of the secretariat become intimately involved in proposal development, supplementary change, and implementation steps in the WHO budgetary process.

Representatives of IGOs are primarily involved in the planning and implementation of joint projects. They lobby and occasionally speak at meetings of WHO policy-making bodies.[24] WHO has formal working agreements with six different IGOs. Furthermore, an average of seven joint committee meetings with IGOs have been held each year, an average of eleven IGO representatives attended the winter Executive Board meetings as observers, and an average of fourteen IGOs were represented at the World Health Assembly meetings. However, IGO representatives become only secondarily involved in each step in the WHO budget process.

Representatives of NGOs are involved in the planning and implementation of projects. They also attend and participate in meetings of WHO policy-making bodies. These organizations are usually technical agencies in the health field or federations of professional associations, and most maintain regular contact with members of the WHO secretariat.[25] The representatives of NGOs contribute technical suggestions, nominate experts for advisory panels, and, in general, provide a link with the scientific community. Many disseminate information on WHO's technical work. However, their involvement in the WHO budgetary process is of secondary importance.

One of the more interesting facets of WHO activities involves the organization's use of medical experts to generate advice on specific public health topics.[26] To facilitate this practice, WHO established subject matter panels, one for each of its major medical concerns. Panel members are appointed by the Director-General and are usually the world's foremost experts on the subject in question. These panelists are consulted on an individual basis by members of the secretariat, both in person and by mail; come together in small groups for specific expert committee meetings; and sometimes meet in less formal scientific or study groups. The expert committees usually gather in Geneva for a week or two and work with members of the secretariat in preparing a monograph. Over the years, an average of fifteen expert committees, twelve scientific group meetings, and four study groups have met annually. Experts may become informally involved in specific aspects of the planning and implementation of budget items, but they are not intimately involved in the WHO budget process.

Summary and Conclusions

Three parts of the framework for analysis have been used to orient the description of the WHO budget process. It was noted that the five steps in the process are spread over a forty-five month period, and details of each step were discussed, as were the types of inputs. Furthermore, the role of various types of policy-makers was discussed, and several impressionistic conclusions concerning their involvement were drawn. This description will provide the basis for subsequent analysis of a more theoretical nature.

5

Policy-Making Rules

The budgeting of appropriations ... is a highly complex process. Nevertheless, ... it would appear that the realized behavior of the process follows quite simple laws.

—Otto A. Davis,
M.A.H. Dempster,
and Aaron Wildavsky

The focus in this chapter will be on the behavior of policy-makers in regard to the regular budget total in the World Health Organization during the first twenty-one years of its existence. Actions on the budget total at the five steps in the budget process will be analyzed. First, a brief history of activity at each step will be presented. Next, plausible policy-making rules describing behavior at the steps will be posited, followed by a discussion of statistical techniques used in the empirical examination of the rules. Finally, the policy-making rules will be evaluated using data from 1951-69.[1]

History of Budgetary Behavior in WHO

To obtain a historical view of budgetary policy-making behavior in WHO, data on the regular budget total as approved at each step were collected for 1949-69. Several interesting patterns emerged. As might be expected, major changes occurred during the proposal development step. Modifications at the executive body or assembly steps were frequent but small in magnitude. There were numerous supplementary changes which always involved relatively small net additions. Data on the implementation step indicated that the budget total had never been overspent. Finally, there appears to have been a change in the general pattern of behavior in about the middle of the era.

In the budget proposal, the Director-General has focused upon justification of the increase over the prior year. The marginal increment over the preceding year's anticipated expenses was usually broken down in detail and presented as cost-of-living increases, needed to maintain staff and activities at the level of the prior year, and program increases which expanded activities of the organization. The cost-of-living increase usually varied from 3 to 5 percent, while the proposed total increment averaged 14.7 percent more than expenses anticipated for the prior year and 15.2 percent more than the budget level originally approved by the Assembly for the preceding year.[2]

Behavior at the proposal development step is best described as incremental. The Director-General made marginal adjustments to one of four prior actions to determine the proposed budget total: Assembly budget total for the prior year; budget total recommended for the prior year by the Executive Board; budget total proposed by the Director-General for the prior year; or anticipated expenses for the prior year known at the time of the proposal development step. The proposal development action is the Director-General's responsibility; and it seems reasonable to view his calculation of the percentage of change as a rational one based on consideration of a variety of organizational, external, and leadership factors.

The Executive Board rarely recommended a change in the Director-General's budget proposal. Significant changes were suggested for only five of the twenty-one years, with no significant cut being recommended after 1958. Cuts for 1951, 1952, 1957, and 1958 were related to socialist countries withdrawing from and then rejoining WHO. The only significant addition occurred in 1967 because of an Executive Board recommendation for a smallpox eradication program per a specific resolution of the Assembly.[3]

Behavior at this step is incremental in orientation, with policy-makers arriving at the recommended budget total by calculating a marginal adjustment in the budget total proposed by the Director-General for the current year. Executive Board action could also be based on: Assembly budget total for the prior year, budget total recommended by the Executive Board for the prior year, or anticipated expenses for the prior year known at the time of the executive body step. Since the Executive Board consisted of twenty-four individuals, each with one vote, and since a vote was always called on the budget issue, this step in the budget process is best described as legislative in nature. It seems reasonable to view the percentage of change as a result of a bargaining process engaged in by policy-makers.

The World Health Assembly gives final approval to the budget, and accordingly, any major changes to the Director-General's proposal are officially made at the assembly step. During nine of the first ten years, the Assembly made or upheld cuts in the Director-General's proposed budget total. After 1958, the Assembly made no net cut. The practice since 1958 has been to approve the Director-General's proposal as submitted or to add special new programs, such as malaria eradication, to it.[4]

Behavior at this step is incremental in orientation with the budget total arrived at by policy-makers calculating a marginal adjustment in the budget total recommended by the Executive Board. Other plausible prior actions upon which Assembly action could be based are: Assembly budget total for the prior year, budget total proposed by the Director-General for the current year, and anticipated expenses for the prior year known at the time of the assembly step. This step in the budget process is best described as legislative in orientation, and it seems reasonable to view the percentage of change as the result of a bargaining process engaged in by policy-makers.

During fifteen of the years under study, the budget total increased through supplementary appropriations averaging 3.7 percent for the twenty-one year period. During the first five years, automatic transfers forward of unspent portions of the budget accounted for most supplementary increases. In 1957, a supplementary addition was necessitated by an increase in the UN-wide salary scale. After 1958, a change in the practice of including all available casual income in the original appropriation resolution made casual income available on a regular basis for financing supplementary appropriations. The result was supplementary additions in nine of the last eleven years included in the study.[5]

Supplementary additions have been ranging from buildings to special assistance for emergency health crises in member-states. They were always justified on the basis of special external or leadership circumstances. Because casual income was always available to provide needed revenue, there was no increase in assessments for any year because of supplementary additions. Only once was the Director-General's proposal for supplementary additions not approved as presented.

Behavior at this step is incremental in nature, with the budget total arrived at by policy-makers calculating a marginal adjustment in the budget total recommended by the Assembly. The only other plausible prior action on which the budget total could be based at this step is the one at the supplementary change step for the prior year.[6] Since the ultimate authority for approval of supplementary additions lies with the Assembly, and since the Assembly is best described as a legislative policy-making body, this step must be considered legislative in nature. Furthermore, it seems reasonable to view the percentage of change as the result of a bargaining situation.

During the implementation step, an attempt is made to prudently expend the budget. However, a major concern has been, and will continue to be, not to overspend it.[7] The behavior at this step is incremental in orientation, with the expenditure total arrived at by policy-makers calculating a marginal change from the budget total after the supplementary change step. The only other plausible prior action on which the expenditure total could be based is the budget total after the implementation step for the prior year.[8] The implementation action is the Director-General's responsibility, and it seems reasonable to view activity at this step as being oriented toward trying to rationally expend the budget.

Plausible Rules

The brief description of policy-making in WHO offers several suggestions regarding specification of policy-making rules. Rules for each step will be stated as equations focusing on the budget total as the dependent variable. The overview indicates the budget process is incremental and provides suggestions as to which prior actions serve as the basis for marginal adjustments at each step in the process. Rules appear to be basically linear, being either temporally stable or subject to a step change during the period under investigation.

The basic idea of incrementalism is that actions are arrived at by making marginal changes from prior actions. The basic rule of incremental policy-making built upon in this study is: $Y_{it} = b_i X_{it} + e_{it}$, where Y is an action; X is a prior action; b is a fixed parameter, with $b - 1.0$ being the incremental change; and e is a stochastic variate which takes into account circumstances not contained in the remainder of the equation. The i refers to the specific action and t to the time period in question.

There are several ramifications to this incremental formulation. The analysis will involve time series data. The only endogenous variable in the equation is the dependent variable, Y_{it}. The independent variables, X_{it} and e_{it}, are considered to be predetermined.[9] The parameter b_i is the net result of various inputs into the policy-making process. The independent variables are additive; action is based on an incremental change from a prior action, and circumstances may then dictate addition of a special adjustment. Finally, the incremental process is viewed as basically a linear one.[10] The possibility that relationships are curvilinear will be discussed later in the chapter.[11]

A temporally stable rule uses the same parameter value for the entire time period. Suppose the activity of the Executive Board is a temporally stable incremental process based on assembly action on the budget total for the prior year. Stated as a stochastic equation, the policy-making rule is: $EB_t = bA_{t-1} + e_t$, where EB_t is the executive body's recommended budget total for the year; A_{t-1} is the assembly's budget total for the prior year; b is a fixed percentage used for the entire time period; and e_t is a random error term taking into account circumstances not otherwise contained in the equation. This rule can be stated in the following manner: the executive body's recommended budget total for a year is a fixed percentage of the assembly's budget total for the prior year, plus a stochastic disturbance.

The apparent shift in the WHO pattern of behavior in the middle of the era under study suggests the possibility of step changes in rules. Under step change conditions, the budgetary process is approximated by linear rules where the equation's parameter values, or the entire equation, are permitted to change to reflect different circumstances during the period under consideration. To illustrate a change in the equation's parameters, the above-mentioned dynamic stochastic equation would be restated in the following manner: $EB_t = a_j A_{t-1} + u_t$, where EB_t is the executive body's recommended budget total for the year; A_{t-1} is the assembly's budget total for the prior year; a_j is a fixed percentage for political epoch j (with $j = 1, 2$); and u_t is a random error term to take into account circumstances not otherwise contained in the equation. That is, the executive body's recommended budget total for a year is a fixed percentage of the assembly's budget total for the prior year, plus a stochastic disturbance, with a step change in the fixed percentage taking place sometime during the period.

It is also possible that one policy-making rule was used in the first and another in the second political epoch. To illustrate a change in rules situation, it will be assumed that the assembly's total for the prior year served as the basis for the executive body action in the first era, and the proposal development total for the current year served as the prior action for the second era. Thus, there are two different stochastic equations to describe policy-making behavior: political epoch 1, $EB_t = cA_{t-1} + v_t$; political epoch 2, $EB_t = dPD_t + w_t$, where EB_t is the executive body's recommended budget total for the year; A_{t-1} is the assembly's budget total for the prior year; PD_t is the proposal development total for the year; c is a fixed percentage for the first political epoch; d is a fixed percentage for the second political epoch; and v_t and w_t are random error terms to take into account circumstances not otherwise contained in the equations.

If a step change did take place, exactly when did it occur and what caused it? It appears that the shift point was related to one, or a combination, of the following: change in the executive head starting with the 1955 budget; return of the U.S.S.R. and other socialist countries (which first affected the 1957 budget); influx of new nations in the early 1960s (which will be treated as first significantly affecting the 1963 budget); and pressure for limited budget growth by the United States and other western countries (which first significantly affected the 1965 budget).[12] To examine these possible shift points, parameters in each plausible rule—and policy-making rules themselves—will be allowed to change beginning with 1955, 1957, 1963, and 1965. The possibility of multiple shift points exists, but analysis in this study will be limited to one shift point.

The budget total at each of the five steps in the policy-making process could conceivably serve as the prior action for any rule. To this is added a sixth type of plausible prior action: anticipated expenses for the prior year known at the time of the step in question. Anticipated expenses consist of the assembly approved budget total for the prior year plus supplementary changes known at the time of the step. It is reasonable to assume that only the most recent occurrence of each type of prior action would be used in a policy-making rule. As suggested in the overview of budgetary actions, a total of sixteen prior actions seems plausible as the basis for rules at the five steps (see Table 6).

TABLE 6   PLAUSIBLE PRIOR ACTIONS

Action	Plausible Prior Actions
Proposal Development Total (PD_t)	Prior Year's Assembly Total (A_{t-1})
	Prior Year's Executive Body Total (EB_{t-1})
	Prior Year's Proposal Development Total (PD_{t-1})
	Prior Year's Anticipated Expenses $(AE\,(pd)_{t-1})$
Executive Body Total (EB_t)	Prior Year's Assembly Total (A_{t-1})
	Prior Year's Executive Body Total (EB_{t-1})
	Current Proposal Development Total (PD_t)
	Prior Year's Anticipated Expenses $(AE\,(eb)_{t-1})$
Assembly Total (A_t)	Prior Year's Assembly Total (A_{t-1})
	Current Executive Body Total (EB_t)
	Current Proposal Development Total (PD_t)
	Prior Year's Anticipated Expenses $(AE\,(a)_{t-1})$
Supplementary Change Total (SC_t)	Current Assembly Total (A_t)
	Prior Year's Supplementary Change Total (SC_{t-1})
Implementation Total (I_t)	Current Supplementary Change Total (SC_t)
	Prior Year's Implementation Total (I_{t-1})

As can be seen from Table 6, four actions could plausibly serve as the basis for calculation at each of the first three steps: the prior action in time at the proposal development, executive body, and assembly steps; and anticipated expenses for the prior year at the time of the step under consideration. There are two plausible prior actions for the supplementary change and implementation steps: the action for the prior step in time and the action for the prior year at the step itself. The rules at each step describe policy-making on the budget total for that step and differ only in regard to the prior action which serves as the basis. Each rule will be examined under temporally stable conditions for the entire period under study. It will also be examined under conditions where the parameter in the equation, or the equation itself, will be permitted to take a step change.

Statistical Considerations

Three interrelated problems arise in the analysis of these policy-making rules. The first involves selection of appropriate techniques for estimating parameters for rules. The second concerns a determination of shift points in step change versions of plausible rules and an examination of whether chosen step change versions provide significantly better fits than temporally stable versions of the same rules. Finally, the problem of selection criteria for choosing the plausible policy-making rule which best describes data at each step must be faced. In all work involving tests of significance, the $p = .01$ level has arbitrarily been selected for use.

The first problem faced was the selection of the parameter estimation technique. The statement of the incremental budgetary rules called for estimation of an equation with an a priori specification of $Y_t = bX_t + e_t$, whereas the commonly used regression techniques, like ordinary least squares (OLS), estimate an equation specified as $Y_t = a + bX_t + e_t$. Thus, the use of normal regression techniques imposes an additional parameter (the intercept) on the rules. The problem is that substantive concerns should dictate the use of parameter estimation techniques rather than parameter estimation techniques dictating substantive statements.

There appear to be three strategies for dealing with the

inclusion of the intercept when using a technique like OLS for the estimation of parameters. First, it is possible to simply ignore the intercept, a strategy which should be avoided whenever possible. Second, it is possible to interpret the intercept as the starting level for the data (e.g., the budgetary base). This strategy was attempted; but in preliminary analysis, it was discovered that the intercept was frequently a negative figure. Because it is not meaningful to have a negative budget, it was not satisfactory to interpret a negative intercept as the starting level for the data. Third, it is sometimes possible to give a substantive interpretation to the intercept. In the WHO case, this might involve arguing that after utilizing the basic incremental rule, the policy-makers introduced an adjustment (e.g., for a reserve fund or hedge factor) which is a fixed sum across all years. However, such an interpretation forces an unwanted substantive modification for methodological reasons, and was therefore rejected for use in the current work.

Furthermore, in the preliminary analysis of WHO data, it was noted that the use of the OLS technique presented practical problems by confusing predictions which were made to years outside the data base used to estimate the parameters. For example, there had always been an increase in the amount of the budget at certain steps in the budget process; yet, in estimating parameters, the OLS technique sometimes yielded a regression coefficient of less than one and a large positive intercept. Likewise, at certain steps, there had always been a cut in the amount of the budget total; yet the OLS technique yielded a regression coefficient of greater than one and a large negative intercept. Because the net effect is appropriate, no practical problem exists with the predictions as long as the range of values of the data remains within the bounds of the data utilized in estimating the parameters. However, when the values of the data increase greatly, as they do in long-term budget projections, undesirable artifacts are created. The intercept no longer adequately corrects predictions, and rules which should be providing cuts end up providing increases, and vice versa.

It was decided that for the purposes of the analysis the OLS technique would be constrained so that no intercept was permitted.[13] Therefore, the basic parameter estimation technique which was utilized was constrained least squares, with the intercept being forced through the origin to eliminate it. The specific least squares procedure which was used calculated the total sum of squares from zero (instead of the mean) with everything else being calculated in the same manner as in the OLS technique. The interested reader is referred to the SPSS computer program documentation and an econometrics text such as Christ's *Econometric Models and Methods* for details concerning the derivation and properties of the constrained least squares estimates.[14] The primary advantage of the constrained least squares technique is that it allows one to obtain substantively pleasing parameter estimates.

Although the estimates obtained using the constrained least squares technique have desirable properties, there are three aspects of these procedures which should be noted concerning the comparison of the constrained and ordinary least squares estimates. First, the entire concept of variance is changed because the sum of squares is calculated from zero instead of the mean. There is no problem in comparing the coefficients of determination for rules which are estimated utilizing constrained least squares, but these estimates cannot be directly compared to ordinary least squares estimates of coefficients of determination. Because only coefficients of determination estimated by constrained least squares techniques are compared, and because other criteria for goodness of fit are utilized, this is not a significant problem in this research. Second, given the generally increasing budget data, the values for the later years in the data set are further from zero and hence weighted more heavily. However, with this type of data the budget values for the earliest and latest years in the data set tend to be further from the mean and hence weighted more heavily by the OLS technique. Careful examination of the data indicates that this aspect of the constrained least squares technique does not present any major problems. Third, when using constrained least squares, the mean value for the estimated residuals is no longer zero, although it was always quite close for all estimates. This means that the familiar standard error of the estimate is no longer an entirely satisfactory alternative measure of goodness of fit. Because of this, a measure called the average deviation (explained in more detail later in this chapter) is calculated.

For all of the analyses, it was assumed that the disturbances were independently distributed with zero mean and a constant but unknown variance independent of other predetermined variables. Furthermore, it was assumed the error terms were normally distributed.[15]

One assumption about the error terms is that they are serially uncorrelated. When this assumption is incorrect, estimates of regression coefficients may be inefficient and biased.[16] Therefore, the null hypothesis that estimated residuals are mutually independent was tested. The appropriate test for this hypothesis uses the Durbin-Watson d statistic.[17] However, it is only appropriate when lagged endogenous variables are not included in the equation.[18] When lagged endogenous variables are involved, the Geary test is used.[19] The null hypothesis was rejected in favor of the alternative hypothesis of autocorrelation if d was outside the .01 bounds established by Theil and Nagar or if Geary's test was outside the .01 bounds established by Habibagahi and Pratschke.[20] In the event this procedure indicated that estimated residuals were autocorrelated, it was assumed disturbances obeyed a first order autoregression scheme and the generalized least squares technique,[21] with the intercept forced through the origin, was used.

If it can be established that there is no autocorrelation problem and the equation system is recursive in the technical sense, then the single equation technique applied to each equation in turn is identical to the simultaneous full-information maximum likelihood method, and estimates will have the desirable attributes of that technique.[22] Technically, a recursive system must fulfill two requirements: independent variables must be predetermined for each equation, and estimated error terms in different equations must be uncorrelated.[23] The first requirement was met by the set of specified equations. The second was tested as part of the selection criteria.

Finally, the standard error of the regression coefficient and the F test were used as measures of reliability of parameter estimates. The standard error of the regression coefficient is the standard deviation of the regression coefficient estimated from the sample. The smaller the estimated standard error, the more accurate the estimated regression coefficient will be.[24] The F statistic, of course, indicates the significance of the regression coefficient.[25] Although this information is examined, it tells little, since the bivariate budget rules and data produce such significant regression coefficients. This information is reported mainly to conform to established econometric practices.

There are two special problems involved in analysis of step change versions of policy-making rules: determination of the appropriate shift point and determination of whether a step change version provides a statistically better fit than the temporally stable version of the rule. To determine the shift point in each rule, the following procedure was used. First, parameter estimates for each of the rules for each subperiod before and after the four hypothesized shift points were calculated. Second, the best fitting step change version for each rule was selected. It was identified as that version which provided the smallest summed squared deviations from actual data for the entire 1951-69 period. The summing process proceeded in the following manner: the estimated summed squared deviations for a given rule for each of the possible first subperiods were added, on a pairwise basis, to the estimated summed squared deviations of all plausible rules at that step for the appropriate second subperiod. This approach not only allowed a step change to take place in rules, but also allowed the basic rule to change.

To answer the question of whether a step change version provided a significantly better fit than a temporally stable version of the same policy-making rule, it was asked if both groups of observations belonged to the same regression model by stating the null hypothesis that the sets of coefficients in the two linear regressions are equal. The appropriate test of this null hypothesis is the one designed by Chow.[26] Using Chow's procedure, the sum of squares of residuals assuming equality and sum of squares without assuming equality are obtained. The ratio of the difference in goodness of fit, adjusted for corresponding degrees of freedom, is distributed as the F ratio under the null hypothesis. The normal table of values was then used for determining the appropriate F value. If the F value was significant at the .01 level, the null hypothesis was rejected; and the step change version of the rule was utilized in further analysis.

Having specified techniques for the estimation of parameters and selection of the most pleasing version of each of the basic incremental budget rules, one is faced with the problem of criteria for selecting the most satisfactory rule at each step. Three criteria were used for the determination of empirical fit, with the rule at each step which ranked highest according to those criteria being selected. The use of a test of significance was rejected as an overall test of each rule because it would tell very little. Given the nature of the data, all of the rules provided good enough fits to be significant, according to a test of significance. The primary interest here is in determining the best fit among alternative rules rather than in whether or not the fit of any one rule was statistically significant. In the analysis, the three criteria which were used converged in their selection of rules; not once did one criterion contradict another, although some discriminated more clearly than others.

The first criterion specified that disturbances in the selected equations should be uncorrelated with disturbances in equations in other steps in the system. This is one of the assumptions of the recursive system, and to find that it does not hold indicates a rule is incorrectly specified. In order to examine this assumption of uncorrelated disturbances, the null hypothesis that estimated residuals in different equations are mutually independent was tested. Estimated error terms of rules under consideration were correlated, using the product moment correlation coefficient, on a pairwise basis with appropriate estimated errors in rules accepted at prior steps in the budget process. David's .01 levels of significance for the two tailed test for $df = n - k$, with $k = 1$, were used to determine acceptance or rejection of the null hypothesis.[27] From among the rules at each step which met this criterion, the one which provided the best fit was selected. This test reinforced the other selection criteria, and in this study the same rules would have been accepted had this criterion not been used.

The second criterion was the adjusted r^2. Because of small sample size, the coefficient of determination is susceptible to over estimation of the amount of variance explained; and because of potential differences in degrees of freedom, different r^2 values may not be directly comparable. The following formula, therefore, was used to adjust the coefficient of determination: $r^2 = r^2 - \dfrac{k-1}{n-k}(1-r^2)$, where n is the number of observations and k is the number of explanatory variables.[28] However, because the step change version involves two linear equations, it was not just a matter of counting the number of explanatory variables to arrive at the k value for the adjustment to r^2 when a step change version of the rules was involved. Because the following regression equation produces identical estimates of variance as the OLS step change version of the rules, it was used as the basis for determining the k value for the adjustment of the coefficient of determination: $Y_t = a + b_1 X_t + b_2 Z_t + b_3 W_t + u_t$, where a, b_1, b_2, and b_3 are the estimated coefficients; Y_t is the dependent variable; X_t is the independent variable; Z_t is a dummy variable to distinguish between two periods in the step change model, with 0 representing the first subperiod and 1 representing the second subperiod; W_t is an interaction variable arrived at by multiplying X_t and Z_t; and u_t is the error term. For the constrained least squares estimates, the intercept (a), the dummy variable (Z_t), and the parameter for the dummy variable (b_2) are simply dropped from the equation. The k value for the adjusted r^2 for step change versions of the rules was, therefore, equal to 2.[29] Given the nature of the time series budgetary data and the constrained least squares technique of calculating variance, it can be expected that all of the estimated coefficients of determination will be abnormally high, especially when compared with the coefficients of determination which political scientists are used to observing (which are usually calculated utilizing cross sectional data and the ordinary least squares technique). The adjusted r^2 was used simply as a measure of relative goodness of fit to determine which of two or more alternative rules provided the better fit.

It might be noted that Stromberg argues that because the mean of the estimated error terms does not always equal zero when the constrained least squares estimation procedure is used, an adjustment in calculation of variance is required.[30]

His proposed adjustment yields the same result as the r^2 by calculating the variance explained as the sum of squares due to the regression line over the total sum of squares. His adjustment was tried on the WHO calculations, and it was found that they made no difference, at least to the fourth decimal place, for the r^2 measure.

The third selection criterion used was the average deviation, which is the mean of the absolute values of the residuals.[31] This measure, which in these circumstances gives a more straightforward understanding of the adequacy of the fit of a rule than the adjusted r^2, should be reasonably small given the range of the data used. The standard error of the estimate is normally used for this purpose when the ordinary least squares technique has been used. However, when the constrained least squares technique is used, the mean of the estimated residuals is no longer equal to zero; and it seems that the standard error of the estimate is no longer exactly appropriate. Therefore, the average deviation was used in the analysis.

Empirical Findings

In order to empirically examine plausible policy-making rules, data were collected on the regular budget total for each step in the WHO budget process for the 1951-69 period. The data source was the *Official Records of the World Health Organization*. Results of the data analysis will be discussed on a step-by-step basis with the detailed statistical findings presented in tables in Appendix B.[32]

The least squares technique, with the intercept forced through zero, was used to estimate parameters for all rules except two in the implementation step. For those two rules, the generalized least squares technique, with the intercept forced through zero, was used to estimate parameters. Tests for autocorrelated residuals and significance of regression coefficients indicated all parameter estimates in the analysis were acceptable. The Chow F test indicated that step change and rule change alternatives did not provide significantly better fits than temporally stable versions of rules. This means that although there appeared to be a change in the pattern of behavior during the middle of the time period, the results of the Chow F tests indicated that any change was not statistically significant. Selection criteria, therefore, were used to differentiate between temporally stable rules at each step.

The item of analysis at the first step was the budget total proposed by the Director-General of WHO (PD_t). The first of the selection criteria, correlation of error terms with those in prior equations, was not relevant because this is the first equation in the recursive system. Measures of goodness of fit were, therefore, used to decide the rule to accept. The most variance in the PD_t variable was explained by the A_{t-1} - PD_t temporally stable rule. The adjusted r^2 was .9982, and the average deviation was $985,000, an adequate fit when the actual data range from approximately $8 million to $61 million is noted. The following rule was accepted for the proposal development step: $PD_t = b_1 A_{t-1} + e_{1t}$, where PD_t is the proposal development budget total for the year; A_{t-1} is the assembly's budget total for the prior year; b_1 is a fixed percentage used for the entire time period; and e_{1t} is a random error term to take into account circumstances not otherwise contained in the equation. That is, the proposal development budget total for a given year (PD_t) is a fixed percentage (b_1) of the assembly's budget total for the prior year (A_{t-1}), plus a stochastic disturbance (e_{1t}).

At the second step, the analysis focused on the budget total recommended by the executive body (EB_t). The only temporally stable rule with estimated error terms uncorrelated with those of the rule accepted at the proposal development step was the PD_t - EB_t rule. This rule was also accepted according to criteria for goodness of fit. The adjusted r^2 was .9996, and the average deviation was $368,000, an adequate fit when the actual data range from approximately $7 million to $61 million is noted. The following rule was accepted for the executive body step: $EB_t = b_2 PD_t + e_{2t}$, where EB_t is the executive body budget total for the year; PD_t is the proposal development budget total for the year; b_2 is a fixed percentage used for the entire time period; and e_{2t} is a random error term to take into account circumstances not otherwise contained in the equation. That is, the executive body's budget total for a given year (EB_t) is a fixed percentage (b_2) of the proposal development budget total for the year (PD_t), plus a stochastic disturbance (e_{2t}).

The item of analysis at the third step was the budget total approved by the assembly (A_t). The only temporally stable rule with estimated error terms uncorrelated with those of either the rule accepted at the proposal development or executive body steps was the EB_t - A_t rule. This rule was also accepted according to criteria for goodness of fit. The adjusted r^2 was .9997, and the average deviation was $306,000, an adequate fit given the range of actual data from approximately $7 million to $61 million. The following rule was accepted for the assembly step: $A_t = b_3 EB_t + e_{3t}$, where A_t is the assembly budget total for the year; EB_t is the executive body budget total for the year; b_3 is a fixed percentage used for the entire time period; and e_{3t} is a random error term to take into account circumstances not otherwise contained in the equation. Otherwise stated, the assembly budget total for a given year (A_t) is a fixed percentage (b_3) of the executive body budget total for the year (EB_t), plus a stochastic disturbance (e_{3t}).

At the next step, the budget total after action on supplementary changes (SC_t) was focused upon. The only temporally stable rule with estimated error terms uncorrelated with those of one of the rules accepted at the proposal development, executive body, or assembly steps was the A_t - SC_t rule. This rule was also accepted according to criteria for goodness of fit. The adjusted r^2 was .9997, and the average deviation was $420,000, an adequate fit given the range of actual data from approximately $8 million to $62 million. The following rule was accepted for the supplementary change step: $SC_t = b_4 A_t + e_{4t}$, where SC_t is the supplementary change budget total for the year; A_t is the assembly budget total for the year; b_4 is a fixed percentage used for the entire time period; and e_{4t} is a random error term to take into account circumstances not otherwise contained in the equation. That is, the supplementary change budget total for a given year (SC_t) is a fixed percentage (b_4) of the assembly budget total for the year (A_t), plus a stochastic disturbance (e_{4t}).

The item of analysis at the final step was the total expenditure figure for the year (I_t). The only temporally stable rule with estimated error terms uncorrelated with those of one of the rules accepted at the proposal development, executive body, assembly, or supplementary change steps was the SC_t - I_t

rule. This rule was also accepted according to criteria for goodness of fit. The adjusted GLS estimate of r^2 was .9998, and the average deviation was a very respectable $143,000. The following rule was accepted for the implementation step: $I_t = b_5 SC_t + e_{5t}$, where I_t is the implementation budget total for the year; SC_t is the supplementary change budget total for the year; b_5 is a fixed percentage used for the entire time period; and e_{5t} is a random error term to take into account circumstances not otherwise contained in the equation. Otherwise stated, the implementation budget total for a given year (I_t) is a fixed percentage (b_5) of the supplementary change budget total for the year (SC_t), plus a stochastic disturbance (e_{5t}).

Miscellaneous Considerations

Would different rules have been accepted if the ordinary least squares technique had been used to estimate parameters? To determine the answer to this question, all rules were estimated using ordinary least squares. Other statistical criteria remained the same. The only difference in the rules accepted was that step changes were allowed to take place at the proposal development and implementation steps, according to the criterion of Chow's F test.

Is the fit provided by the rules impressive? To answer this question, two additional criteria of fit were developed: ability of rules to generate actual increases for each year, as reflected in the adjusted r^2 when actual increments and rule predicted increments were correlated at each step, and the ability of the rule predicted deviation from the trend to generate actual deviation from the trend, as reflected in the adjusted r^2 when deviations from the actual trend and rule predicted deviations from the actual trend were correlated, with the trend estimated by using the simple autoregression model. The sensitivity of ordinary least squares versions of the temporally stable accepted rules was the following in regard to increases for each year: $A_{t-1}-PD_t$ rule, r^2 was .77; PD_t-EB_t rule, r^2 was .96; EB_t-A_t rule, r^2 was .95; A_t-SC_t rule, r^2 was .95; and SC_t-I_t rule, r^2 was .99. The sensitivity of these same rules in regard to deviations from the actual trend for each year was: $A_{t-1}-PD_t$ rule, r^2 was .58; PD_t-EB_t rule, r^2 was .87; EB_t-A_t rule, r^2 was .87; A_t-SC_t rule, r^2 was .83; and SC_t-I_t rule, r^2 was .98.

Should the rules have been stated in nonlinear form? If the rules were actually curvilinear, a significant autocorrelation problem with residuals should have developed, or Chow's F test should have indicated step changes were appropriate. Nevertheless, a decision was made to explore whether a reasonable effort could uncover a better fitting curvilinear version of rules. Analysis of plots of data and residuals from linear equations suggested that a polynomial regression model might work better. The basic polynomial regression equation is: $Y_t = a + b_1 X_t + b_2 X_t^2 + , \ldots, b_k X_t^k + e_t$, where Y_t is the dependent variable; X_t is the independent variable; a is the intercept; $b_1, b_2, \ldots, b_k$ are fixed parameters; and e_t is a random error term to take into account circumstances not otherwise contained in the equation. The ordinary least squares technique is used to estimate each succeeding parameter; and, for this analysis, it was arbitrarily decided to allow k to take on the value of five.[33] Polynomial versions of rules do not improve upon the adjusted variance explained by ordinary least squares versions of plausible policy-making rules.[34]

Summary and Conclusions

This chapter examined rules of behavior used by policy-makers at the steps in the policy-making process. The analysis led to interesting findings. First, incremental policy-making rules provided quite good fits to actual WHO behavior from 1951 to 1969. Second, the rules were temporally stable. Results for the entire system can be summarized in Diagram 5.

A simple set of recursive equations describes behavior regarding the budget total in the WHO policy-making process. Because of the timing of the WHO budget cycle, the system of equations works so that the most recent action serves as the precedent for the succeeding action. The conclusion is: $Y_{it} = b_i X_{it} + e_{it}$, where Y_{it} is the budget total at a step in the policy-making process; X_{it} is the budget total at the prior step in time in the policy-making process; b_i is a fixed percentage for the step in question; and e_{it} is a random error term to take into account circumstances not otherwise contained in the equation. The i refers to the specific step in question and the t to the time period in question. It is concluded that, for all steps

DIAGRAM 5   SYSTEM OF POLICY-MAKING RULES

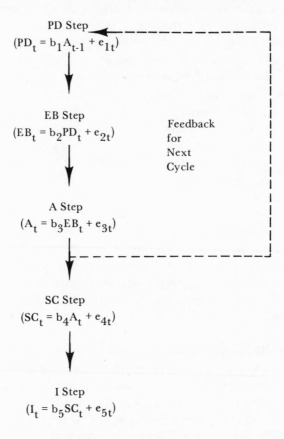

PD Step
$$(PD_t = b_1 A_{t-1} + e_{1t})$$

EB Step
$$(EB_t = b_2 PD_t + e_{2t})$$

Feedback
for
Next
Cycle

A Step
$$(A_t = b_3 EB_t + e_{3t})$$

SC Step
$$(SC_t = b_4 A_t + e_{4t})$$

I Step
$$(I_t = b_5 SC_t + e_{5t})$$

in the budgetary process, the budget total at time t (Y_{it}) is a fixed percentage (b_i) of the budget total for the prior step in time (X_{it}), plus a stochastic disturbance (e_{it}).

6

Computer Model

The process of simulation involves constructing a theory, or model, of a system that prescribes the system's processes. . . .By carrying out the processes postulated in the theory, a hypothetical stream of behavior is generated that can be compared with the stream of behavior of the original system.

—*G.P.E. Clarkson*
and H.A. Simon

In this chapter, a model will be developed for the budget-making process, with findings from Chapter 5 serving as its basis. A discussion of the logic involved and details of the model will be presented. Parameter estimation techniques will be discussed, and data from the 1951-69 period will be used to estimate parameters for the model. Finally, data from 1970-74 will be used to examine the model's validity.

Logic of the Model

Because of the convenience involved in the generation of random numbers and the ease and accuracy of calculation contained in a computer model,[1] the model will be stated as a computer simulation. In designing the simulation, the goals are to reflect the actual WHO budget process and, at the same time, to set up experiments of theoretical interest. Experiments will be made possible by building factors of interest into policy-making rules contained in the model.

Five steps in the policy-making process were presented in the framework for analysis in Chapter 2. In the computer model, each step is treated as a submodel. By linking the submodels together, a dynamic model is developed which allows the tracing, through sensitivity analysis, of the impact of each step, or elements within the steps, on the endogenous variables in the budget model.

Three types of inputs were mentioned in the framework for

analysis in Chapter 2. In the model, the single rule at each step (identified in Chapter 5) is decomposed to reflect the impact of organizational, external, and leadership inputs. Specifically, the rule at each step is rewritten as an identity of the following form: $Y_{it} = X_{it} + ZORG_{it} + ZE_{it} + ZL_{it}$, where Y is the budget total at the step under consideration; X is the budget total at the prior step in time; $ZORG$ is the incremental change from the prior step in time due to organizational inputs; ZE is the incremental change from the prior step in time due to external inputs; ZL is the incremental change from the prior step in time due to leadership inputs; i is the subscript for the step in question; and t is the subscript for the time period involved.

Next, behavioral rules need to be specified at each step to generate values for $ZORG_{it}$, ZE_{it}, and ZL_{it}. In the development of these behavioral rules, the following simple assumption served as the beginning point: $Z_{jit} = b_{ji}X_{it} + e_{jt}$, where Z is the incremental change; b is a fixed percentage of change; X is the budget total for the prior step in time in the budget process; e is a stochastic disturbance; j is the subscript for the type of incremental change in question (i.e., organizational, leadership, external); i is the subscript for the step in question, and t is the subscript for the time period involved.

Incremental change variables for which rules are desired, and relevant budget total variables from the prior step in the budget process, must now be specified. For WHO, the relevant variables are as follows:

Incremental Change Variable	Budget Total Variable From Prior Step
$PDORG_t$	A_{t-1}
PDE_t	A_{t-1}
PDL_t	A_{t-1}
$EBORG_t$	PD_t
EBE_t	PD_t
EBL_t	PD_t
$AORG_t$	EB_t
AE_t	EB_t
AL_t	EB_t
$SCORG_t$	A_t

$$SCE_t \qquad\qquad\qquad A_t$$
$$SCL_t \qquad\qquad\qquad A_t$$
$$IORG_t \qquad\qquad\qquad SC_t$$
$$IE_t \qquad\qquad\qquad SC_t$$
$$IL_t \qquad\qquad\qquad SC_t$$

where PD is the proposal development step; EB is the executive body step; A is the assembly step; SC is the supplementary change step; I is the implementation step; ORG is organizational factors; E is external factors; and L is leadership factors. Behavioral equations generated from this list are concerned with incremental changes only, while identities are concerned with budget totals for the various steps.

Thus, the model is developed as a block recursive system of equations, with fifteen possible endogenous variables generated by behavioral rules and five endogenous variables generated by identities. When all rules are linked together, they form a dynamic, self-contained computer model which produces the budget total at each step.

The Computer Model

The computer model contains five different submodels, each with a set of equations representing policy-making activity at a step in the budget process. As seen from Diagram 6, the model completes each step in turn. It can be recycled and run through additional time periods as desired.

In specifying the WHO model, any behavioral equations which had not been used in the 1951-69 time period were dropped. As seen from Table 7, the model has fifteen endogenous variables, twelve behavioral equations, and five identities. Information required to start the simulation is presented at the end of the table. (A more detailed flowchart is presented in Diagram 7.)

The computer program in Appendix C translates actions contained in the flowchart into instructions for the computer. The program is written in Fortran IV and is operational on the CDC 6600 Computer at Indiana University's Wrubel Computing Center.

Taken as a whole, the model reflects the idea that a complex process is broken into a series of less complex problems, which

DIAGRAM 6   OVERVIEW OF COMPUTER MODEL

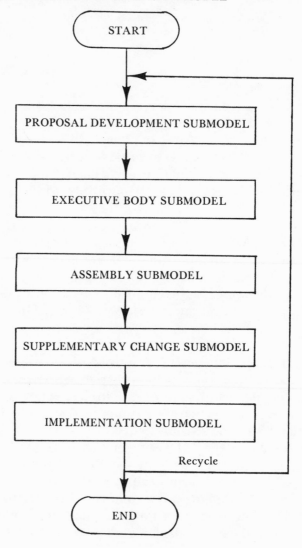

are then solved individually and sequentially. Thus, division of the model into submodels and the breakdown of submodels into smaller elements reflect the tendency to partition complex problems into manageable subproblems. The incrementalism of the model is reflected in the fact that each problem is handled as a marginal change from a prior action.

DIAGRAM 7   DETAILED FLOWCHART OF COMPUTER MODEL

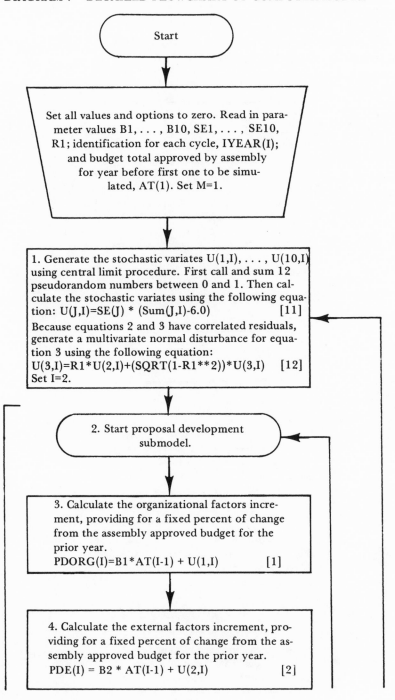

Start

Set all values and options to zero. Read in parameter values B1, . . . , B10, SE1, . . . , SE10,
R1; identification for each cycle, IYEAR(I);
and budget total approved by assembly
for year before first one to be simulated, AT(1). Set M=1.

1. Generate the stochastic variates U(1,I), . . . , U(10,I)
using central limit procedure. First call and sum 12
pseudorandom numbers between 0 and 1. Then calculate the stochastic variates using the following equation: $U(J,I)=SE(J) * (Sum(J,I)-6.0)$ [11]
Because equations 2 and 3 have correlated residuals,
generate a multivariate normal disturbance for equation 3 using the following equation:
$U(3,I)=R1*U(2,I)+(SQRT(1-R1**2))*U(3,I)$ [12]
Set I=2.

2. Start proposal development
submodel.

3. Calculate the organizational factors increment, providing for a fixed percent of change
from the assembly approved budget for the
prior year.
$PDORG(I)=B1*AT(I-1) + U(1,I)$ [1]

4. Calculate the external factors increment, providing for a fixed percent of change from the assembly approved budget for the prior year.
$PDE(I) = B2 * AT(I-1) + U(2,I)$ [2]

87

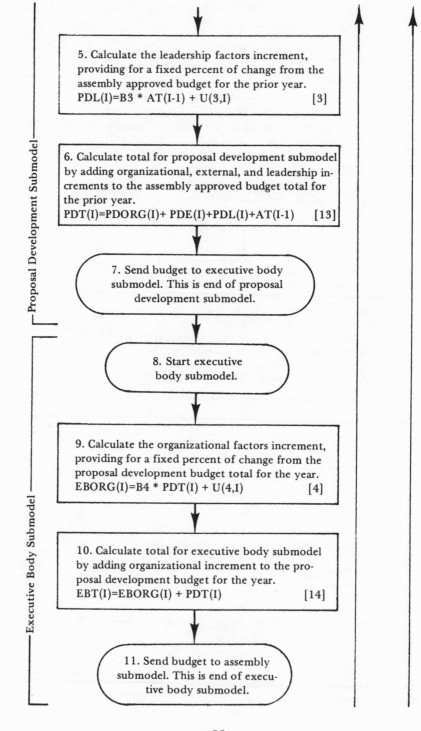

Proposal Development Submodel

5. Calculate the leadership factors increment, providing for a fixed percent of change from the assembly approved budget for the prior year.
PDL(I)=B3 * AT(I-1) + U(3,I)   [3]

6. Calculate total for proposal development submodel by adding organizational, external, and leadership increments to the assembly approved budget total for the prior year.
PDT(I)=PDORG(I)+ PDE(I)+PDL(I)+AT(I-1)   [13]

7. Send budget to executive body submodel. This is end of proposal development submodel.

Executive Body Submodel

8. Start executive body submodel.

9. Calculate the organizational factors increment, providing for a fixed percent of change from the proposal development budget total for the year.
EBORG(I)=B4 * PDT(I) + U(4,I)   [4]

10. Calculate total for executive body submodel by adding organizational increment to the proposal development budget for the year.
EBT(I)=EBORG(I) + PDT(I)   [14]

11. Send budget to assembly submodel. This is end of executive body submodel.

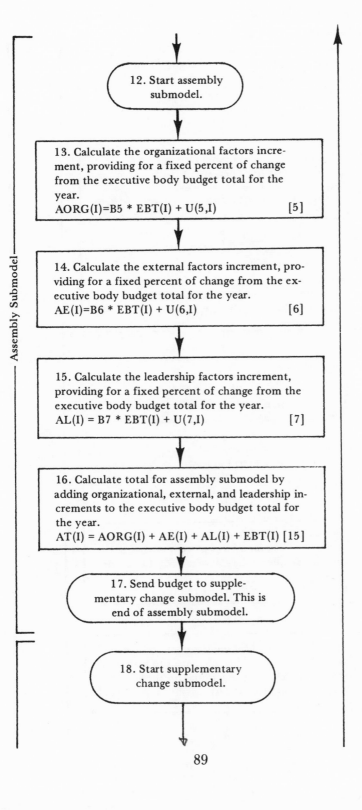

12. Start assembly submodel.

13. Calculate the organizational factors increment, providing for a fixed percent of change from the executive body budget total for the year.
AORG(I)=B5 * EBT(I) + U(5,I)   [5]

14. Calculate the external factors increment, providing for a fixed percent of change from the executive body budget total for the year.
AE(I)=B6 * EBT(I) + U(6,I)   [6]

15. Calculate the leadership factors increment, providing for a fixed percent of change from the executive body budget total for the year.
AL(I) = B7 * EBT(I) + U(7,I)   [7]

16. Calculate total for assembly submodel by adding organizational, external, and leadership increments to the executive body budget total for the year.
AT(I) = AORG(I) + AE(I) + AL(I) + EBT(I) [15]

17. Send budget to supplementary change submodel. This is end of assembly submodel.

18. Start supplementary change submodel.

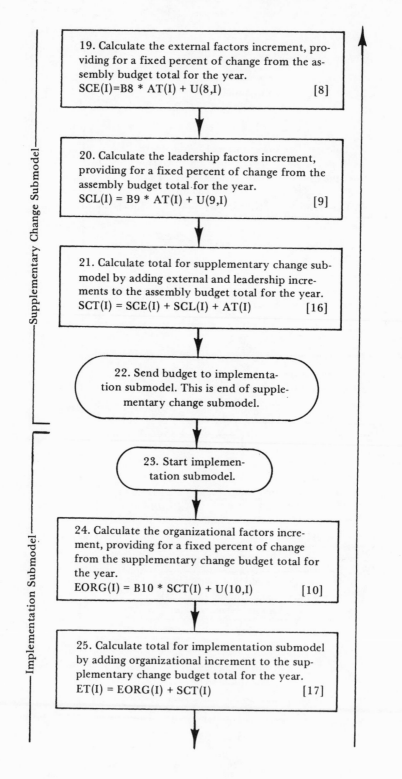

19. Calculate the external factors increment, providing for a fixed percent of change from the assembly budget total for the year.
$$SCE(I) = B8 * AT(I) + U(8,I) \qquad [8]$$

20. Calculate the leadership factors increment, providing for a fixed percent of change from the assembly budget total for the year.
$$SCL(I) = B9 * AT(I) + U(9,I) \qquad [9]$$

21. Calculate total for supplementary change submodel by adding external and leadership increments to the assembly budget total for the year.
$$SCT(I) = SCE(I) + SCL(I) + AT(I) \qquad [16]$$

22. Send budget to implementation submodel. This is end of supplementary change submodel.

23. Start implementation submodel.

24. Calculate the organizational factors increment, providing for a fixed percent of change from the supplementary change budget total for the year.
$$EORG(I) = B10 * SCT(I) + U(10,I) \qquad [10]$$

25. Calculate total for implementation submodel by adding organizational increment to the supplementary change budget total for the year.
$$ET(I) = EORG(I) + SCT(I) \qquad [17]$$

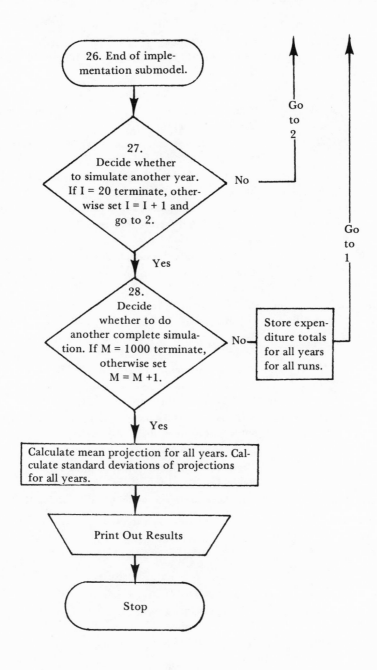

26. End of imple-mentation submodel.

27. Decide whether to simulate another year. If I = 20 terminate, other-wise set I = I + 1 and go to 2.

No → Go to 2

Yes

28. Decide whether to do another complete simula-tion. If M = 1000 terminate, otherwise set M = M +1.

No → Store expen-diture totals for all years for all runs. → Go to 1

Yes

Calculate mean projection for all years. Calculate standard deviations of projections for all years.

Print Out Results

Stop

TABLE 7   VARIABLES, PARAMETERS, EQUATIONS, IDENTITIES, AND STARTING INFORMATION USED IN THE COMPUTER MODEL*

Endogenous Variables

PDORG(I)	Organizational factors increment in proposal development submodel for period I.
PDE(I)	External factors increment in proposal development submodel for period I.
PDL(I)	Leadership factors increment in proposal development submodel for period I.
PDT(I)	Proposal development submodel total for period I.
EBORG(I)	Organizational factors increment in executive body submodel for period I.
EBT(I)	Executive body submodel total for period I.
AORG(I)	Organizational factors increment in assembly submodel for period I.
AE(I)	External factors increment in assembly submodel for period I.
AL(I)	Leadership factors increment in assembly submodel for period I.
AT(I)	Assembly submodel total for period I.
SCE(I)	External factors increment in supplementary change submodel for period I.
SCL(I)	Leadership factors increment in supplementary change submodel for period I.
SCT(I)	Supplementary change submodel total for period I.
EORG(I)	Organizational factors increment in implementation submodel for period I.
ET(I)	Implementation submodel total for period I.

Exogenous Variables

$U(1, I), \ldots, U(10, I)$	Stochastic variates for the ten behavioral equations for period I.

Status Variables

I	Time period subscript.
IYEAR(I)	Actual year for subscript I.
J	Equation number.
SUM(J,I)	Total of pseudorandom numbers.

Parameters

$B1, \ldots, B10$	Incremental change parameters for the first ten behavioral equations.

TABLE 7—*Continued.*

SE1, . . . ,SE10   Standard errors of estimate for behavioral equations 1 through 10. To be used as parameters in behavioral equation 11 to generate stochastic variates $U1, \ldots, U10$.

R1   Correlation between estimated residuals for equations 2 and 3. To be used as a parameter in equation 12 to generate multivariate stochastic variate $U(3,I)$.

Behavioral Equations

$$PDORG(I) = B1 * AT(I-1) + U(1,I) \tag{1}$$
$$PDE(I) = B2 * AT(I-1) + U(2,I) \tag{2}$$
$$PDL(I) = B3 * AT(I-1) + U(3,I) \tag{3}$$
$$EBORG(I) = B4 * PDT(I) + U(4,I) \tag{4}$$
$$AORG(I) = B5 * EBT(I) + U(5,I) \tag{5}$$
$$AE(I) = B6 * EBT(I) + U(6,I) \tag{6}$$
$$AL(I) = B7 * EBT(I) + U(7,I) \tag{7}$$
$$SCE(I) = B8 * AT(I) + U(8,I) \tag{8}$$
$$SCL(I) = B9 * AT(I) + U(9,I) \tag{9}$$
$$EORG(I) = B10 * SCT(I) + U(10,I) \tag{10}$$
$$U(J,I) = SE(J) * (SUM(J,I) - 6.0) \tag{11}$$
$$U(3,I) = R1 * U(2,I) + (SQRT(1 - R1**2)) * U(3,I) \tag{12}$$

Identities

$$PDT(I) = PDORG(I) + PDE(I) + PDL(I) + AT(I-1) \tag{13}$$
$$EBT(I) = EBORG(I) + PDT(I) \tag{14}$$
$$AT(I) = AORG(I) + AE(I) + AL(I) + EBT(I) \tag{15}$$
$$SCT(I) = SCE(I) + SCL(I) + AT(I) \tag{16}$$
$$ET(I) = EORG(I) + SCT(I) \tag{17}$$

Required Starting Information

AT(1)   Actual assembly total for year before first one to be simulated.

IYEAR(I)   Actual year.

B1, . . . , B10   Incremental change parameters for the first ten behavioral equations.

SE1, . . . , SE10   Standard errors of estimate for behavioral equations 1 through 10. To be used as parameters in behavioral equation 11 to generate stochastic variates.

TABLE 7—*Continued.*

$R1$ Correlation between estimated residuals for equations 2 and 3. To be used as a parameter in equation 12 to generate multivariate stochastic variate $U(3,I)$.

*Notation matches that used in the FORTRAN IV program in Appendix C and Diagram 7. It should be noted that elsewhere in the book the labels I, E, and AE are used to mean different things than they mean here. The context in which the terms are used and the specific definitions which are offered should eliminate any confusion.

The portion of the program generating stochastic disturbances is of special interest. These disturbances represent factors not otherwise contained in the incremental change from the prior step and are assumed to be independently distributed with zero mean and a constant but unknown finite variance which is independent from other variables in the equation.[2] Furthermore, it is assumed error terms are normally distributed and disturbances in each block are uncorrelated with those in preceding blocks.[3] When components of these random disturbances are also independent of those of other random disturbances in the same bloc, generation of stochastic variates follows directly from a general routine for a univariate normal distribution. When random disturbances are correlated with other random disturbances in the same block, a routine for generating a multivariate normal distribution for those stochastic variates is used.

To generate the univariate normal disturbances for each time period the Central Limit procedure is followed. First, twelve numbers are called and summed from the computer's pseudorandom number generator. The program then subtracts 6.0 from that sum and multiplies the result by the estimated standard error of estimate for that equation. The equation used is: $U_{it} = se_i(sum_{it} - 6.0)$, where U_{it} is the stochastic disturbance for the ith equation for the tth time period, and sum_{it} is the total of twelve pseudorandom numbers supplied by the computer. This routine is represented by behavioral equation 11 in the computer model.[4]

To generate the multivariate normal distribution, a second routine is used. Since only the estimated error terms of equations 2 and 3 turned out to be significantly correlated, the routine will be demonstrated for the instance when two variables are involved. In this case, one of the variables generated by the normal routine is transformed according to the following equation: $MU_{1t} = p \cdot U_{2t} + [\sqrt{(1-p^2)}] \cdot U_{1t}$, where MU_{1t} is the multivariate disturbance for the tth time period; U_{1t} is the normal disturbance for the tth time period; U_{2t} is the other normal disturbance for the tth time period; and p is the estimated correlation coefficient between the two disturbances. This routine is represented by behavioral equation 12 in the computer model.[5]

Estimation of Parameters

The first step in the estimation of parameters was collection of data for the 1951-69 period. Data were collected from the *Official Records of the World Health Organization.* The breakdown of the budget total at each step into organizational, leadership, and external increments involved a careful reading of documents and a coding of data into appropriate categories. This procedure was surprisingly straightforward, and when a second coder performed a reliability check on a randomly selected sample of 20 percent of the years, no differences in coding were discovered.[6]

A total of twenty-one parameters was estimated for the twelve specified behavioral equations. Parameters $B1, \ldots, B10$, incremental change parameters for the first ten behavioral equations, were estimated by regression coefficients when variables were regressed on each other in accordance with the specification of rules. Parameters $SE1, \ldots, SE10$, used to generate stochastic disturbances in behavioral equation 11, were estimated by the standard error of estimate from the same process which generated the estimates for parameters $B1, \ldots, B10$. Parameter $R1$, used in behavioral equation 12 to generate the multivariate stochastic variable $U(3,1)$, was estimated by the product moment correlation coefficient when estimated residuals for behavioral equations two and three were correlated.

The estimation procedure followed precedents set in Chapter 5, the basic estimation technique being least squares, with the intercept forced through the origin.[7] In the event this procedure yielded estimates with autocorrelated residuals, the generalized least squares technique was used, with the intercept

TABLE 8 PARAMETERS FOR BEHAVIORAL EQUATIONS IN MODEL

Equation Number	Regressor	Regressand	b (S.E.) F Test Value	r^2	S.E. Estimate / Mean	Durbin-Watson	p	Correlation of Error Terms with Error Terms in Prior Equations 1	2	3	4	5	6	7	8	9	p
1[a]	$AT(I{-}1)$	$PDORG(I)$	.0888 (.0042) 446.01	.9612	487 / 44	2.73	>.01										
2[a]	$AT(I{-}1)$	$PDE(I)$	.0143 (.0056) 6.49	.2651	650 / 19	2.17	>.01	.01									>.01
3[a]	$AT(I{-}1)$	$PDL(I)$	.0131 (.0056) 5.52	.2347	645 / 105	1.48	>.01	.09	.65								$r_{23} <.01$
4[a]	$PDT(I)$	$EBORG(I)$	.0055 (.0049) 1.24	.0644	638 / -142	1.90	>.01	-.19	.44	.13							all >.01
5[b]	$EBT(I)$	$AORG(I)$	-.0003 (.0012) .07	.0040	221 / -42	2.17	>.01	-.35	-.09	-.11	-.05						all >.01

6[a]	EBT(I) AE(I)	.0007 (.0010) .54	.0293	126 20	1.34 >.01	.36	-.08	-.13	-.01	.05					all >.01
7[a]	EBT(I) AL(I)	.0028 (.0036) .60	.0321	473 49	1.88 >.01	.08	-.08	.11	-.04	.04	-.01				all >.01
8[a]	AT(I) SCE(I)	.0153 (.0042) 13.42	.4272	543 160	1.88 >.01	.14	-.23	.00	-.43	.13	-.04	-.04	.41		all >.01
9[a]	AT(I) SCL(I)	.0050 (.0015) 10.92	.3776	197 3	1.67 >.01	.04	.25	.21	.40	-.05	-.14	-.14	-.16	-.19	all >.01
10[b]	SCT(I) EORG(I)	-.0131 (.0034) 15.03	.4692	198 -42	1.27 >.01	-.32	.16	-.22	.24	-.10	-.11	-.24	-.30	-.30	all >.01

[a]The LS technique with the intercept forced through the origin was used for estimation.
[b]The GLS technique with the intercept forced through the origin was used for estimation.

again being forced through zero. The Durbin-Watson d statistic was used to determine autocorrelation of residuals. The Pearson Product Moment Correlation Coefficient and David's levels of significance were used to examine independence of error terms in various equations. The results of the estimation procedure are presented in Table 8.[8] The least squares procedure was used to estimate sixteen parameters, generalized least squares was used to estimate four parameters, and ordinary least squares was used to estimate the other parameter ($R1$). It should be noted that none of the estimated error terms are significantly autocorrelated or correlated across blocks. Furthermore, the only correlated error terms within blocks are between equations 2 and 3. While the estimation procedure does not offer an optimal solution to all problems, on balance it appears to be adequate.

There are two major disadvantages to the estimates. First, error terms do not have a mean of zero. This situation forced a decision on whether or not to add the mean to equation 11. The decision not to do so allows for a more theoretically pleasing model. Second, some of the estimates of regression coefficients (equations 4-7) result in low r^2 and F values. In those cases, there was very little linear increment, and changes are considered exogenous and random. Since the computer model has a procedure for generating random disturbances which utilizes the standard error of estimate from those equations, it was decided that the estimates would be used. However, there are possible specification errors in these equations, and future research should examine them more closely.

Validity of the Model

There is little agreement on how to validate a computer model.[9] The crucial test is the model's ability to predict actual behavior in a future time period.[10] Because the model was developed with only knowledge of the period from 1951 to 1969, it seems reasonable to examine its validity by asking about its ability to predict total expenditure figures after 1969. At this writing, expenditure data for WHO are available for 1970, 1971, 1972, 1973, and 1974. Two basic questions will be asked about the computer model: how accurately does it predict the actual WHO expenditure figure for each of those years, and is the fit provided by the computer model better than the fit of a naive alternative model?

To obtain the predictions, one thousand runs of the computer model were made for 1970-80. Parameters estimated from 1951-69 data and the actual assembly total for 1969 were used. The pseudorandom number generator produced a different set of stochastic disturbances in each run. The model used approximately 2,200,000 different pseudorandom numbers and generated a reasonable estimate of the range of probable impact of stochastic disturbances. The mean estimate was accepted as the predicted expenditure total, and the standard deviation was used as an estimate of the probable range of variation.[11]

The actual expenditure totals for 1969-74, mean predicted expenditure totals for 1970-80, and the standard deviations of the model predictions for 1970-80 are presented in Table 9.[12] In percentage terms, the mean prediction for 1970 was off by 2.6 percent, for 1971 by 3.3 percent, for 1972 by 2.6 percent, for 1973 by 3.0 percent, and for 1974 by 2.2 percent. Even though the model overestimated expenditures for each year, it nevertheless provides reasonable estimates.

TABLE 9   FIT OF COMPUTER MODEL ($000)

Year	Actual Expenditures	Mean Predicted Expenditures	s of 1000 Model Predictions
1969	$ 61,687		
1970	67,190	$ 68,904	$ 1,663
1971	75,196	77,664	2,315
1972	85,218	87,459	3,044
1973	95,547	98,415	3,719
1974	108,406	110,808	4,373
1975		124,733	5,294
1976		140,395	6,155
1977		158,146	7,055
1978		178,050	8,071
1979		200,417	9,186
1980		225,600	10,475

Would a simpler, self-contained, naive model provide as good a fit?[13] For an answer, the predictive ability of a simple cell model (First Order Markov Model) was considered.[14] This model can be stated symbolically as follows: $Y_t = a + bY_{t-1}$, where Y_t is the expenditure total for a given year; a is an intercept; and b is a fixed mean percentage. Data for 1951-69 were used to estimate parameters, using the ordinary least squares technique.[15] The actual 1969 expenditure total was used as a starting point, and the model was allowed to move forward in a self-contained manner, generating expenditure totals for 1970-80. The results are presented in Table 10.

TABLE 10   FIT OF SIMPLE CELL MODEL ($000)

Year	Actual Expenditures	Computer Model Mean Predicted Expenditures	Cell Model Predictions
1969	$ 61,687		
1970	67,190	$ 68,904	$ 69,664
1971	75,196	77,664	78,665
1972	85,218	87,459	88,817
1973	95,547	98,415	100,269
1974	108,406	110,808	113,188
1975		124,733	127,762
1976		140,395	144,203
1977		158,146	162,750
1978		178,050	183,673
1979		200,417	207,276
1980		225,600	231,903

Predictions of this simple cell model were off by 3.7 percent for 1970, 4.6 percent for 1971, 4.2 percent for 1972, 4.9 percent for 1973, and 4.4 percent for 1974. In each case, the computer model was more accurate than the simple cell model. In predicting the $46,719,000 increase in expenditures during the five-year (1970-74) period, the computer model was off by 5.1 percent, while the simple cell model was off by 10.2 percent. Given the nature of budgetary data and the well-known predictive ability of the cell model, the predictive ability of the computer model is impressive.[16]

Summary and Conclusions

The computer model of the budget process in WHO contains twelve behavioral equations and five identities. There are behavioral equations generating organizational changes at the proposal development, executive body, assembly, and implementation steps; external and leadership changes are provided at the proposal development, assembly, and supplementary change steps. Ten behavioral equations provide for a stochastic disturbance and incremental changes from the prior step in time in the budget process. Two behavioral equations generate stochastic disturbances. Five identities add generated increments to the budget total from the prior step and form a budget total for the step in question. The model is self-contained and can be run forward to any point in time. Only the stochastic disturbances, based on the pseudorandom number generator in the computer, are exogenous variables. The model is a reasonable representation of the WHO budget process since it provides a good fit to actual WHO expenditure totals for 1970-74 and a better fit than a plausible alternative cell model.

7

Counterfactual Analysis

To be theoretical in nature, the ranking [of variable sets] would have to specify how much more potent each set of variables is than those below it on [the] scale, and the variables themselves would have to be causally linked to specific forms . . . of behavior.

—James N. Rosenau

The model is a simulation containing variables and statements relating the variables.[1] It can be executed on a computer, and the results indicate what will happen, given the circumstances specified in the model. Alternative results can be obtained by altering values of variables, or specifications of relationships, and running the model again. In this chapter, sensitivity analysis of this type will be used to examine the difference it would have made if steps in the policy-making process, types of inputs, and policy-making rules had not been included in the expenditure calculations.

Research Design

In order to evaluate the steps in the policy-making process, types of inputs, and policy-making rules, a series of pretest-posttest experiments will be undertaken.[2] The pretest-posttest research design can be diagramed as follows:

$$O_1 \quad X \quad O_2$$

where O_1 is the pretreatment observation; X is a treatment; and O_2 is the post-treatment observation.

For analysis, the O_1 will be the 1969 expenditure total for a run of the basic computer model; X will be the elimination of relevant incremental coefficients and random disturbances; and O_2 will be the 1969 expenditure total for the run after relevant changes have been made in the computer model. Since each experiment will be replicated one thousand times, analysis will involve a comparison of one thousand observations before and after treatment. The same set of potential random disturbances utilized in the basic model will be used, but salient factors to be examined will be eliminated by setting incremental coefficients and standard errors of estimate for relevant equations to zero.

Even though the pretest-posttest design is generally not considered a good laboratory research design, for this problem with the computer model it is the strongest possible design. To illustrate this point, let us consider challenges to experimental validity which Campbell and Stanley advance as rival plausible hypotheses.[3] Challenges from what they call history, maturation, testing, instrumentation, experimental mortality, interaction of selection and maturation, intra-session history, interaction of testing and treatment, interaction of selection and treatment, reactive effects of experimental arrangements, and multiple-treatment interference are controlled by the closed, self-contained computer model itself. Selection is controlled by the research design which uses identical cases before and after treatment. Statistical regression is controlled to the extent that the pseudorandom number generator of the computer does not have a bias in generating random numbers.[4]

In most research efforts, the posttest only control group design would be considered a better research design.[5] It can be diagramed in the following manner:

$$R \quad X \quad O$$

$$R \qquad O$$

In this design, randomization is used to control confounding effects and to eliminate sources of invalidity.

It would have been possible to use the posttest only control group design by utilizing a different set of random numbers for the treatment group and control group, thereby generating independent samples. However, since the pretest-posttest design controlled all probable confounding factors, there is no advantage to using the posttest only control group design. Indeed, there is even a disadvantage. To the extent that the pseudorandom number generator exhibits a bias in identification of random numbers to be used in treatment and control groups, the two groups have not been equated through randomization. Because the pretest-posttest design does not allow the possibility of even this slight amount of "noise" in the experiment, it appears to be a slightly better design for our study.

In analyzing the pretest-posttest experiments, the focus will be on the difference between pretest and posttest expenditures for 1969. This is interpreted as the net effect of the factor in question. The total of the annual projections for the entire 1951-69 period will also be examined. The difference in totals for the 1951-69 period will be interpreted as the net effect of the factor from 1951 to 1969.

Because of custom, a correlated t value for examination of the difference between means will be reported.[6] For those with interest in testing the null hypothesis that there is no difference in means, the significance using the two-tailed test at the .01 level will be reported. However, with an n as large as one thousand, statistical significance is not as important as substantive significance, indicated in this case by the absolute value of the difference.

Steps in the Policy-Making Process

In order to evaluate the impact of steps in the policy-making process, the model was run one thousand times for 1951 to 1969 without each step. The estimated expenditures for each of those runs are plotted in Chart 1, together with the estimated expenditure total for the basic model. As seen from the chart, trends in expenditure totals are similar, except for the estimates without the proposal development step. The elimination of submodels without a compound multiplier effect (supplementary change and implementation submodels) produces a result only slightly different from the basic model. The other submodels, which have a compound multiplier effect, because their product is used in calculations for subsequent years, differ most markedly from the basic model.

Detailed results of the runs are presented in Table 11. The data demonstrate that the real growth in the simulated expenditure total was accounted for by the proposal

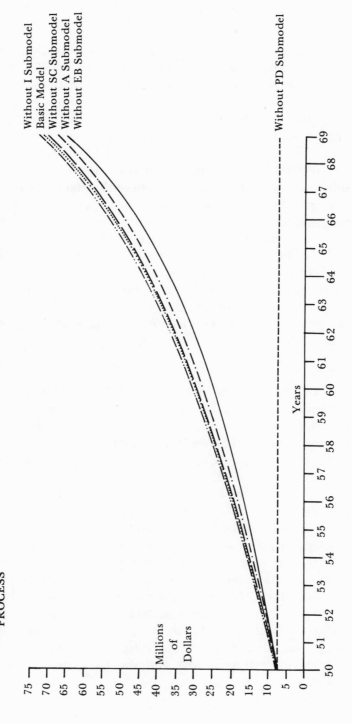

CHART 1 MEAN EXPENDITURES FOR 1951-69 FOR SENSITIVITY ANALYSIS OF STEPS IN THE POLICY-MAKING PROCESS

development step. The model without this step differed by -87.6 percent from the basic model in regard to the 1969 projection. The executive body had a positive impact, with a -9.6 percent difference when the model without this step was compared with the basic model. The assembly step also had a positive impact, with the 1969 expenditure estimate differing by -6.3 percent from the one for the basic model. The data also reflect the slightly positive impact of the supplementary change submodel, with the difference between the model without this step and the basic model being -2.0 percent for the 1969 projection. The implementation submodel has a slightly negative impact, with the difference between the model without this step and the basic model being 1.3 percent for the 1969 estimate. It is interesting to note the standard deviation of estimates is small when the proposal development submodel is dropped. This demonstrates that most of the impact of exogenous disturbances is located in the proposal development submodel.

Inputs

In order to evaluate, one by one, the impact of different types of inputs into the policy-making process, the model was run one thousand times for 1951-69 without each type of input. The mean expenditures for each experiment for 1951-69 are plotted in Chart 2, together with the expenditure totals for the basic model. As seen from the chart, the trend for the model without organizational factors is almost level and differs greatly from the trend for the basic model. Trends for models without external and leadership factors are almost identical, with both differing greatly from the basic model. These two sets of inputs have had an almost identical impact over time.

The detailed estimates are presented in Table 12. The difference for 1969 between the model without organizational factors and the basic model was -80.9 percent. The difference for 1969 between the model without external factors and the basic model was -24.2 percent. The difference between the model without leadership factors and the basic model was -23.9 percent.

TABLE 11   SENSITIVITY ANALYSIS OF STEPS IN THE POLICY-MAKING PROCESS ($000)

	1969 Mean	1969 Standard Deviation	1951-69 Total of Means	Comparisons with Basic Model			
				1969 Difference	1951-69 Difference Total of Means	1969 t value	1969 two tailed p (df=999)
Basic Model	$71,607	$28,505	$574,661				
Without PD Submodel	8,863	3,891	157,047	-$62,744	-$417,614	-74.01	<.01
Without EB Submodel	64,749	23,926	535,973	-6,858	-38,688	-18.57	<.01
Without A Submodel	67,097	25,630	548,606	-4,510	-26,055	-13.91	<.01
Without SC Submodel	70,175	27,951	563,169	-1,432	-11,492	-57.68	<.01
Without I Submodel	72,562	28,885	582,282	955	7,621	70.52	<.01

TABLE 12   SENSITIVITY ANALYSIS OF INPUTS ($000)

	1969 Mean	1969 Standard Deviation	1951-69 Total of Means	Comparisons with Basic Model			
				1969 Difference	1951-69 Difference Total of Means	1969 t value	1969 two tailed p (df=999)
Basic Model	$71,607	$28,505	$574,661				
Without ORG Factors	13,669	7,734	200,119	-$57,938	-$374,542	-80.32	<.01
Without E Factors	54,299	17,386	472,139	-17,308	-102,522	-37.43	<.01
Without L Factors	54,507	15,154	476,730	-17,100	-97,931	-24.07	<.01

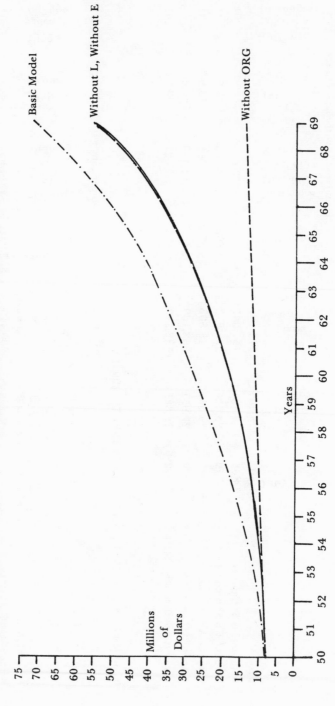

CHART 2   MEAN EXPENDITURES FOR 1951-69 FOR SENSITIVITY ANALYSIS OF INPUTS

Policy-Making Rules

In order to evaluate the impact of policy-making rules, the model was run one thousand times for 1951-69 without each rule. The estimated expenditures for 1951-69 are plotted in Chart 3, together with the expenditure total for the basic model. As can be seen from the chart, equation 1, providing for organizational increments at the proposal development step, is the most important equation. Also important are: equation 2, providing for external increments in the proposal development submodel; 3, providing for leadership increments in the proposal development submodel; 4, providing for organizational increments in the executive body submodel; and 7, providing for leadership increments at the assembly step.

Detailed results of the runs are presented in Table 13. It is striking to note the following differences from the basic model: equation 1, -79.3 percent; equation 2, -22.0 percent; equation 3, -18.9 percent; equation 4, -9.6 percent; equation 7, -5.6 percent. None of the other equations differ by more than ±1.5 percent. Interestingly, the standard deviation of estimates is small when the equation providing for organizational factors at the proposal development step is dropped, demonstrating the impact of exogenous factors contained in this policy-making rule.

Summary and Conclusions

An attempt has been made in this chapter to evaluate the impact of steps in the policy-making process, types of inputs, and policy-making rules. By far, the greatest impact was made by the proposal development step, with only minor impact being exhibited by other steps. Furthermore, organizational factors had the major effect on the growth of expenditures, while external and leadership factors made a substantial impact. The organizational factors rule at the proposal development step was isolated as being by far the major rule in the entire budget process, with four other rules having a noticeable impact on the expenditures during the nineteen years under examination.

CHART 3   MEAN EXPENDITURES FOR 1951-69 FOR SENSITIVITY ANALYSIS OF POLICY-MAKING RULES

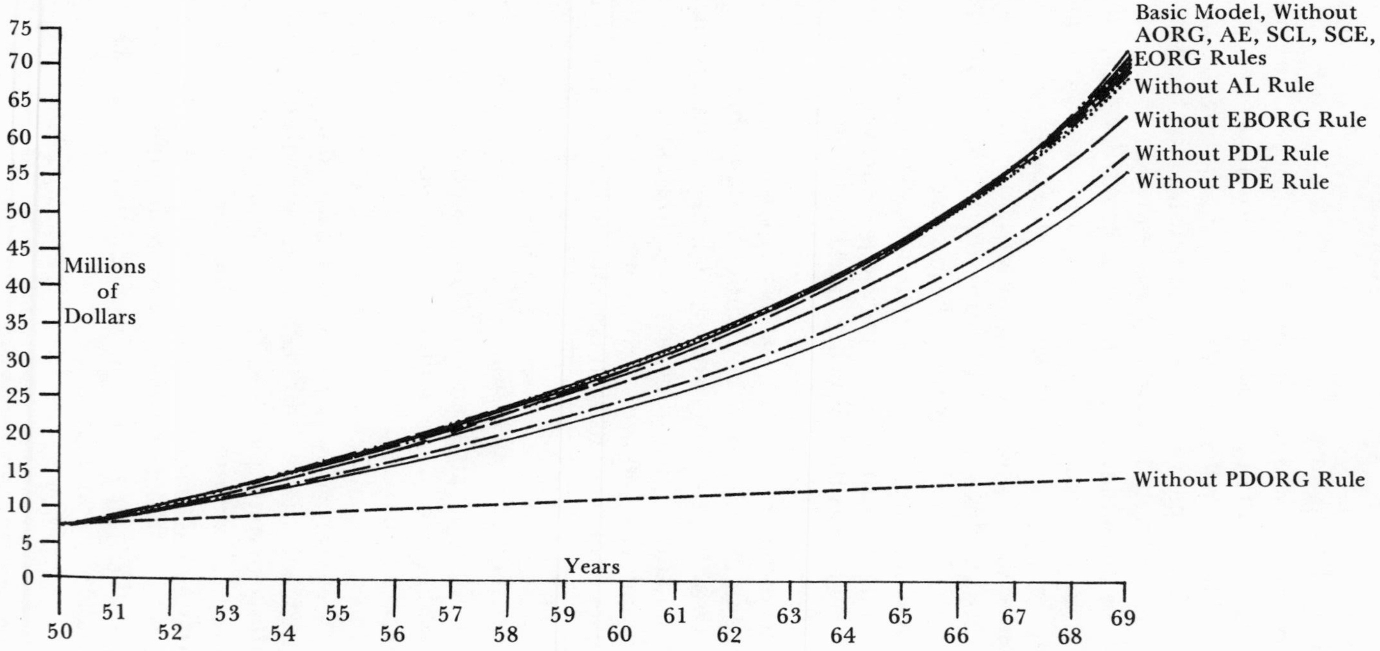

TABLE 13   SENSITIVITY ANALYSIS OF POLICY-MAKING RULES ($000)

	Equation Number	1969 Mean	1969 Standard Deviation	Total of 1951-69 Means	Comparisons with Basic Model			
					1969 Difference	Difference Total of 1951-69 Means	1969 t value	1969 two tailed p (df=999)
Basic Model		$71,607	$28,505	$574,661				
Without PDORG	1	14,808	9,124	208,217	-$56,799	-$366,444	-86.44	<.01
Without PDE	2	55,878	17,858	483,850	-15,729	-90,811	-34.90	<.01
Without PDL	3	58,040	17,298	499,011	-13,567	-75,650	-20.93	<.01
Without EBORG	4	64,749	23,926	535,973	-6,858	-38,688	-18.57	<.01
Without AORG	5	72,048	28,322	577,308	441	2,647	3.32	<.01
Without AE	6	70,653	28,192	569,239	-954	-5,422	-13.17	<.01
Without AL	7	67,572	26,087	551,273	-4,035	-23,388	-14.35	<.01
Without SCE	8	70,526	28,091	565,986	-1,081	-8,675	-51.39	<.01
Without SCL	9	71,257	28,365	571,844	-350	-2,817	-46.23	<.01
Without EORG	10	72,562	28,885	582,282	955	7,621	70.52	<.01

8

Alternative Futures

---

*. . . it is increasingly clear that the global order will be evolved
out of global experience. . . .*

—*Chadwick F. Alger*

An attempt will be made in this chapter to examine possible
futures for the World Health Organization.[1] Simplifying
assumptions will be made about the future, and ramifications
for 1970-80 will be examined by the computer model. If the
assumptions contained in a scenario are accepted, then the
projected expenditure total will result. A discussion of general
considerations regarding the future will be followed by the
presentation of scenarios to be simulated. The research design
guiding analysis will be discussed, and results of the computer
simulation will then be reported. Finally, speculation on the
likely occurrence of each scenario will be provided.

General Considerations

In the development of plausible futures for WHO, an
assumption will be made that the future will involve an
extension, or slight modification, of past behavioral practices.
The computer model describes how expenditures were arrived
at in the past, and there is no reason to believe a drastic change
will occur during the 1970-80 era. Indeed, there is every reason
to believe the future will develop through a series of
incremental changes from the past.

Therefore, before proceeding further, five obvious
forecasting strategies that will not be used are considered. First,
no projections based on rational calculations of needs in the
health area will be made. No such rational calculations have
been made in the past, and there is no indication they will be
made in the near future. Indeed, the needs are so great, and the
willingness of developed countries to provide multilateral

technical assistance is so limited, it is doubtful the expenditure total for WHO will ever be the result of calculations designed to fulfill the world's needs in the health field.

Second, no projections will be made which state the WHO budget as a fixed percent of the world's GNP. There has apparently been no such relationship in the past, and there is little reason to believe there will be one in the near future. The so-called "one percent goal" for aid-flows to lesser developed countries has been consistently ignored in the past, and it is probable that it will be ignored as a strategy in the future.[2]

Third, no projections based on potential major scientific or technological breakthroughs will be made. It is hard to imagine that the 1970s will produce any "medical miracles" with a greater impact on WHO than those occurring during the past two decades.

Fourth, no projections based on the impact of possible major disasters will be made. In the past, natural disasters have not significantly affected the WHO budget total, and there is little reason to believe they will in the near future. It seems reasonable to assume natural disasters will be handled, as in the past, by major powers on an ad hoc basis.

Fifth, no projections will be made which assume a step change in policy-making rules during 1970-80. Such a step change would reflect a drastic and sudden alteration in the political circumstances surrounding the decisions on the WHO budget total.[3] It is difficult to estimate if and when such a sudden change would take place.

However, just because no projections are based on these factors (exogenous to the computer model), it does not mean they are totally ignored in the projections. The impact of some of these items could be absorbed by organizational slack contained in usual incremental changes. The impact of other items may be included in stochastic disturbances generated by the model. As long as assumptions regarding the distribution of disturbances and size of standard errors are reasonable ones, the range of variation generated by repeated replications of each scenario should contain an adequate estimate of the possible impact of exogenous factors. Indeed, the computer model adequately handles two devaluations of the dollar in this manner.

As in the past, the major influence on future expenditures will undoubtedly be international politics. The most salient dimension of politics, for the determination of the WHO budget total, is the so-called "north-south" or "rich nation-poor nation" conflict. In WHO, this conflict is between a loose alignment of lesser developed countries, organized elsewhere as the Group of Seventy-Seven, and a loose coalition of developed countries, organized around the Geneva Group.[4] The conflict is over allocation of resources and focuses upon the WHO expenditure total.

Participants in this struggle understand that the complexity of the WHO budget process means larger problems are broken down into manageable subproblems, which are faced and solved sequentially, as in the computer model. Therefore, they develop general strategies which provide them with basic bargaining positions which can be used throughout the policy-making process. In the foreseeable future, these strategies will be the result of choices regarding the percentage requested for organizational factors in the proposal development step and of types of input factors allowed to influence the expenditure total.

As Chapter 7 clearly demonstrated, a crucial action in the WHO budget process relates to the incremental change in what has been labeled organizational factors at the proposal development step. The importance of this action has not escaped policy-makers in WHO, and for a few years the World Health Assembly gave the Director-General instructions on the "general order of magnitude" to follow in arriving at the organizational factors' increment at the proposal development step.[5] For example, the following was adopted by the World Health Assembly in 1967:

[The Twentieth World Health Assembly] recommends to the Director-General that as a general orientation in preparing his proposed programme and budget estimates for 1969 he should, taking account of the views expressed by delegates during the discussions at the Twentieth World Health Assembly, propose an increase in the programme such as will give a budget increase of an order of magnitude of about 9 percent, provided that no unusual and unforeseen developments occur which would result in additional resources being required by the organization. . . .[6]

In the past few years, this requested increment has turned out to be approximately 9 percent (the estimate used in the computer model for $B1$ is 8.88 percent). However, representatives of most lesser developed countries prefer at least an 11 percent increment, and representatives of most major powers appear to prefer a 7 percent increment for these factors. The 9 percent order of magnitude recommendation has been a compromise. In the development of scenarios for the future, 7.0 percent, 8.88 percent, and 11.0 percent increments will be provided for organizational factors at the proposal development step.

Furthermore, in the past, each type of input factor (organizational, external, and leadership) has been included in calculations in the WHO budget process. However, there is currently some debate over whether this practice should be continued. There now appears to be pressure from certain major powers to include external and leadership factors within the normal organizational growth pattern represented in the organizational increments. There is little debate over whether there should be normal organizational growth; although, as noted earlier, there is debate over how large some of the organizational increments should be.

There may be a change in the way the input factors are handled in the WHO budget process. In order to examine the ramifications of these probable changes, four combinations of input factors will be built into scenarios: organizational factors; organizational and external factors; organizational and leadership factors; and organizational, external, and leadership factors.

Alternative Scenarios

What would be the result if the organizational increment in the proposal development step were set at 7 percent, and only organizational increments were used in the model's calculations? For an answer, the following scenario will be simulated.

Scenario 1: Expenditure totals between 1970 and 1980 will be the result of the pattern of events contained in the basic computer model, with the organizational increment in the proposal development submodel set at 7 percent and only organizational rules being used in budgetary calculations.

This scenario will produce the lowest expenditure total of any scenario to be considered. It represents a major victory for those who desire a cutback in the budget growth of WHO. It involves the elimination of special consideration for external and leadership factors and reduction of normal organization growth. Since this scenario involves a major cut in the WHO growth rate, its acceptance would probably alienate many representatives of lesser developed countries. Scenario one could probably come about only as a compromise resulting from a major crisis concerning the status of the economic and social program of the entire United Nations system. It is one of the least likely of the scenarios considered.

The second scenario also allows for a 7 percent organizational increment at the proposal development step, but it provides for use of organizational and external factors in budgetary calculations.

Scenario 2: Expenditure totals between 1970 and 1980 will be the result of the pattern of events contained in the basic computer model, with the organizational increment in the proposal development submodel set at 7 percent and only organizational and external rules being used in budgetary calculations.

This scenario also represents a victory for policy-makers attempting to slow down the growth rate of the expenditure total. The adoption of this strategy would be contested vigorously by representatives of lesser developed countries.

The third scenario provides for a 7 percent organizational increment at the proposal development step and use of organizational and leadership factors in budgetary calculations.

Scenario 3: Expenditure totals between 1970 and 1980 will be the result of the pattern of events contained in the basic computer model, with the organizational increment in the proposal development submodel set at 7 percent and only organizational and leadership rules being used in budgetary calculations.

This scenario would probably result from the same general circumstances, and produce the same general results, as scenario two. In fact, scenarios two and three represent the same general type of compromise. In each case, the organizational increment in the proposal development step is lowered to 7 percent, and one other set of factors is eliminated. However, it is unlikely this scenario would be maintained for any length of time. Representatives of the United States would probably veto use of leadership increments, and the situation would quickly change to that described by scenario one. If the Director-General then again added the use of external factors, the situation would be described by scenario two.

The fourth scenario provides for a 7 percent organizational increment at the proposal development step and use of all inputs.

Scenario 4: Expenditure totals between 1970 and 1980 will be the result of the pattern of events contained in the basic computer model, with the organizational increment in the proposal development submodel set at 7 percent.

This scenario would represent a victory for those concerned with a slowing down of the growth rate in WHO. The change to this scenario, from present practices, would be a highly contested one since the rate used for the organizational increment at the proposal development step is a major issue.

The fifth scenario provides for continuation of the current rate of approximately 9 percent for the organizational increment at the proposal development step, and use of only organizational factors in budgetary calculations.

Scenario 5: Expenditure totals between 1970 and 1980 will be the result of the pattern of events contained in the basic computer model, with the organizational increment in the proposal development submodel set at 8.88 percent and only organizational rules being used in budgetary calculations.

This scenario again represents a victory for those desiring cuts in the growth of the WHO expenditure total. It is the most likely of the scenarios which involve elimination of external and leadership factors since it does not also involve a percentage change for organizational factors at the proposal development step.

The sixth scenario provides for continuation of the current rate of approximately 9 percent for the organizational increment at the proposal development step, and use of organizational and external factors in budgetary calculations.

Scenario 6: Expenditure totals between 1970 and 1980 will be the result of the pattern of events contained in the basic computer model, with the organizational increment in the proposal development submodel set at 8.88 percent and only organizational and external rules being used in budgetary calculations.

This scenario represents a minor victory for policy-makers trying to curb the growth of the WHO expenditure total. It could be brought about quietly in a de facto manner, unlike the change in the organizational factors' increment at the proposal development step. Since leadership increments have always required the cooperation of the Director-General and representatives of the United States, it would appear that either party would have unilateral ability to eliminate leadership increments. Scenario six appears to be the most likely of the changes from past practices; and indeed, there is already some indication that this strategy is currently being used in WHO.

The seventh scenario provides for an organizational increment of approximately 9 percent at the proposal development step, and use of organizational and leadership factors in budgetary calculations.

Scenario 7: Expenditure totals between 1970 and 1980 will be the result of the pattern of events contained in the basic computer model, with the organizational increment in the proposal development submodel set at 8.88 percent and only organizational and leadership rules being used in budgetary calculations.

This scenario represents a minor victory for those attempting to slow down growth of the expenditure total. It could appease those desiring a cut in the growth rate and can be accomplished in a quiet, de facto, easily reversible manner by the Director-General. The problem with this scenario is that it is unlikely it would continue for long. Once the Director-General initiated scenario seven, representatives from the United States would probably veto use of leadership increments, and the situation would quickly change to that described by scenario five. If the Director-General then added back the use of external factors, the situation would be described by scenario six.

The eighth scenario involves extension of the past pattern of events.

Scenario 8: Expenditure totals between 1970 and 1980 will be the result of the pattern of events contained in the basic computer model, with the organizational increment in the proposal development submodel set at 8.88 percent.

This scenario is a plausible one because it represents a logical compromise between the position of most lesser developed countries which calls for a faster growth rate, and the position of certain major powers which calls for a slower growth rate. It has the advantage of representing the status quo and requires no changes in past practices.

The ninth scenario provides for an 11 percent organizational increment at the proposal development step, and use of only organizational factors in budgetary calculations.

Scenario 9: Expenditure totals between 1970 and 1980 will be the result of the pattern of events contained in the basic computer model, with the organizational increment in the proposal development submodel set at 11 percent and only organizational rules being used in budgetary calculations.

This scenario represents a possible compromise between representatives of lesser developed and developed countries. It would give developed countries the sought-after reduction in the growth rate because elimination of external and leadership factors would more than compensate for the increase in the organizational increment at the proposal development step. At the same time, it would give lesser developed countries a symbolic victory because the highly visible organizational increment at the proposal development step would be increased. This scenario would also have the virtue of greatly simplifying the current complex set of policy-making rules, replacing them with a simpler 11 percent growth rule and three minor organizational increment rules.

The tenth scenario provides for an 11 percent organizational increment at the proposal development step and use of organizational and external factors in budgetary calculations.

Scenario 10: Expenditure totals between 1970 and 1980 will be the result of the pattern of events contained in the basic computer model, with the organizational increment in the proposal development submodel set at 11 percent and only organizational and external rules being used in budgetary calculations.

This scenario will produce approximately the same results as scenario eight which represents the past pattern of events. It could come about by lesser developed countries raising the organizational factors increment at the proposal development step and major powers eliminating leadership additions. This scenario, which would essentially preserve the status quo, could represent the highest budget level which will actually be reached because the United States can be expected to eliminate leadership additions if the organizational increment at the proposal development step is increased to 11 percent.

The next scenario provides for an 11 percent organizational increment at the proposal development step, and use of organizational and leadership factors in budgetary calculations.

Scenario 11: Expenditure totals between 1970 and 1980 will be the result of the pattern of events contained in the basic computer model, with the organizational increment in the proposal development submodel set at 11 percent and only organizational and leadership rules being used in budgetary calculations.

This scenario will produce about the same results as scenarios eight and ten; it will maintain the expenditure pattern of the status quo. The scenario could result from a situation where lesser developed countries raise the organizational growth rate; and the Director-General, worried about the reaction of certain developed countries, decides to neutralize the change by absorbing external factors in organizational slack, eliminating the use of external rules. However, this scenario is unlikely to be maintained since the United States would probably then eliminate use of leadership increments, and the situation would revert to the one described by scenario nine. If the Director-General then reversed his action and started using external rules again, there would be a scenario ten situation.

The last scenario provides for an 11 percent organizational increment at the proposal development step and the use of all types of inputs.

Scenario 12: Expenditure totals between 1970 and 1980 will be the result of the pattern of events contained in the basic computer model, with the organizational increment in the proposal development submodel set at 11 percent.

This scenario will produce the highest expenditure total. It represents a major victory for lesser developed countries and could come about only as a result of a major change in the position of certain major powers, an unlikely event in the foreseeable future. If the United States does not change its current strategy toward WHO, it will undoubtedly eliminate leadership increments, and the situation would revert to the one described by scenario ten.

There are a number of other scenarios which could be considered. For example, a series of scenarios providing for a 6 percent, 8 percent, 10 percent, or 12 percent organizational increment at the proposal development step could be considered. However, in the author's opinion the twelve scenarios discussed here probably represent the most likely alternatives while at the same time adequately representing the range of likely future expenditures.

Research Design

An overview of analysis to be undertaken is presented in Table 14. (Throughout this chapter and in Appendix D, the

TABLE 14   ANALYSIS OF ALTERNATIVE FUTURES

Input Factors

		ORG	ORG,E	ORG,L	ORG, E, L
	7%	Scenario 1	Scenario 2	Scenario 3	Scenario 4
	8.9%	Scenario 5	Scenario 6	Scenario 7	Scenario 8
	11%	Scenario 9	Scenario 10	Scenario 11	Scenario 12

Organizational Factors Increment at Proposal Development Step

8.88 percent projections are listed as 8.9 percent projections to facilitate a smoother presentation. For the same reason, ORG represents organizational factors; E represents external factors; and L represents leadership factors.) Because of interest in the range of variation in estimates, one thousand replications of each scenario will be carried out. For each scenario the random number generator will be started at a different place, producing independent samples.

As in the past, the trend will be plotted for each set of projections. A detailed analysis for 1980 will then be performed. In this analysis, the focus will be on the means and standard deviations of projections. Total expenditures for the eleven-year period for each scenario will also be examined.

For those interested in tests of significance, a fixed effects two-way analysis of variance model will be used to calculate an overall F value to test the null hypothesis that there are no differences between the means of the twelve scenarios.[7] If the null hypothesis is rejected, an examination will be conducted of all possible post hoc comparisons, using the t test to determine which pairwise comparisons differ significantly in regard to the means. Since there is an equal n of one thousand in each cell, there will be no test for homogeneity of variance.[8] However, with an n as large as one thousand, tests of significance are not very meaningful.

Results

The projected mean expenditure estimates for each scenario for 1970-80 are plotted in Chart 4. Estimates for 1980 ranged from a low of approximately $135 million to a high of about $280 million. There appear to be three major groupings of scenarios: (1) scenarios two (7 percent, ORG and E), three (7 percent, ORG and L), and five (8.9 percent, ORG); (2) scenarios four (7 percent, ORG, E, and L), six (8.9 percent, ORG and E), seven (8.9 percent, ORG and L), and nine (11 percent, ORG); and (3) scenarios eight (8.9 percent, ORG, E, and L), ten (11 percent, ORG and E), and eleven (11 percent, ORG and L). Scenarios one (7 percent, ORG) and twelve (11 percent, ORG, E, and L) appear to be quite distinct. Actual expenditures for 1970-74 appear to follow most closely the pattern of scenarios in the second group (scenarios four, six, seven, and nine).

CHART 4   PROJECTION OF ALTERNATIVE FUTURES FROM 1970
TO 1980

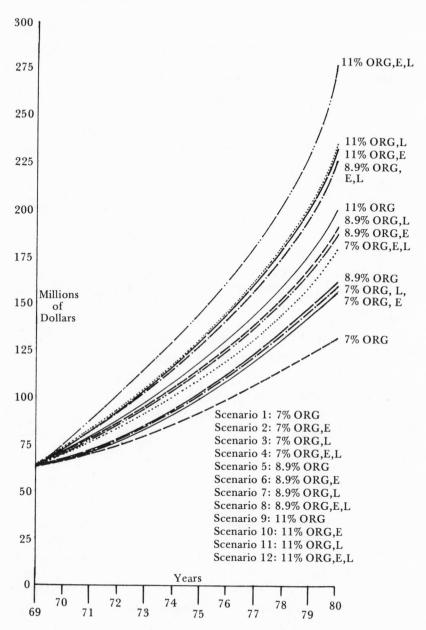

Details of the projections for 1980 are presented in Table 15. The table contains the mean expenditure projection and standard deviation for each scenario for 1980; the range of plus and minus three standard deviations, within which 99.7 percent of the projections for 1980 fall; and estimated expenditure figures for the 1970-80 period. The estimates for 1980 range from a low of $133,764,000 for scenario one, to a high of $277,558,000 for scenario twelve. These figures represent the best estimates of the probable upper and lower bounds for the year 1980. It is estimated that the total spent for the 1970-80 era will be between $1,049,297,000 and $1,684,493,000.

As mentioned earlier, the actual trend for 1970-74 seems to be following the general trend of scenarios four, six, seven, and nine. If this grouping is used as a gauge for what is likely to happen, a range is obtained which is bracketed on one end by the projection for 1980 for scenario four of $187,215,000 and on the other end by the projection for 1980 for scenario nine of $200,285,000. For the entire 1970-80 period, a low estimate for scenario four of $1,303,792,000 and a high estimate for scenario nine of $1,351,345,000 are projected.

The overall F test for the fixed effects two-way analysis of variance, and F values for rows, columns, and interaction are all significant well beyond the .01 level (see Appendix D).[9] Large values of F were a function of the large n, which influences degrees of freedom for the error estimate of the mean square. This result underlines the earlier statement about the limited meaningfulness of tests of significance when the n is large.

Since the overall F value is significant, it is appropriate to proceed with the post hoc pairwise statistical analysis (see Appendix D for details). There were only three pairs which were not statistically different: (1) scenario two (7 percent, ORG and E) and scenario three (7 percent, ORG and L); (2) scenario six (8.9 percent, ORG and E) and scenario seven (8.9 percent, ORG and L); and (3) scenario ten (11 percent, ORG and E) and scenario eleven (11 percent, ORG and L).[10]

Using absolute differences in dollars as a gauge of similarity of results, scenarios two (7 percent, ORG and E), three (7 percent, ORG and L), and five (8.9 percent, ORG) were within

TABLE 15 PROJECTIONS FOR 1980

	1980 Mean Projection	s	1980 Projection -3 s	1980 Projection +3 s	Total of Annual Means 1970-80
Scenario 1 (7%, ORG)	$133,764	$4,308	$120,840	$146,688	$1,049,297
Scenario 2 (7%, ORG and E)	158,351	6,128	139,967	176,735	1,171,173
Scenario 3 (7%, ORG and L)	158,368	6,536	138,760	177,976	1,166,793
Scenario 4 (7%, ORG, E, and L)	187,215	9,280	159,375	215,055	1,303,792
Scenario 5 (8.9%, ORG)	161,790	4,743	147,561	176,019	1,180,156
Scenario 6 (8.9%, ORG and E)	191,012	6,942	170,186	211,838	1,317,975
Scenario 7 (8.9%, ORG and L)	191,585	7,302	169,679	213,491	1,316,400
Scenario 8 (8.9%, ORG, E, and L)	225,600	10,475	194,175	257,025	1,470,591
Scenario 9 (11%, ORG)	200,285	5,255	184,520	216,050	1,351,345
Scenario 10 (11%, ORG and E)	235,813	7,712	212,677	258,949	1,510,352
Scenario 11 (11%, ORG and L)	236,092	8,354	211,030	261,154	1,506,647
Scenario 12 (11%, ORG, E, and L)	277,558	10,894	244,876	310,240	1,684,493

NOTE: A comparison of scenarios 2 and 3, 6 and 7, or 10 and 11 may suggest an error in the results because the scenarios with the organizational and leadership factors (scenarios 3, 7, and 11) produce higher 1980 mean projections; whereas the scenarios with the organizational and external factors (scenarios 2, 6, and 10) produce higher estimates of the Total of Annual Means 1970-80. However, the figures presented in the table are correct. These seemingly inconsistent findings are the result of the fact that certain parameters have a long-term multiplier effect because of their location in the model. This effect is reflected in scenarios 3, 7, and 11. Had the projections been made for just a few more years, scenarios 3, 7, and 11 would have also produced the highest Total of Annual Means.

$3.5 million of each other for the 1980 projection. Scenarios four (7 percent, ORG, E, and L), six (8.9 percent, ORG and E), and nine (11 percent, ORG) were within $13.1 million of each other. Scenarios eight (8.9 percent, ORG, E, and L), ten (11 percent, ORG and E), and eleven (11 percent, ORG and L) were within $10.5 million of each other.

Which Scenario?

The scenarios were treated as *if, then* statements. The results were interpreted as the ramification of a set of assumptions. It is also appropriate to ask the likelihood of occurrence of each scenario.

One obvious means of proceeding involves turning to the history of WHO. Since parameters contained in the model are the equivalent of full information maximum likelihood estimates, the computer model provided the best single estimate for the past. Turning to the past to help guess which scenario is most likely leads to scenario eight which involves simply running the basic computer model forward in time.

Another approach is to classify each year from 1951 to 1969 into one of twelve categories, or scenarios (see Table 16). However, with a history of only nineteen years, it is not meaningful to assign probabilities of occurrence to the scenarios. The most that can be done is to describe the past, looking for trends and other information which will give insight for the future.

In the table, all organizational increments at the proposal development step of less than 8.0 percent are classified as 7 percent, those between 8.0 percent and 10.0 percent as 8.9 percent, and those greater than 10.0 percent as 11 percent decisions. It is no surprise that the most frequently occurring alternative is scenario eight (8.9 percent, ORG, E, and L). Interestingly, the years using the 8.9 percent organizational increment at the proposal development step (scenarios five through eight) are all recent. The other years (1951-60) use 7 percent and 11 percent alternatives.

It is also appropriate to add information on the 1970, 1971, 1972, 1973, and 1974 actions in WHO. For 1970, the organizational increment at the proposal development step was 7.9 percent, with organizational and external factors being

TABLE 16   PAST USES OF ALTERNATIVE SCENARIOS

Organizational Increment at Proposal Development Step	Scenario		Years Involved	Percent of Cases
7% (≤7.99%)	ORG	(Scenario 1)	1954, 1956	10.5
	ORG, E	(Scenario 2)	1951, 1959	10.5
	ORG, L	(Scenario 3)		0.0
	ORG, E, L	(Scenario 4)		0.0
8.9% (≥8.00% and ≤10.00%)	ORG	(Scenario 5)	1968	5.3
	ORG, E	(Scenario 6)	1969	5.3
	ORG, L	(Scenario 7)		0.0
	ORG, E, L	(Scenario 8)	1961, 1962, 1963, 1964, 1966, 1967	31.6
11% (≥10.01%)	ORG	(Scenario 9)		0.0
	ORG, E	(Scenario 10)	1952, 1953, 1958, 1960	21.0
	ORG, L	(Scenario 11)		0.0
	ORG, E, L	(Scenario 12)	1955, 1957, 1965	15.8

used in budgetary calculations. For 1971, the organizational increment at the proposal development step was 8.3 percent, with organizational, leadership and external factors being used in budgetary calculations. For 1972, the organizational increment at the proposal development step was 7.8 percent, with organizational and external factors being used in budgetary calculations. For 1973, the organizational increment at the proposal development step was 8.7 percent, with organizational and external factors being used in budgetary calculations. For 1974, the organizational increment at the proposal development step was 7.6 percent, with organizational and external factors being used in budgetary calculations.[11]

Although the past conditions and shapes the future, it does not completely determine it. The future will probably be an extension, or modification, of the past; but we can really only speculate about it. In this regard, any scenario including leadership factors is unlikely to be used on a regular basis because of current pressure for budget cuts from the United States government. The U.S. government could probably cut out leadership increments and can be expected to eliminate scenarios three (7 percent, ORG and L), four (7 percent, ORG, E, and L), seven (8.9 percent, ORG and L), eight (8.9 percent, ORG, E, and L), eleven (11 percent, ORG and L), and twelve (11 percent, ORG, E, and L). Furthermore, scenario one (7 percent, ORG) seems unlikely without a major crisis since lesser developed nations have the power, and could be expected, to block the drastic cut represented by this scenario. Thus, there are five scenarios which seem most likely to occur: (1) scenario two (7 percent, ORG and E); (2) scenario five (8.9 percent, ORG); (3) scenario six (8.9 percent, ORG and E); (4) scenario nine (11 percent, ORG); and (5) scenario ten (11 percent, ORG and E). Among these, the least likely to occur are scenarios two, nine, and ten. Each involves a change in the highly symbolic organizational increment at the proposal development step, with scenario two representing a victory for those desiring budget cuts and scenarios nine and ten a victory for lesser developed nations. Nevertheless, these three scenarios represent likely alternatives for the future.

The least likely to occur of the two other alternatives is

scenario five. Scenario six is the most likely because it involves the least controversial change from past practice in WHO. It is the author's guess that if scenario six does not develop, scenario five will.

Summary and Conclusions

There are a multiplicity of futures which could be simulated. Each parameter could be set at any value, and the computer model could be run forward to any point in time. Furthermore, any step change (or changes) in policy-making rules could be introduced at any time. The scenarios simulated in this chapter merely represent plausible alternatives which could occur in the future. Nevertheless, the projections yield some extremely interesting results. The WHO expenditure total for 1980 will probably fall between $133,764,000 and $277,558,000, with a total of between $1,049,297,000 and $1,684,493,000 being spent for the 1970-80 era. It is the author's judgment that between $1,180,156,000 and $1,317,975,000 will be spent for the 1970-80 period, and the expenditures for 1980 should be between $161,790,000 and $191,012,000. It seems probable, unless there is a major change in the political situation, that the growth rate will decrease from that observed during the first twenty-one years of the World Health Organization.

9

Contributions and Implications

---

*Out of the process of developing, integrating, and testing . . .
bodies of theory, it is to be expected that ideas will spring which
probably would never be conceived without the frame of
reference provided by the theory.*

—*Harold Guetzkow*

This volume represents an attempt to contribute to the
development of a general behavioral theory of policy-making
and, as noted earlier, grows out of and hopefully contributes to
five different social science research traditions. This chapter
will be both conclusion and commencement; it will attempt
not only to fit the present study into broader contexts, but will
also suggest how its frame of reference could be modified to
examine other phenomena.

Contributions to Literature

The contribution of this study to the recent literature of
quantitative international politics is twofold. It first extended
quantitative research to a new area of concern—budgetary
phenomena in international organizations. Second, it
demonstrated that a variety of econometric techniques could be
used to tackle the complex problem of policy formulation in
international politics. The study arrives at a set of behavioral
generalizations and states them in the form of a computer
simulation model. The model itself is novel and represents a
conceptual way of organizing a complex policy-making
process. Furthermore, the model permits the formulation of
numerical solutions which in turn allow statements to be made
about the relative impact of theoretical factors built into the
model itself. It also permits the specification of alternative
scenarios of the future and the analysis of their eventual
ramifications. Although no new measurement or data analytic

techniques have been used in this study, several infrequently used time-series techniques have been utilized to estimate parameters for specified stochastic equations. The implication is that these, and other, econometric techniques are potentially useful in different areas of quantitative international politics.

The book makes a contribution to the study of policy-making in international politics by developing a new framework for analysis. The framework grows out of the work of Snyder, Bruck and Sapin, Frankel, Deutsch, Hilsman, Rosenau, and Allison and represents a new way of conceiving policy-making in international governmental organizations. With slight modifications, it would be relevant for the general study of policy-making in international politics. Whereas the ideas of system, process, decomposability, issue-areas, steps in the policy-making process, types of policy-makers, types of inputs, and policy-making rules are not new in the social sciences, their combination into a single framework for analysis of policy-making in the international politics field is original.

Furthermore, the mode of applying the framework demonstrates a manner of approaching a research problem which may be of relevance in the general study of policy-making in international politics. The framework was used to raise questions, order data, and to describe the WHO budget process. A model was then built and was used to examine a series of *if, then* statements regarding alternative pasts and futures. Most importantly, specifications of the model dictated the use of statistical techniques, instead of the other way around. The success of this research approach suggests it is of potential relevance for other areas of policy-making.

The book extends prior work in the field of behavioral budgetary theory in three ways. First, a new political setting, international governmental organizations, is considered. Second, the number of steps included in the analysis has been expanded to encompass actions from the development of the proposal for action to the expenditure of funds. Third, a new way of conceptualizing the impact of input factors is presented.

The findings support the general model of Davis, Dempster, and Wildavsky in that incremental rules describe the behavior of policy-makers in regard to the budget total in WHO. The principal finding is that there exists an overall rule which involves a fixed percentage of change from action at the prior step in the budget process. Furthermore, it was found that the budget-balancing routine of Crecine and the step change alternatives of Davis, Dempster, and Wildavsky were not relevant for WHO.

The study also provides a new way of conceptualizing the impact of organizational, external, and leadership factors. One school of thought, represented by Davis, Dempster, and Wildavsky, utilizes organizational variables, claiming that any linear change from these variables is due to organizational factors. This view necessitates the addition of exogenous variables (sometimes dummy variables) to put nonorganizational factors into the analysis. The other school of thought, represented by the early work of Davis, correlated nonorganizational variables with budgetary totals, arguing that the portion of the budget accounted for by this linear relationship was due to nonorganizational factors.[1] The position taken in this book holds that prior actions serve as the basis for calculations. But not all change from those prior actions is the result of organizational factors just because the prior action is an organizational one.

The position has been adopted that organizational, external, and leadership factors all influence the magnitude of the fixed percentage of change from the prior action. For example, a 13 percent change from a prior organizational action could represent a 9 percent change due to organizational factors, 2 percent change due to external factors, and 2 percent change due to leadership factors, instead of a 13 percent change due to organizational factors. Given this line of thought, it seems reasonable to decompose the total amount of change from the prior step, contained in the endogenous variable, into the portion based on each of the input factors, and then have policy-making rules for each of the organizational, external, and leadership based actions. This, of course, assumes that decomposition of this sort is possible for the researcher. Furthermore, it assumes that decomposed actions are again added together to arrive at the total amount of change.

The book also applies to international organizational phenomena a number of ideas regarding policy-making which were developed in the organization theory literature. It must be concluded that organization theory is relevant for the study of international organizations, and nothing was discovered which leads us to believe international organizations are essentially different from other organizations in regard to policy-making. It was found that ideas of decomposability, satisficing, organizational constraints, and computer simulation methodology, developed in organization theory by scholars such as Simon, March, and Cyert, are relevant to the study of international governmental organizations. A variety of other organization theory questions could easily be studied in international organizations.

It is in the field of international organizations where this study made its biggest contribution. It first demonstrated the potential utility of ideas derived from quantitative international politics, policy-making in international politics, behavioral budgetary theory, and organization theory to the study of international organizations. Furthermore, a new conceptual framework for analysis of policy-making was created and applied to WHO activities. The framework provided perspective on budgetary activities in WHO, oriented description of the budget process, gave guidance for the selection and testing of alternative plausible policy-making rules, provided the elements essential for developing a computer simulation model, and set up sensitivity analysis of the past and future. The computer model is the most important contribution of the book. It is an empirically tested theoretical statement about budget-making in international governmental organizations. When considered together with the work of Alker, et al., it represents a possible beginning for a general theory of policy-making in international organizations.

Policy Implications

This study was not designed for the purpose of generating policy recommendations. Nevertheless, there are implications which follow from the simulation of alternative futures. The most important contribution is the demonstration of how models can be used to systematically evaluate *if, then* statements. There appear to be a number of practical problems facing policy-makers which could be handled in this general manner.

Implications for managers of the WHO program relate to the tremendous increase in resources which will be available in the future. It has been estimated that between $1,049,297,000 and $1,684,493,000 will be spent from regular budget funds during the period 1970-80. When these figures are compared with $478,448,000, the total spent from regular budget funds during the 1949-69 era, it becomes apparent that between two and three times as much will be spent in the decade of the 1970s as in the two prior decades. Even allowing for inflation, the increase in available resources will be substantial. Problems in recruitment, subcontracting, and planning will need to be recognized and solved. The type of questions raised by studies such as the Jackson Report will gain even greater salience in the future, and modern management concerns should immediately be attended to by the WHO staff.[2]

Implications for the political strategy of those who desire to slow down growth of the WHO program are quite obvious. These policy-makers, currently from developed countries, will want to change the policy-making parameters so that little increase is made in the budget total. They may, for example, want to eliminate special leadership increments, force externally dictated increments to be absorbed within normally dictated organizational increments, and attempt to lower increments for organizational factors. It is obvious that these policy-makers fail to constitute a majority, and their best strategy would lay in influencing the Director-General during the proposal development step.

Implications for the political strategy pursued by those who desire to speed up the growth of the WHO program are also quite obvious. These policy-makers, usually from lesser developed countries, will want to increase the percentage of leadership and external increments, while maintaining or increasing the percentage of organizational increments. They may also want to force the making of crucial decisions at the World Health Assembly where they control the policy-making situation.

Ramifications for the political strategy of the Director-General are not as obvious. In the future, the magnitude of stakes involved may intensify the conflict over the budget total. If this happens, the Director-General may no longer be able to recommend successful compromises between positions involving faster and slower growth. He may need to choose sides, thereby greatly decreasing his chances for re-election. Regardless of the strategy the Director-General chooses to follow, it seems his choice will be a controversial one.

Suggestions for Further Research

This book represents only a beginning. There are a number of ways in which the study could be extended to other concerns. For example, both the theoretical and methodological approaches presented here could be utilized in a general examination of policy-making. Studies involving policy-making in international politics, behavioral budgetary theory, and organization theory could be undertaken. However, subsequent discussion will consider only possible extensions of the study which deal with international organizational phenomena. These considerations fall into four categories: tests involving other budgetary theories; extensions to other aspects of the budget-finance issue-area; extensions to other issue-areas; and extensions to other international organizations.

It was demonstrated that the incremental model was quite accurate in predicting expenditure totals for WHO. It was also shown that the model was more accurate in its predictions than a simple, naive, first-order Markov model. Nevertheless, it has not been shown that the model predicts WHO expenditure totals more accurately than other budgetary theories. If the incremental model does predict better, then we will have more faith in it than we now have.

One plausible alternative is the "share of the pie" model of Natchez and Bupp.[3] This model argues that budget totals are calculated as a share of the larger pie. The idea could be developed that there is a pie, or budget total, for the entire United Nations system, and the WHO total is calculated as a share of that larger pie. To test this model's ability to predict, it would be necessary to make the model dynamic in some way, and the parameter producing the share of the pie would need to be specified and estimated. Data on the total for the United Nations system would also need to be collected.

A second plausible alternative for testing is a reaction model. Variations of this model have been employed by Richardson, Choucri and North, and others to study arms races.[4] In this tradition, the increase in the budget total is seen as a reaction to actions by an adversary. However, for our purposes another variation of the reaction model, advanced by Manser, Naylor, and Wertz, seems more appropriate. In this model, which has been applied at the state level in America, one of the key factors influencing the increase in the budget total is the budget total of the prior year for neighboring states.[5] This neighborhood model could be applied to WHO by conceiving of agencies like the Food and Agriculture Organization, the International Labour Organisation, and the United Nations Educational, Scientific and Cultural Organization as neighbors. To test this model's ability to predict, it would need to be made dynamic in some way; and parameters producing reactions would need to be estimated. Data for other agencies would also need to be collected.

There are a number of other aspects of the budget-finance issue-area in need of exploration. For example, focus on the budget total may have masked a number of subtleties in the budget process which would be uncovered by focusing on allocations at the account, administrative unit, program, country, or regional levels. This would be in the tradition of Crecine, Jackson, Stromberg, Kanter, Natchez and Bupp, and Manser, Naylor, and Wertz. The incremental model could be fitted at these different levels of aggregation, and a series of empirical tests involving other theories could be conducted.

Focusing upon the income side of the budget and asking questions about "who pays?" should also produce interesting results. The work of Olson, Olson and Zeckhauser, Russett, Russett and Sullivan, Ruggie, and Loehr, from the public goods literature, should serve as a valuable source of ideas for such an enterprise.[6]

The inclusion of other issue-areas is also a potentially valuable future step. One logical way to begin would be to adapt the model of Alker and his associates to task expansion actions in the program area or to election-appointment actions within WHO. The Alker model could use prior task expansion actions, or individual background characteristics of prior appointees, for matching purposes. An attempt could also be made to develop linkages between the Alker model and the one developed in this book. The result would be a new model of policy-making in different issue-areas in international governmental organizations.

Since the aim is to develop a theory of how policy is made in international organizations, and not just a theory of how policy is made in WHO, it is imperative for future analyses to include other international organizations. Not only should other international governmental agencies (e.g., the Food and Agriculture Organization, International Labour Organisation, United Nations Educational, Scientific and Cultural Organization, Organization of American States, United Nations, and the European Common Market) be included, but the transnational politics critique of Keohane and Nye should be taken seriously; and international nongovernmental organizations, such as the Red Cross, and multinational corporations, such as General Motors, should also be studied.[7] Only by the comparative method can it be ascertained that the results obtained are not specific to the agency being studied; and only in this way can a general theory of policy-making in international organizations be developed.

However, extension of policy-making research to other organizations should proceed within the loose paradigm presented in the first two chapters of this book. The empirical orientation of Snyder, Deutsch, Hilsman, Rosenau, Allison, Wildavsky, Crecine, Simon, Cyert and March, and Alker has raised a number of interesting questions, techniques for studying them, and some preliminary answers. What is needed is consolidation, refinement, and systematic extension of prior work. It is not necessary to start all over again by collecting all available data and correlating it in all possible ways. What is needed is more formal reasoning based on prior work on policy-making. Such an approach facilitates the development of a theory of policy-making in international politics. It allows us to accumulate knowledge and have the impact of studies exceed their particular content.

Appendix A

Simplified Flowchart Showing Major Action Involved in WHO Regular Budget Cycle

DIAGRAM 8 SIMPLIFIED FLOWCHART SHOWING MAJOR ACTION INVOLVED IN WHO REGULAR BUDGET CYCLE

Headquarters Secretariat	Director-General	Regional Secretariat	Member-States	International Organizations

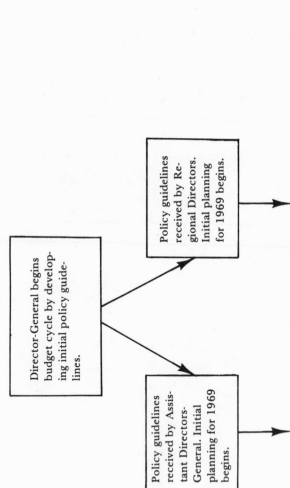

Director-General begins budget cycle by developing initial policy guidelines.

Policy guidelines received by Regional Directors. Initial planning for 1969 begins.

Policy guidelines received by Assistant Directors-General. Initial planning for 1969 begins.

MONTH 1 (September 1966)

MONTH 2 (October 1966)

140

MONTH 3
(November
1966)

MONTH 4
(December
1966)

MONTH 5
(January
1967)

MONTH 6
(February
1967)

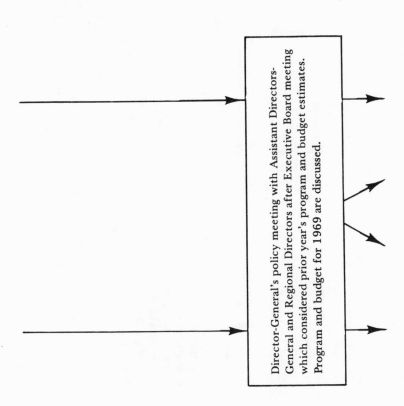

Director-General's policy meeting with Assistant Directors-General and Regional Directors after Executive Board meeting which considered prior year's program and budget estimates. Program and budget for 1969 are discussed.

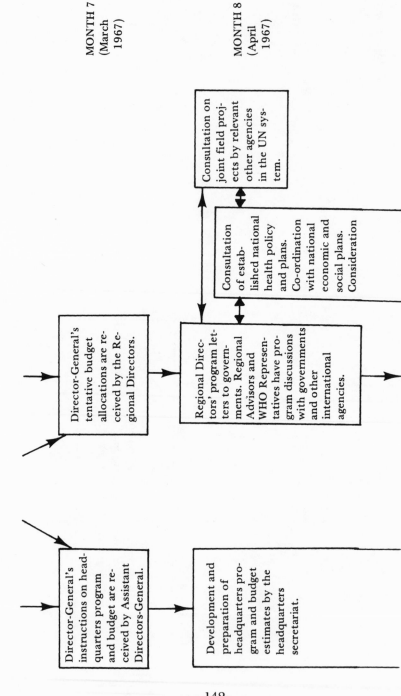

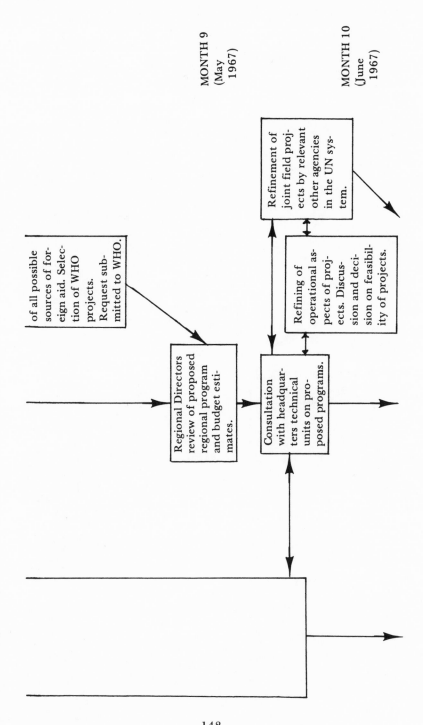

MONTH 9
(May
1967)

MONTH 10
(June
1967)

of all possible sources of foreign aid. Selection of WHO projects. Request submitted to WHO.

Regional Directors review of proposed regional program and budget estimates.

Consultation with headquarters technical units on proposed programs.

Refinement of joint field projects by relevant other agencies in the UN system.

Refining of operational aspects of projects. Discussion and decision on feasibility of projects.

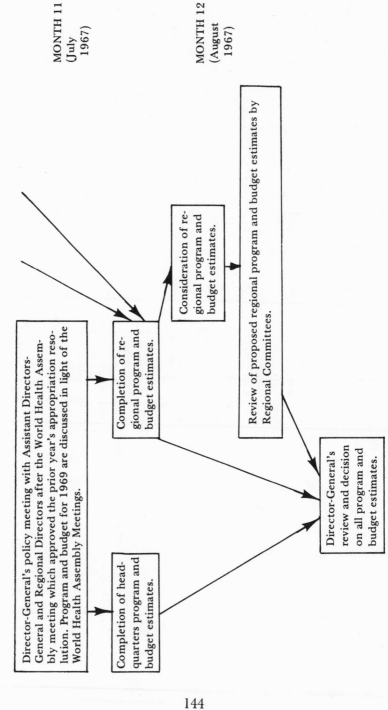

MONTH 11
(July
1967)

MONTH 12
(August
1967)

Director-General's policy meeting with Assistant Directors-General and Regional Directors after the World Health Assembly meeting which approved the prior year's appropriation resolution. Program and budget for 1969 are discussed in light of the World Health Assembly Meetings.

Completion of regional program and budget estimates.

Consideration of regional program and budget estimates.

Review of proposed regional program and budget estimates by Regional Committees.

Director-General's review and decision on all program and budget estimates.

Completion of headquarters program and budget estimates.

MONTH 13
(September 1967)

MONTH 14
(October 1967)

MONTH 15
(November 1967)

United Nations General Assembly begins. Matters affecting the UN and the specialized agencies may be considered (decided).

Consolidation and production of Director-General's proposed program and budget document.

145

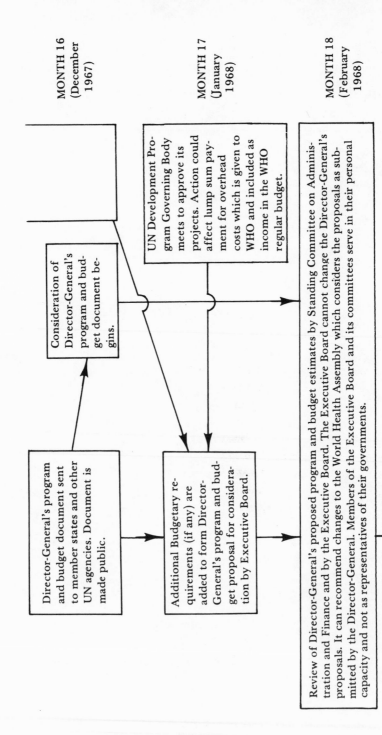

MONTH 16
(December
1967)

MONTH 17
(January
1968)

MONTH 18
(February
1968)

Consideration of Director-General's program and budget document begins.

UN Development Program Governing Body meets to approve its projects. Action could affect lump sum payment for overhead costs which is given to WHO and included as income in the WHO regular budget.

Director-General's program and budget document sent to member states and other UN agencies. Document is made public.

Additional Budgetary requirements (if any) are added to form Director-General's program and budget proposal for consideration by Executive Board.

Review of Director-General's proposed program and budget estimates by Standing Committee on Administration and Finance and by the Executive Board. The Executive Board cannot change the Director-General's proposals. It can recommend changes to the World Health Assembly which considers the proposals as submitted by the Director-General. Members of the Executive Board and its committees serve in their personal capacity and not as representatives of their governments.

MONTH 19
(March
1968)

MONTH 20
(April
1968)

Director-General's policy meeting with Assistant Directors-General and Regional Directors after the Executive Board meeting. Program and budget for 1969 may be discussed. Program and budget for following year will be discussed.

Report of Executive Board's recommendations on Director-General's program and budget proposals is sent to member states and other UN agencies. Document is made public.

Consideration of report of Executive Board and Director-General's program and budget proposals. Development of governmental position for World Health Assembly meetings.

Additional budgetary requirements (if any) are added to form the Director-General's program and budget proposal for consideration by the World Health Assembly.

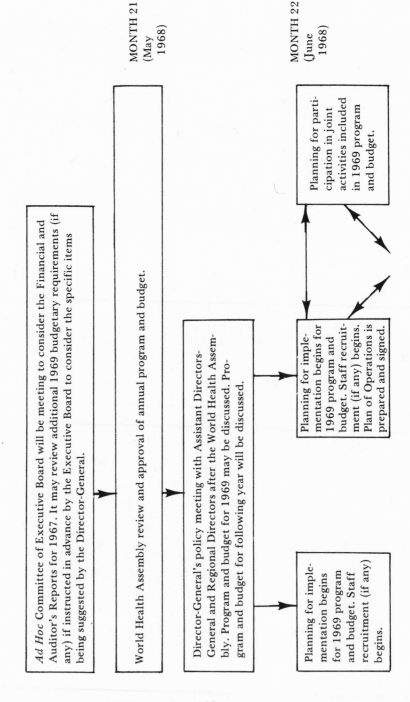

MONTH 21
(May
1968)

MONTH 22
(June
1968)

Ad Hoc Committee of Executive Board will be meeting to consider the Financial and Auditor's Reports for 1967. It may review additional 1969 budgetary requirements (if any) if instructed in advance by the Executive Board to consider the specific items being suggested by the Director-General.

World Health Assembly review and approval of annual program and budget.

Director-General's policy meeting with Assistant Directors-General and Regional Directors after the World Health Assembly. Program and budget for 1969 may be discussed. Program and budget for following year will be discussed.

Planning for implementation begins for 1969 program and budget. Staff recruitment (if any) begins.

Planning for implementation begins for 1969 program and budget. Staff recruitment (if any) begins. Plan of Operations is prepared and signed.

Planning for participation in joint activities included in 1969 program and budget.

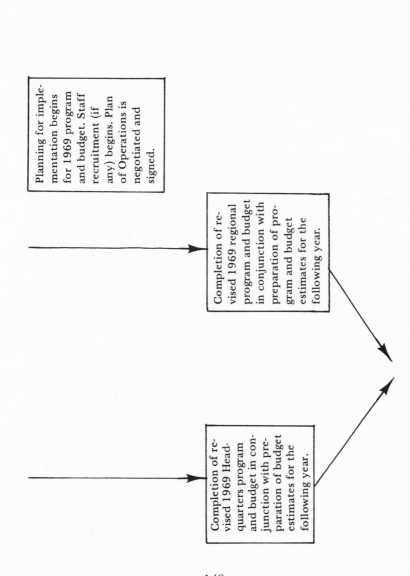

MONTH 23
(July
1968)

Planning for imple-
mentation begins
for 1969 program
and budget. Staff
recruitment (if
any) begins. Plan
of Operations is
negotiated and
signed.

Completion of re-
vised 1969 regional
program and budget
in conjunction with
preparation of pro-
gram and budget
estimates for the
following year.

MONTH 24
(August
1968)

Completion of re-
vised 1969 Head-
quarters program
and budget in con-
junction with pre-
paration of budget
estimates for the
following year.

149

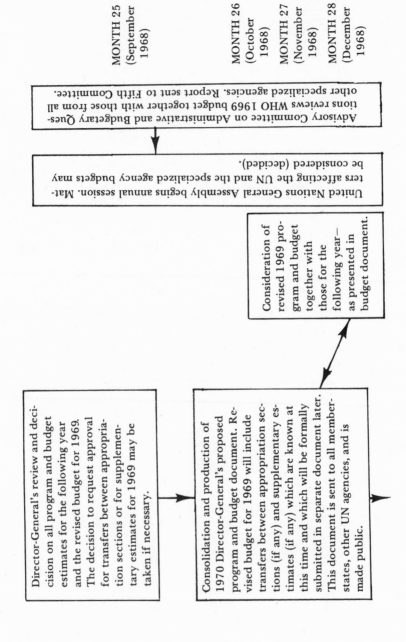

MONTH 25
(September
1968)

MONTH 26
(October
1968)

MONTH 27
(November
1968)

MONTH 28
(December
1968)

Advisory Committee on Administrative and Budgetary Questions reviews WHO 1969 budget together with those from all other specialized agencies. Report sent to Fifth Committee.

United Nations General Assembly begins annual session. Matters affecting the UN and the specialized agency budgets may be considered (decided).

Consideration of revised 1969 program and budget together with those for the following year—as presented in budget document.

Director-General's review and decision on all program and budget estimates for the following year and the revised budget for 1969. The decision to request approval for transfers between appropriation sections or for supplementary estimates for 1969 may be taken if necessary.

Consolidation and production of 1970 Director-General's proposed program and budget document. Revised budget for 1969 will include transfers between appropriation sections (if any) and supplementary estimates (if any) which are known at this time and which will be formally submitted in separate document later. This document is sent to all member-states, other UN agencies, and is made public.

150

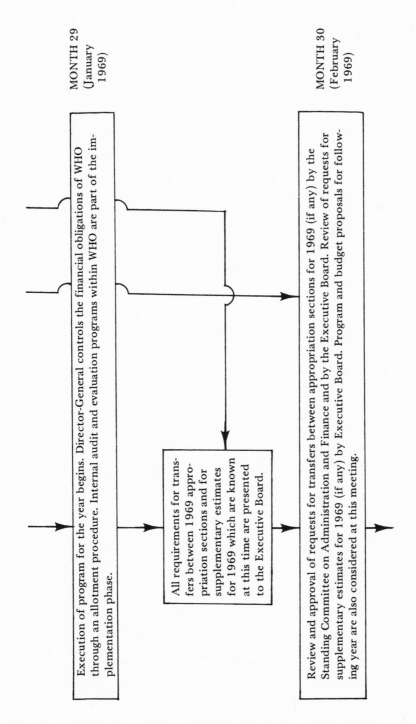

MONTH 29
(January
1969)

Execution of program for the year begins. Director-General controls the financial obligations of WHO through an allotment procedure. Internal audit and evaluation programs within WHO are part of the implementation phase.

All requirements for transfers between 1969 appropriation sections and for supplementary estimates for 1969 which are known at this time are presented to the Executive Board.

MONTH 30
(February
1969)

Review and approval of requests for transfers between appropriation sections for 1969 (if any) by the Standing Committee on Administration and Finance and by the Executive Board. Review of requests for supplementary estimates for 1969 (if any) by Executive Board. Program and budget proposals for following year are also considered at this meeting.

151

Director-General's policy meeting with the Assistant Directors-General and the Regional Directors after the Executive Board meeting. Program and budget for the second succeeding year are discussed. Program and budget for 1969 and 1970 may be discussed if appropriate.

Report of Executive Board meeting contains recommendations on supplementary estimates for 1969 by Executive Board.

Consideration of supplementary estimates for 1969 as contained in the report of the Executive Board meeting.

Additional requirements for transfers between 1969 appropriation sections (if any) and for supplementary estimates (if any) are formalized for Health Assembly.

152

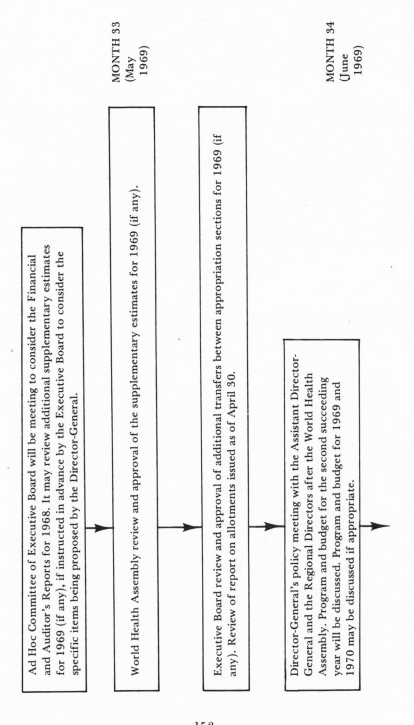

MONTH 33
(May
1969)

Ad Hoc Committee of Executive Board will be meeting to consider the Financial and Auditor's Reports for 1968. It may review additional supplementary estimates for 1969 (if any), if instructed in advance by the Executive Board to consider the specific items being proposed by the Director-General.

World Health Assembly review and approval of the supplementary estimates for 1969 (if any).

Executive Board review and approval of additional transfers between appropriation sections for 1969 (if any). Review of report on allotments issued as of April 30.

MONTH 34
(June
1969)

Director-General's policy meeting with the Assistant Director-General and the Regional Directors after the World Health Assembly. Program and budget for the second succeeding year will be discussed. Program and budget for 1969 and 1970 may be discussed if appropriate.

MONTH 35
(July
1969)

MONTH 36
(August
1969)

MONTH 37
(September
1969)

Director-General's review and decision on additional transfers
between 1969 appropriation sections (if any) which may be submitted by mail to Executive
Board members.

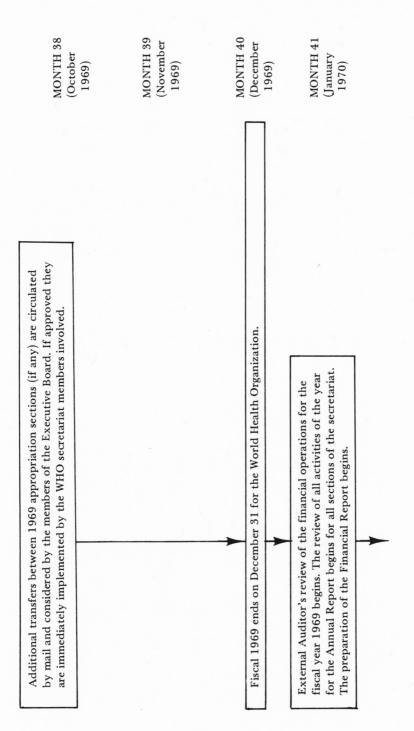

MONTH 38
(October
1969)

MONTH 39
(November
1969)

MONTH 40
(December
1969)

MONTH 41
(January
1970)

Additional transfers between 1969 appropriation sections (if any) are circulated by mail and considered by the members of the Executive Board. If approved they are immediately implemented by the WHO secretariat members involved.

Fiscal 1969 ends on December 31 for the World Health Organization.

External Auditor's review of the financial operations for the fiscal year 1969 begins. The review of all activities of the year for the Annual Report begins for all sections of the secretariat. The preparation of the Financial Report begins.

155

MONTH 42
(February
1970)

MONTH 43
(March
1970)

MONTH 44
(April
1970)

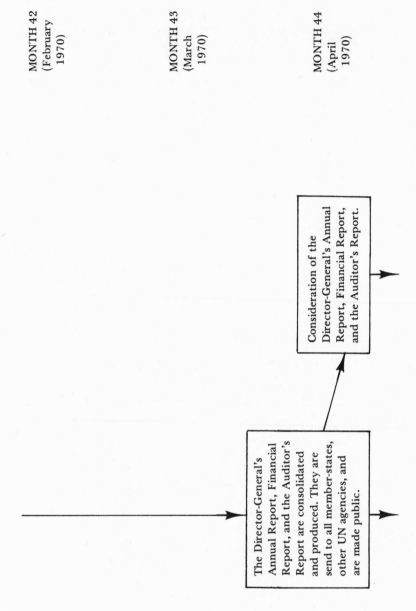

The Director-General's Annual Report, Financial Report, and the Auditor's Report are consolidated and produced. They are send to all member-states, other UN agencies, and are made public.

Consideration of the Director-General's Annual Report, Financial Report, and the Auditor's Report.

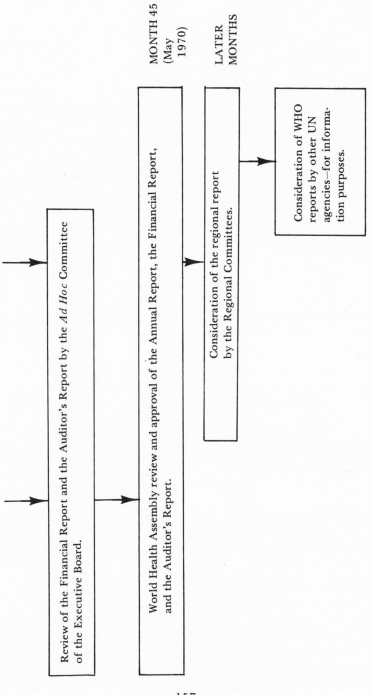

Review of the Financial Report and the Auditor's Report by the *Ad Hoc* Committee of the Executive Board.

World Health Assembly review and approval of the Annual Report, the Financial Report, and the Auditor's Report.

MONTH 45 (May 1970)

Consideration of the regional report by the Regional Committees.

LATER MONTHS

Consideration of WHO reports by other UN agencies—for information purposes.

Appendix B

Details of Empirical Examination of Plausible Policy-Making Rules

TABLE 17   FIT OF ALTERNATIVE RULES AT PROPOSAL DEVELOPMENT STEP (PD_t)

	Rules	Independent Variable(s)		Regression Coefficient	Std. Error Regression Coefficient (F Value)	r^2	Durbin-Watson or Turnovers	Significance	Chow's F	Significance	r^2 on Total	Average Deviation (\$000)
Temporally Stable Rules	PD.1*	A_{t-1}	1951-69	1.1165	.0113 (9837.2)	.9982	1.90	>.01			.9982	985
	PD.2*	EB_{t-1}	1951-69	1.1198	.0157 (5106.4)	.9965	1.88	>.01			.9965	1224
	PD.3*	PD_{t-1}	1951-69	1.1280	.0158 (5091.2)	.9965	10	>.01			.9965	1214
	PD.4*	$AE(pd)_{t-1}$	1951-69	1.1123	.0115 (9342.5)	.9981	1.98	>.01			.9981	1021
Step Change Rules	PD.5*	A_{t-1}	1951-64	1.1528	.0203 (3234.0)	.9960	2.47	>.01	1.624	>.01	.9984	910
	*	A_{t-1}	1965-69	1.1053	.0142 (6038.3)	.9994	1.98	>.01				

PD.6*	EB_{t-1}	1951-64	1.1678	.0323 (1303.5)	.9901	2.34	>.01	1.375	>.01	.9968	1161
*	EB_{t-1}	1965-69	1.1055	.0141 (6131.1)	.9994	2.08	>.01				
PD.7*	PD_{t-1}	1951-56	1.0224	.0457 (500.0)	.9901	4	>.01	.732	>.01	.9966	1099
*	PD_{t-1}	1957-69	1.1318	.0180 (3971.2)	.9970	7	>.01				
PD.8*	$AE(pd)_{t-1}$	1951-64	1.1477	.0213 (2908.6)	.9956	2.36	>.01	1.443	>.01	.9983	993
*	$AE(pd)_{t-1}$	1965-69	1.1015	.0142 (6045.2)	.9993	2.38	>.01				
PD.9*	A_{t-1}	1951-64	1.1528	.0203 (3234.0)	.9960	2.47	>.01	1.733	>.01	.9984	918
*	PD_{t-1}	1965-69	1.1192	.0141 (6262.2)	.9994	3	>.01				

*The LS technique with the intercept forced through the origin was used for estimation.

TABLE 18   FIT OF ALTERNATIVE RULES AT EXECUTIVE BODY STEP (EB_t)

Temporally Stable Rules	Independent Variable(s)	Regression Coefficient	Std. Error Reg. Coeff. (F Value)	r^2	Durbin-Watson or Turnovers	Significance	Chow's F	Significance	r^2 on Total	Average Deviation (000$)	r between e's PD	
EB.1*	A_{t-1} 1951-69	1.1224	.0134 (6997.5)	.9974	2.12	>.01			.9974	1075	.92	<.01
EB.2*	EB_{t-1} 1951-69	1.1258	.0173 (4238.0)	.9958	2.02	>.01			.9958	1347	.94	<.01
EB.3*	PD_t 1951-69	1.0055	.0049 (41563.4)	.9996	8	>.01			.9996	368	.17	>.01
EB.4*	$AE(eb)_{t-1}$ 1951-69	1.1061	.0097 (13130.8)	.9986	2.45	>.01			.9986	866	.90	<.01

Step Change Rules												
EB.5*	A_{t-1} 1951-64	1.1450	.0205 (3120.5)	.9959	2.14	>.01	.379	>.01	.9975	1064	.96	<.01
*	A_{t-1} 1965-69	1.1155	.0243 (2113.8)	.9981	2.28	>.01					.97	<.01
EB.6*	EB_{t-1} 1951-56	1.0231	.0477 (460.0)	.9893	4	>.01	.528	>.01	.9959	1265	.84	>.01
*	EB_{t-1} 1957-69	1.1293	.0200 (3177.6)	.9962	5	>.01					.96	<.01
EB.7*	PD_t 1951-62	.9863	.0082 (14438.7)	.9992	1.48	>.01	1.054	>.01	.9996	398	-.40	>.01
*	PD_t 1963-69	1.0083	.0074 (18404.9)	.9997	2.37	>.01					.42	>.01
EB.8*	$AE(eb)_{t-1}$ 1961-64	1.1238	.0148 (5769.3)	.9978	2.65	>.01	.458	>.01	.9986	788	.90	<.01
*	$AE(eb)_{t-1}$ 1965-69	1.1007	.0172 (4080.1)	.9990	2.52	>.01					.96	<.01

*The LS technique with the intercept forced through the origin was used for estimation.

TABLE 19   FIT OF ALTERNATIVE RULES AT ASSEMBLY STEP (A_t)

Temporally Stable Rules	Independent Variable(s)	Regression Coefficient	Std. Error Reg. Coefficient (F Value)	r^2	Durbin-Watson or Turnovers	Significance	Chow's F	Significance	r^2 on Total	Average Deviation (000$)	r between e's PD	r between e's EB	Significance
A.1*	A_{t-1} 1951-69	1.1261	.0138 (6676.6)	.9973	8	>.01			.9973	1109	.86	.55	PD, EB <.01
A.2*	EB_t 1951-69	1.0032	.0043 (55539.6)	.9997	1.93	>.01			.9997	306	-.12	-.04	PD, E >.01
A.3*	PD_t 1951-69	1.0087	.0063 (25475.2)	.9993	1.97	>.01			.9993	606	.09	.61	EB <.01
A.4*	$AE(a)_{t-1}$ 1951-69	1.1070	.0096 (13176.5)	.9986	1.83	>.01			.9986	844	.87	.39	PD <.01

Step Change Rules											
A.5* A_{t-1} 1951-64	1.1598	.0211 (3026.3)	.9957	6	>.01					.82	.97	PD, EB <.01
* A_{t-1} 1965-69	1.1158	.0237 (2226.2)	.9982	3	>.01	.854	>.01	.9975	1133	.11	.95	PD, EB >.01
A.6* EB_t 1951-62	1.0248	.0138 (5497.5)	.9980	1.44	>.01					-.11	-.07	PD, EB >.01
* EB_t 1963-69	1.0001	.0005 (3,375,056.9)	1.0000	3.00	>.01	1.889	>.01	.9997	293	.17	.72	PD, EB >.01
A.7* PD_t 1951-54	.9561	.0276 (1199.8)	.9975	2.22	>.01					.86	.55	PD, EB >.01
* PD_t 1955-69	1.0096	.0068 (22149.5)	.9994	2.04	>.01	.594	>.01	.9993	563	-.12	-.04	PD, E >.01
A.8* $AE(a)_{t-1}$ 1951-64	1.1396	.0141 (6495.3)	.9980	1.63	>.01					.09	.61	EB <.01
* $AE(a)_{t-1}$ 1965-69	1.0970	.0155 (5005.1)	.9992	2.82	>.01	1.819	>.01	.9988	783	.87	.39	PD <.01

*The LS technique with the intercept forced through the origin was used for estimation.

TABLE 20 FIT OF ALTERNATIVE RULES AT SUPPLEMENTARY CHANGE STEP (SC_t)

		Independent Variable	Regression Coefficient	Std. Error Reg. Coeff. (F Value)	r^2	Durbin-Watson or Turnovers	Significance	Chow's F	Significance	r^2 on Total	Average Deviation (000$)	r between e's PD	EB	A	Significance
Temporally Stable Rules	SC.1*	A_t 1951-69	1.0203	.0042 (60080.3)	.9997	1.79	>.01			.9997	420	-.06	-.28	.27	PD, EB, A >.01
	SC.2*	SC_t 1951-69	1.1273	.0111 (10361.0)	.9983	8	>.01			.9983	959	.77	.33	.35	PD <.01
Step Change Rules	SC.3*	A_t 1951-62	1.0334	.0086 (14500.0)	.9992	1.55	>.01	.668	>.01	.9997	402	-.03	-.31	.29	PD, EB, A >.01
	*	A_t 1963-69	1.0184	.0059 (29782.1)	.9998	1.87	>.01					-.08	-.23	-.18	PD, EB, A >.01
	SC.4*	SC_t 1951-64	1.1561	.0192 (3623.3)	.9964	4	>.01	1.002	>.01	.9984	995	.67	-.01	.46	PD <.01
	*	SC_t 1965-69	1.1183	.0162 (4746.2)	.9992	2	>.01					.91	.76	-.78	PD, EB, A <.01

*The LS technique with the intercept forced through the origin was used for estimation.

TABLE 21   FIT OF ALTERNATIVE RULES AT IMPLEMENTATION STEP (I_t)

		Independent Variable	Regression Coefficient	Std. Error Reg. Coeff. (F Value)	r^2	Durbin-Watson or Turnovers	Significance	Chow's F	Significance	r^2 on Total	Average Deviation ($000)	r between e's				Significance
												PD	EB	A	SC	
Temporally Stable Rules	I.1**	SC_t 1951-69	.9870	.0034 (85911.1)	.9998	1.27	>.01			.9998	143	-.14	.24	-.22	-.41	PD, EB, A, SC >.01
	I.2*	I_{t-1} 1951-69	1.1304	.0114 (9885.9)	.9982	8	>.01			.9982	940	.79	.38	.31	.26	PD <.01
Step Change Rules	I.3*	SC_t 1951-62	.9712	.0029 (11248.2)	.9999	1.04	>.01	.526	<.01	.9999	138	.09	.20	.21	-.23	PD, EB, A, SC >.01
	**	SC_t 1963-69	.9903	.0062 (25242.6)	.9998	1.18	>.01					-.24	.36	-.34	-.45	PD, EB, A, SC >.01
	I.4*	I_{t-1} 1951-54	1.1036	.0483 (440.1)	.9933	2	>.01	.951	<.01	.9983	824	.96	-.85	.46	.91	PD, EB, A, SC >.01
	*	I_{t-1} 1955-69	1.1326	.0119 (9118.0)	.9985	7	>.01					.78	.44	.31	.33	PD <.01

*The LS technique with the intercept forced through the origin was used for estimation.
**The GLS technique with the intercept forced through the origin was used for estimation.

Appendix C

Fortran IV Program
for Computer Model

```
          PROGRAM BUDGET (INPUT,OUTPUT,TAPE 60 = INPUT,TAPE 61 = OUTPUT,PUNC
         1H)
C         PROGRAM FOR BUDGETARY POLICY-MAKING IN WHO
          DIMENSION  PDORG(20), PDL(20), PDE(20), EBORG(20), EBT(20),
         Z AORG(20), AL(20), AE(20), SCL(20), SCE(20), SCT(20), EORG(20),
         Z ET(20), IYEAR(20), U(10,20), R(10,20,12),SE(10), SUM(10,20),
         Z PDT(20),AT(20),X(20,1000),ESUM(20),EMEAN(20),SY(20),Z(20),
         7 STD(20),RINC(120)
C         INPUT SECTION
          READ (60,100)   (IYEAR(I), I = 1,20)
      100 FORMAT (20I2)
          READ (60,110) B1,B2,B3,B4,B5,B6,B7,B8,B9,B10
      110 FORMAT (10F5.4)
          READ (60,120) (SE(I), I = 1,10)
      120 FORMAT (10F5.0)
          READ (60,130) AT(1)
      130 FORMAT (F5.0)
C         ZERO OUT ARRAYS
          DO 140 I = 1,20
          ESUM(I) = 0.0
          EMEAN(I) = 0.0
          SY(I) = 0.0
          Z(I) = 0.0
          STD(I) = 0.0
          DO 140  M = 1,1000
      140 X(I,M) = 0.0
C         SET M FOR SIMULATION RUN
          M = 1
C         GENERATE THE VALUES FOR THE STOCHASTIC VARIATE
      200 DO 220 I = 1,20
          DO 220 J = 1,10
          SUM(J,I) = 0.0
          DO 215 K = 1,12
          R(J,I,K) = RANF(N)
      215 SUM(J,I) = SUM(J,I) + R(J,I,K)
      220 U(J,I) = SE(J) * (SUM(J,I) - 6.0)
C         GENERATE MULTIVARIATE NORMAL DISTRIBUTION
          R1 = .6551
          DO 250 I = 1,20
      250 U(3,I) = R1 * U(2,I) + (SQRT(1-R1**2)) * U(3,I)
C         SET I FOR SIMULATION RUN
          I = 2
C         PROPOSAL DEVELOPMENT SUBMODEL
C         CALCULATE ORGANIZATIONAL FACTORS INCREMENT
      300 PDORG(I) = B1 * AT(I-1) + U(1,I)
C         CALCULATE EXTERNAL FACTORS INCREMENT
          PDE(I) = B2 * AT(I-1) + U(2,I)
C         CALCULATE LEADERSHIP FACTORS INCREMENT
          PDL(I) = B3 * AT(I-1) + U(3,I)
C         CALCULATE TOTAL FOR PROPOSAL DEVELOPMENT SUBMODEL
          PDT(I) = AT(I-1) + PDORG(I) + PDE(I) + PDL(I)
C         SEND BUDGET TO EXECUTIVE BODY SUBMODEL
C         EXECUTIVE BODY SUBMODEL
C         CALCULATE ORGANIZATIONAL FACTORS INCREMENT
          EBORG(I) = B4 * PDT(I) + U(4,I)
C         CALCULATE TOTAL FOR EXECUTIVE BODY SUBMODEL
          EBT(I) = PDT(I) + EBORG(I)
C         SEND BUDGET TO ASSEMBLY SUBMODEL
C         ASSEMBLY SUBMODEL
C         CALCULATE ORGANIZATIONAL FACTORS INCREMENT
          AORG(I) = B5 * EBT(I) + U(5,I)
C         CALCULATE EXTERNAL FACTORS INCREMENT
          AE(I) = B6 * EBT(I) + U(6,I)
C         CALCULATE LEADERSHIP FACTORS INCREMENT
          AL(I) = B7 * EBT(I) + U(7,I)
C         CALCULATE TOTAL FOR ASSEMBLY SUBMODEL
          AT(I) = EBT(I) + AORG(I) + AE(I) + AL(I)
C         SEND BUDGET TO SUPPLEMENTARY CHANGE SUBMODEL
C         SUPPLEMENTARY CHANGE SUBMODEL
C         CALCULATE EXTERNAL FACTORS
          SCE(I) = B8 * AT(I) + U(8,I)
```

```
C       CALCULATE LEADERSHIP FACTORS
        SCL(I) = B9 * AT(I) + U(9,I)
C       CALCULATE TOTAL FOR SUPPLEMENTARY CHANGE SUBMODEL
        SCT(I) = AT(I) + SCE(I) + SCL(I)
C       SEND BUDGET TO IMPLEMENTATION SUBMODEL
C       IMPLEMENTATION SUBMODEL
C       CALCULATE ORGANIZATIONAL FACTORS INCREMENT
        EORG(I) = B10 * SCT(I) + U(10,I)
C       CALCULATE TOTAL FOR IMPLEMENTATION SUBMODEL
        ET(I) = SCT(I) + EORG(I)
C       SAVE AND SUM EXPENDITURE TOTAL
        X(I,M) = ET(I)
        ESUM(I) = ESUM(I) + X(I,M)
C       CHECK TO SEE IF SIMULATION SHOULD RECYCLE OR TERMINATE
        I = I + 1
        IF (I-20)  300,300,390
  390   M = M + 1
        IF (M - 1000)  200,200,450
C       PUNCH OUT EXPENDITURE TOTALS
  450   I = 1
        DO 458  M = 1,100
        PUNCH 455, X(20,I), X(20,I+1), X(20,I+2), X(20,I+3), X(20,I+4),
      Z X(20,I+5), X(20,I+6), X(20,I+7), X(20,I+8), X(20,I+9)
  455   FORMAT (10F8.0)
        WRITE (61,456) X(20,I), X(20,I+1), X(20,I+2), X(20,I+3), X(20,I+4)
      Z, X(20,I+5), X(20,I+6), X(20,I+7), X(20,I+8), X(20,I+9)
  456   FORMAT (1X,F10.0)
  458   I = I + 10
        DO 460  I = 2,20
        EMEAN(I) = ESUM(I) / 1000
        DO 460  M = 1,1000
        X(I,M) = X(I,M) - EMEAN(I)
        SY(I) = SY(I) + X(I,M)**2
        Z(I) = SY(I) / 999
  460   STD(I) = SQRT(Z(I))
C       PRINT OUT RESULTS
        WRITE (61,500)
  500   FORMAT (1H1,*YEAR    MEAN    STANDARD DEVIATION*)
        DO 510  I = 2,20
  510   WRITE (61,520)  IYEAR(I),EMEAN(I),STD(I)
  520   FORMAT (I5,2F10.0)
        WRITE (61,600)
  600   FORMAT (1H1,*PARAMETERS*)
        WRITE (61,620)  B1,B2,B3,B4,B5,B6,B7,B8,B9,B10
  620   FORMAT (2X,10F8.4)
        WRITE (61,700)
  700   FORMAT (1H1,*STANDARD ERRORS*)
        DO 720  I = 1,10
  720   WRITE (61,730) SE(I)
  730   FORMAT (10F5.0)
        END
```

Appendix D

Details of Analysis of Variance of 1980 Projections

TABLE 22 POST-HOC PAIRWISE COMPARISONS OF 1980 PROJECTIONS

	Scenario 1 (7%, ORG)	Scenario 2 (7%, ORG, E)	Scenario 3 (7%, ORG, L)	Scenario 4 (7%, ORG, E, L)	Scenario 5 (8.9%, ORG)	Scenario 6 (8.9%, ORG, E)
Scenario 1 (7%, ORG)		-72.28	-72.33	-157.14	-82.39	-168.30
Scenario 2 (7%, ORG, E)	-$24,587		-.05	-84.85	-10.11	-96.02
Scenario 3 (7%, ORG, L)	-24,604	-$17		-84.81	-10.06	-95.97
Scenario 4 (7%, ORG, E, L)	-53,451	-28,864	-$28,847		74.75	-11.16
Scenario 5 (8.9%, ORG)	-28,026	-3,439	-3,422	$25,425		-85.91
Scenario 6 (8.9%, ORG,E)	-57,248	-32,661	-32,644	-3,797	-$29,222	
Scenario 7 (8.9%, ORG, L)	-57,821	-33,234	-33,217	-4,370	-29,795	-$573
Scenario 8 (8.9%, ORG, E,L)	-91,836	-67,249	-67,232	-38,385	-63,810	-34,588
Scenario 9 (11%, ORG)	-66,521	-41,934	-41,917	-13,070	-38,495	-9,273
Scenario 10 (11%, ORG, E)	-102,049	-74,462	-77,445	-48,598	-74,023	-44,801
Scenario 11 (11%, ORG, L)	-102,328	-77,741	-77,724	-48,877	-74,302	-45,080
Scenario 12 (11%, ORG, E, L)	-143,794	-119,207	-119,190	-90,343	-115,768	-86,546

NOTE: The t tests are in top triangle. They are marked with a □ if not significant at the .01 level for 11 and 988 degrees of freedom. The absolute difference in dollars is given in the lower triangle ($000).

TABLE 22—*Continued*

	Scenario 7 (8.9%, ORG, L)	Scenario 8 (8.9%, ORG, E, L)	Scenario 9 (11%, ORG)	Scenario 10 (11%, ORG, E)	Scenario 11 (11%, ORG, L)	Scenario 12 (11%, ORG, E, L)
Scenario 1 (7%, ORG)	-169.99	-269.98	-195.56	-300.01	-300.83	-422.73
Scenario 2 (7%, ORG, E)	-97.70	-197.70	-123.28	-227.73	-228.55	-350.45
Scenario 3 (7%, ORG, L)	-97.65	-197.65	-123.23	-227.68	-228.50	-350.40
Scenario 4 (7%, ORG, E, L)	-12.85	-112.85	-38.43	-142.87	-143.69	-265.60
Scenario 5 (8.9%, ORG)	-87.59	-187.59	-113.17	-217.62	-218.44	-340.34
Scenario 6 (8.9%, ORG, E)	-1.69	-101.68	27.26	-131.71	-132.53	-254.43
Scenario 7 (8.9%, ORG, L)		-100.00	-25.58	-130.03	-130.84	-252.75
Scenario 8 (8.9%, ORG, E, L)	-$34,015		74.42	-30.03	-30.85	-152.75
Scenario 9 (11%, ORG)	-8,700	$25,315		-104.45	-105.27	-227.17
Scenario 10 (11%, ORG, E)	-44,228	-10,213	-$35,528		-.82	-122.72
Scenario 11 (11%, ORG, L)	-44,507	-10,492	-35,807	$-279		-121.90
Scenario 12 (11%, ORG, E, L)	-85,973	-51,958	-77,273	-41,745	-$41,466	

NOTE: The *t* tests are in top triangle. They are marked with a □ if not significant at the .01 level for 11 and 988 degrees of freedom. The absolute difference in dollars is given in the lower triangle ($000).

TABLE 23   ANALYSIS OF VARIANCE TABLE FOR 1980 PROJECTIONS

Source	SS	df	MS	F	p
Rows[a]	12,245,294,000,000	2	6,127,147,200,000	105,914.38	<.01
Columns[b]	6,318,604,100,000	3	2,106,201,400,000	36,407.98	<.01
Interaction	142,850,960,000	6	23,808,494,000	411.53	<.01
Error between Cells	692,857,030,000	11,976	57,853,793		
Total	19,408,606,090,000	11,987			

[a]Organizational factors at proposal development step.

[b]Inputs.

Appendix E

1949-69 WHO Data for the Steps in the Budget Process

TABLE 24   DATA FOR THE STEPS IN THE BUDGET PROCESS: WORLD HEALTH ORGANIZATION ($000)

	Proposal Development Step	Executive Body Step	Assembly Step	Supplementary Change Step	Implementation Step
1949	6368	*	5000	6037	5434
1950	8193	8193	7502	7622	7583
1951	7651	7300	7300	7697	7185
1952	8703	7678	7678	8709	8414
1953	8490	8490	8485	8970	8504
1954	8572	8572	8497	8497	8135
1955	10311	10311	9500	9500	9275
1956	9612	9600	10203	10203	9983
1957	12967	12525	12225	12550	12091
1958	14417	13632	13566	13566	13171
1959	14287	14287	14287	14949	14654
1960	16419	16419	16919	16919	16624
1961	18569	18569	18975	19780	19202
1962	21600	21577	23607	24864	24165
1963	29956	29956	29956	30394	29784
1964	34065	34065	34065	34543	33869
1965	38360	38360	38360	39507	33346
1966	42390	42442	42442	44482	43440
1967	49200	51615	51515	52075	51339
1968	55994	55994	56123	56123	55563
1969	60784	60784	60784	62122	61687

*There was no executive body recommendation for 1949.

Notes

Chapter 1

1. For a systematic survey of the literature of quantitative international politics, see Susan D. Jones and J. David Singer, *Beyond Conjecture in International Politics: Abstracts of Data-Based Research* (Ithaca, N.Y.: F.E. Peacock Publishers, 1972).

2. For an introduction to different meanings of the approach and a presentation of the pros and cons involved, see Klaus Knorr and James N. Rosenau, eds., *Contending Approaches to International Politics* (Princeton, N.J.: Princeton University Press, 1969).

3. Richard S. Rudner, *Philosophy of Social Science* (Englewood Cliffs, N.J.: Prentice-Hall, 1966), p. 10.

4. See George P. Murdock, "Anthropology as a Comparative Science," *Behavioral Science* 2(1957):249-54; Arthur L. Kalleberg, "The Logic of Comparison: A Methodological Note on the Comparative Study of Political Systems," *World Politics* 19(1966):69-82; and Gideon Sjoberg, "The Comparative Method in the Social Sciences," *Philosophy of Science* 22(1955):106-17.

5. S. Stevens in Fred N. Kerlinger, *Foundations of Behavioral Research: Educational and Psychological Inquiry* (New York: Holt, Rinehart and Winston, 1966), p. 411.

6. For an overview of this literature, see Richard C. Snyder and James A. Robinson, *National and International Decision-Making* (New York: Institute for International Order, 1961); and James A. Robinson and Richard C. Snyder, "Decision-Making in International Politics," in *International Behavior: A Social-Psychological Analysis*, ed. Herbert C. Kelman (New York: Holt, Rinehart and Winston, 1965), pp. 435-63.

7. See Richard C. Snyder, H.W. Bruck, and Burton Sapin, *Decision-Making as an Approach to the Study of International Politics* Foreign Policy Analysis Series, no. 3 (Princeton, N.J.: Princeton University, Organizational Behavior Section, 1954); Richard C. Snyder, "A Decision-Making Approach to the Study of Political Phenomena," in *Approaches to the Study of Politics*, ed. Roland Young (Evanston, Ill: Northwestern University Press, 1958), pp. 3-38; Richard C. Snyder, H.W. Bruck, and Burton Sapin, eds., *Foreign Policy Decision-Making: An Approach to the Study of International Politics* (New York: The Free Press, 1962), pp. 14-185; Glenn D. Paige, *The Korean Decision* (New York: The Free Press, 1968); and Richard C. Snyder and Glenn D. Paige, "The United States' Decision to Resist Aggression in Korea: The Application of an Analytical Scheme," *Administrative Science Quarterly* 3(1958):341-78.

8. See Joseph Frankel, *The Making of Foreign Policy: An Analysis of*

Decision-Making (New York: Oxford University Press, 1963). Frankel does not call for the re-creation of the decision-making situation in the eyes of the decision-maker. For other critiques of the Snyder, Bruck, and Sapin framework, see Herbert McClosky, "Concerning Strategies for a Science of International Politics," in Snyder, Bruck, and Sapin, *Foreign Policy Decision-Making*, pp. 186-205; Stanley Hoffman, "International Relations: The Long Road to Theory," *World Politics* 11(1959):346-77; and James N. Rosenau, "The Premises and Promises of Decision-Making Analysis," in *Contemporary Political Analysis*, ed. James C. Charlesworth (New York: The Free Press, 1967), pp. 189-211.

9. See David Easton, "An Approach to the Analysis of Political Systems," *World Politics* 9(1957):383-400; idem, *The Political System: An Inquiry into the State of Political Science* (New York: Alfred A. Knopf, 1953); idem, *A Framework for Political Analysis* (Englewood Cliffs, N.J.: Prentice-Hall, 1965); idem, *A Systems Analysis of Political Life* (New York: John Wiley and Sons, 1965).

10. Karl W. Deutsch, *The Nerves of Government* (New York: The Free Press, 1963).

11. Roger Hilsman, "The Foreign-Policy Consensus: An Interim Research Report," *Journal of Conflict Resolution* 3(1959):361-82; idem, *To Move A Nation: The Politics of Foreign Policy in the Administration of John F. Kennedy* (New York: Dell Publishing Co., 1964).

12. Hilsman, *To Move a Nation*, pp. 541-3; 543-4; 548.

13. These article-length publications have been collected in James N. Rosenau, *The Scientific Study of Foreign Policy* (New York: The Free Press, 1971).

14. For a survey of this literature, see Patrick J. McGowan and Howard B. Shapiro, *The Comparative Study of Foreign Policy: A Survey of Scientific Findings* (Beverly Hills, Calif.: Sage Publications, 1973).

15. Graham T. Allison, "Conceptual Models and the Cuban Missile Crisis," *American Political Science Review* 63(1969):689-718; idem, *Essence of Decision: Explaining the Cuban Missile Crisis* (Boston: Little, Brown and Co., 1971); Graham T. Allison and Morton H. Halperin, "Bureaucratic Politics: A Paradigm and Some Policy Implications," *World Politics* 24(1972):40-79.

16. Aaron Wildavsky, *The Politics of the Budgetary Process* (Boston: Little, Brown and Co., 1964); see also Aaron Wildavsky and Arthur Hammann, "Comprehensive Versus Incremental Budgeting in the Department of Agriculture," *Administrative Science Quarterly* 10(1965):321-46. For another foundation for the modern era of budgeting studies, see Richard F. Fenno, Jr., *The Power of the Purse: Appropriations Politics in Congress* (Boston: Little, Brown and Co., 1966).

17. Otto A. Davis, M.A.H. Dempster, and Aaron Wildavsky, "A Theory of the Budgetary Process," *American Political Science Review* 60(1966):529-47; idem, "On the Process of Budgeting: An Empirical Study of Congressional

Appropriations," *Papers on Non-Market Decision Making* 1(1966):63-132; idem, "On the Process of Budgeting II: An Empirical Study of Congressional Appropriations," in *Studies in Budgeting,* ed. R.F. Byrne, et al. (Amsterdam: North-Holland Publishing Co., 1971), pp. 292-376.

18. Otto A. Davis, M.A.H. Dempster, and Aaron Wildavsky, "Towards a Predictive Theory of Government Expenditure I: U.S. Domestic Appropriations" (Paper delivered at the Annual Meeting of the American Political Science Association, New Orleans, La., September 4-8, 1973).

19. John P. Crecine, "A Computer Simulation Model of Municipal Budgeting," *Management Science* 13(1967):786-815; idem, "A Simulation of Municipal Budgeting: The Impact of Problem Environment," in *Simulation in the Study of Politics,* ed. William D. Coplin (Chicago: Markham Publishing Co., 1968), pp. 115-46; idem, *Governmental Problem Solving: A Computer Simulation of Municipal Budgeting* (Chicago: Rand McNally and Co., 1969); idem, *Defense Budgeting: Organizational Adaptation to External Constraints* Memorandum RM-6121-PR (Santa Monica, Calif.: Rand Corporation, 1970); idem, "Defense Budgeting: Organizational Adaptation to Environmental Constraints," in Byrne, *Studies in Budgeting,* pp. 210-61. The first three citations report on the Detroit, Cleveland, and Pittsburgh study and relate the external constraints to the policy-making process.

20. Donald A. Gerwin, *Budgeting Public Funds: The Decision Process in an Urban School District* (Madison: University of Wisconsin Press, 1969); idem, "Towards a Theory of Public Budget Decision-Making," in Byrne, *Studies in Budgeting,* pp. 262-91; John L. Stromberg, *The Internal Mechanisms of the Defense Budget Process, Fiscal 1953-1968* Memorandum RM-6243 (Santa Monica, Calif.: Rand Corporation, 1970); Arnold Kanter, "Congress and the Defense Budget: 1960-1970," *American Political Science Review* 66(1972):129-43; Thomas Anton, *The Politics of State Expenditure in Illinois* (Urbana: University of Illinois Press, 1966); Ira Sharkansky, "Economic and Political Correlates of State Government Expenditures: General Tendencies and Deviant Cases," *Midwest Journal of Political Science* 2(1967):173-92; idem, "Agency Requests, Gubernatorial Support and Budget Success in State Legislatures," *American Political Science Review* 62(1968):1220-31.

21. Stromberg, *Internal Mechanisms;* Kanter, "Congress and the Defense Budget"; Peter B. Natchez and Irvin C. Bupp, "Policy and Priority in the Budgetary Process," *American Political Science Review* 67(1973):951-63.

22. Oliver E. Williamson, "A Rational Theory of the Federal Budgeting Process," *Papers on Non-Market Decision Making* 2(1967): 71-89; John E. Jackson, "Politics and the Budgetary Process," *Social Science Research* 1(1972):35-60; Natchez and Bupp, "Policy and Priority."

23. John Wanat, "Bases of Budgetary Incrementalism," *American Political Science Review,* 68(1974):1221-8.

24. For an overview of organization theory, see James G. March and Herbert A. Simon, *Organizations* (New York: John Wiley and Sons, 1958); James G.

March, ed., *Handbook of Organizations* (Chicago: Rand McNally and Co., 1965); James D. Thompson, *Organizations in Action* (New York: McGraw Hill Book Co., 1967).

25. See Herbert A. Simon, *Administrative Behavior: A Study of Decision-Making Processes in Administrative Organization*, 2nd ed. (New York: The Free Press, 1966); idem, "A Behavioral Model of Rational Choice," *Quarterly Journal of Economics* 60(1955):99-118; idem, "Theories of Decision-Making in Economics and Behavioral Science," *American Economic Review* 69(1959):253-83; Paul Wasserman and Fred S. Silander, *Decision-Making: An Annotated Bibliography* (Ithaca, N.Y.: Cornell University Press, 1958); Paul Wasserman, *Decision-Making: An Annotated Bibliography, Supplement 1958-1963* (Ithaca, N.Y.: Cornell University Press, 1965); Ward Edwards, "The Theory of Decision-Making," *Psychological Bulletin* 51(1954):380-417; idem, "Behavioral Decision Theory," *Annual Review of Psychology* 12(1961):473-98; William J. Gore and Fred S. Silander, "A Bibliographical Essay on Decision-Making," *Administrative Science Quarterly* 4(1969):97-121; Julian Feldman and Hershel E. Kanter, "Organizational Decision-Making," in March, *Handbook of Organizations*, pp. 614-49; Donald W. Taylor, "Decision Making and Problem Solving," in March, *Handbook of Organizations*, pp. 48-86; Herbert A. Simon, "Political Research: The Decision-Making Framework," in *Varieties of Political Theories*, ed. David Easton (Englewood Cliffs, N.J.: Prentice-Hall, 1966), pp. 15-24.

26. Simon, *Administrative Behavior*. See also Kalman J. Cohen and Richard M. Cyert, "Simulation of Organizational Behavior," in March, *Handbook of Organizations*, pp. 305-34; R.M. Cyert and J.G. March, eds., *A Behavioral Theory of the Firm* (Englewood Cliffs, N.J.: Prentice-Hall, 1963); Herbert A. Simon and Allen Newell, "Models: Their Use and Limitations," in *The State of the Social Sciences*, ed. Leonard D. White (Chicago: University of Chicago Press, 1956), pp. 66-83.

27. Daniel Katz and Robert L. Kahn, *The Social Psychology of Organizations* (New York: John Wiley and Sons, 1966); Cyert and March, *Behavioral Theory*.

28. Cyert and March, *Behavioral Theory*.

29. For an overview of the literature on international organizations, see Ronald J. Yalem, "The Study of International Organization, 1920-1965: A Survey of the Literature," *Background* 10(1966):1-56.

30. Chadwick F. Alger, "Research on Research: A Decade of Quantitative and Field Research on International Organizations," *International Organization* 24(1970):416-17.

31. Robert E. Riggs, et al., "Behavioralism in the Study of the United Nations," *World Politics* 22(1970):202-3.

32. See Chadwick F. Alger, "Interaction and Negotiation in a Committee of the United Nations General Assembly," *Peace Research Society (International) Papers* 5(1966):141-60; idem, "Interaction in a Committee of the United Nations General Assembly," in *Quantitative International Politics: Insights and Evidence*, ed. J. David Singer (New York: The Free

Press, 1968), pp. 51-84; idem, "Negotiation, Regional Groups, Interaction, and Public Debate in the Development of Consensus in the United Nations General Assembly" (Paper presented at the Sixth World Congress of Sociology, International Sociology Association, Evian, France, September 1966); John G. Hadwen and Johan Kaufmann, *How United Nations Decisions are Made* (Leyden, The Netherlands: A.W. Sythoff, 1960); Johan Kaufmann, *Conference Diplomacy* (Leyden, The Netherlands: A.W. Sythoff, 1968); Robert O. Keohane, "The Study of Political Influence in the General Assembly," *International Organization* 21(1967):221-37; Hayward R. Alker, Jr., "Dimensions of Conflict in the General Assembly," *American Political Science Review* 58(1964):642-57; Jack E. Vincent, "National Attributes as Predictors of Delegate Attitudes at the United Nations," *American Political Science Review* 67(1968):916-31; idem, "The Convergence of Voting and Attitude Patterns at the United Nations," *Journal of Politics* 31(1969):952-83; idem, "Predicting Voting Patterns in the General Assembly," *American Political Science Review* 65(1971):471-98; Arend Lijphart, "The Analysis of Bloc Voting in the General Assembly: A Critique and a Proposal," *American Political Science Review* 57(1963):902-17; Leroy N. Rieselbach, "Quantitative Techniques for Studying Voting Behavior in the U.N. General Assembly," *International Organization* 14(1960):291-306; Bruce M. Russett, "Discovering Voting Groups in the United Nations," *American Political Science Review* 60(1966):327-39; Richard Pratt and R.J. Rummel, "Issue Dimensions in the 1963 United Nations General Assembly," *Multivariate Behavioral Research* 3(July 1971):251-86; Hayward R. Alker, Jr. and Bruce M. Russett, *World Politics in the General Assembly* (New Haven, Conn.: Yale University Press, 1965); Thomas Hovet, *Bloc Politics in the United Nations* (Cambridge, Mass.: Harvard University Press, 1960); idem, *Africa in the United Nations* (Evanston, Ill.: Northwestern University Press, 1963).

33. See Ernst B. Haas, *Beyond the Nation State: Functionalism and International Organization* (Stanford, Calif.: Stanford University Press, 1964); idem, *The Uniting of Europe: Political, Social, and Economic Forces, 1950-1957* (Stanford, Calif.: Stanford University Press, 1958); Leon N. Lindberg, *The Political Dynamics of European Economic Integration* (Stanford, Calif.: Stanford University Press, 1963); idem, "Decision Making and Integration in the European Community," *International Organization* 19(1965):56-80; Ernst B. Haas and Philippe C. Schmitter, "Economics and Differential Patterns of Political Integration: Projections about Unity in Latin America," *International Organization* 18(1964):705-37; Roger D. Hansen, "Regional Integration: Reflections on a Decade of Theoretical Efforts," *World Politics* 21(1969):242-71; Leon N. Lindberg and Stuart A. Scheingold, *Europe's Would-be Polity: Patterns of Change in the European Community* (Englewood Cliffs, N.J.: Prentice-Hall, 1970); Leon N. Lindberg and Stuart A. Scheingold, eds., *Regional Integration, Theory and Research* (Cambridge, Mass.: Harvard University Press, 1971); Joseph S. Nye, *Peace in Parts: Integration and Conflict in Regional Organization* (Boston: Little, Brown and Co., 1971).

34. See R.W. Cox and H.K. Jacobson, "Decision-Making in International

Organizations: An Interim Report" (Paper presented at the Annual Meeting of the American Political Science Association, New York City, September 2-6, 1969); J. David Singer, *Financing International Organizations: The United Nations Budget Process* (The Hague: Martinus Nijhoff, 1961); John G. Stoessinger, et al., *Financing the United Nations System* (Washington, D.C.: Brookings Institution, 1964); Norman Hill, "The Allocation of Expenses in International Organizations," *American Political Science Review* 21(1927):128-37; Yalem, "The Study of International Organization."

35. Robert W. Cox and Harold K. Jacobson, *The Anatomy of Influence: Decision-Making in International Organization* (New Haven, Conn.: Yale University Press, 1973), pp. 1-36.

36. Claude-Albert Colliard, "La Procedure Budgetaire des Organisations Internationales," *Revue de Science Financiere* 2(1958):237-60; idem, "Les Principes Budgetaries dans les Organisations Internationales," *Revue de Science Financiere* 3(1958):437-60.

37. Stoessinger, et al., *Financing the United Nations System;* Gerard J. Mangone and Anand K. Srivastava, "Budgeting for the United Nations," *International Organization* 12(1958):473-85.

38. Terence Higgins, "The Politics of United Nations Finance," *The World Today* 19(1963):380-89; Inis L. Claude, Jr., "The Political Framework of the United Nations' Financial Problems," *International Organization* 17(1963):831-59.

39. Norbert Kohlhase, "Le rôle des missions permanentes dans le processus de decision budgetaire des Commanautés européenes, de l'OCDE et de l'OIT," in Dotation Carnegie Pour la Paix Internationale, *Les Missions Permanentes Aupres des Organisations Internationales,* vol. 2 (Brussels: Etablissements Emile Bruylant, 1973), pp. 11-189.

40. Edward Miles, "Organizations and Integration in International Systems," *International Studies Quarterly* 12(1968):196-224.

41. Hayward R. Alker, Jr. and Cheryl Christensen, "From Causal Modelling to Artificial Intelligence: The Evolution of a UN Peace Making Simulation," in *Experimentation and Simulation in Political Science,* ed. J. LaPonce and P. Smoker (Toronto: University of Toronto Press, 1972), pp. 177-224; Hayward R. Alker, Jr. and William J. Greenberg, "The UN Charter: Alternate Pasts and Alternate Futures," in *The United Nations: Problems and Prospects,* ed. Edwin H. Fedder (St. Louis: Center for International Studies, University of Missouri-St. Louis, 1971), pp. 113-42.

Chapter 2

1. Leon N. Lindberg and Stuart A. Scheingold, *Europe's Would-be Polity: Patterns of Change in the European Community* (Englewood Cliffs, N.J.: Prentice-Hall, 1970), p. 71; R.W. Cox and H.K. Jacobson, "Decision-Making in International Organizations: An Interim Report" (Paper presented at the Annual Meeting of the American Political Science Association, New York

City, September 2-6, 1969), pp. 9-13; Joseph S. Nye, *Peace in Parts: Integration and Conflict in Regional Organization* (Boston: Little, Brown and Co., 1971), p. 40; William Coplin, *The Functions of International Law* (Chicago: Rand McNally and Co., 1966), pp. 152-5; Chadwick F. Alger, "Decisions to Undertake New Activities in Assemblies and Councils of the UN System," in *The United Nations: Problems and Prospects*, ed. Edwin H. Fedder (St. Louis: Center for International Studies, University of Missouri-St. Louis, 1971), p. 169.

2. Hayward R. Alker, Jr. and Bruce M. Russett, *World Politics in the General Assembly* (New Haven, Conn.: Yale University Press, 1965); Richard Pratt and R. J. Rummel, "Issues Dimensions in the 1963 United Nations General Assembly," *Multivariate Behavioral Research* 6(1971):251-86.

3. For an overview of the issue-area concerns of scholars, see Robert A. Dahl, *Who Governs?* (New Haven, Conn.: Yale University Press, 1961); James N. Rosenau, "Pre-Theories and Theories of Foreign Policy," in *Approaches to Comparative and International Politics,* ed. R. Barry Farrell (Evanston, Ill.: Northwestern University Press, 1966), pp. 27-92; Aaron Wildavsky, "The Analysis of Issue-Contexts in the Study of Decision-Making," *Journal of Politics* 24(1962):717-32.

4. World Health Organization, *Handbook of Resolutions and Decisions of the World Health Assembly and the Executive Board, 1948-72*, vol. 1 (Geneva: World Health Organization, 1973), pp. 437-8. (World Health Organization hereafter cited as WHO.)

5. *Everyman's United Nations*, 8th ed. (New York: United Nations, 1968), p. 24.

6. Chadwick F. Alger, "Interaction and Negotiation in a Committee of the United Nations General Assembly," *Peace Research Society (International) Papers* 5(1966):143.

7. WHO, *Handbook of Resolutions*, vol. 1, p. 1.

8. International Labour Organisation, *Draft Budget, Programme and Budget Proposals, 1967, and Other Financial Questions* (Geneva: International Labour Office, 1966), p. 1.

9. David Easton, *A Framework for Political Analysis* (Englewood Cliffs, N.J.: Prentice-Hall, 1963), pp. 108-17; Karl W. Deutsch, *The Nerves of Government* (New York: The Free Press, 1963), pp. 258-61; Rosenau, "Pre-theories," pp. 42-3; Lindberg and Scheingold, *Europe's Would-be Polity*, pp. 110-6; Nye, *Peace in Parts*, pp. 55-107; Phillippe C. Schmitter, "A Revised Theory of Regional Integration," in *Regional Integration: Theory and Research*, ed. Leon N. Lindberg and Stuart A. Scheingold (Cambridge, Mass.: Harvard University Press, 1971), pp. 246-9.

10. Rosenau discusses five clusters of variables (governmental, systemic, idiosyncratic, role, and societal) which need to be taken into account in the study of foreign policy-making ("Pre-theories," pp. 42-3). In this study, I have changed governmental to organizational, systemic to external, and idiosyncratic and role have been merged to form a leadership category. For the study of IGOs, the societal category is not relevant.

11. International Labour Organisation, *Draft Budget,* p. 11.

12. WHO, *Handbook of Resolutions,* vol. 1, p. 230.

13. For an overview of the literature on leadership, see Dorwin Cartwright, "Influence, Leadership, Control," in *Handbook of Organizations,* ed. James G. March (Chicago: Rand McNally and Co., 1965), pp. 1-47; John R. Raser, *Personal Characteristics of Political Decision-Makers: A Literature Review* (La Jolla, Calif.: Western Behavioral Sciences Institute, 1965); Fred I. Greenstein, "The Impact of Personality on Politics: An Attempt to Clean Away Underbrush," *American Political Science Review* 61(1967):629-41; Daniel Katz and Robert L. Kahn, *The Social Psychology of Organizations* (New York: John Wiley and Sons, 1966); Rosenau, "Pre-Theories," pp. 42-3.

14. WHO, *Handbook of Resolutions,* vol. 1, pp. 216-17.

15. See Dahl, *Who Governs?;* Floyd Hunter, *Community Power Structure: A Study of Decision Makers* (Garden City, N.Y.: Anchor Books, 1963). There are numerous other studies, but these are the major ones regarding who governs. For examples of literature concerned with the behavioral rules used by policy-makers, see the section in Chapter 1 which deals with behavioral budgetary theory.

16. For an alternate scheme for classifying policy-makers in IGOs, see Robert W. Cox and Harold K. Jacobson, *The Anatomy of Influence: Decision-making in International Organization* (New Haven, Conn.: Yale University Press, 1973), pp. 15-36.

17. For general information on how nations organize themselves in work with IGOs, see United States General Accounting Office, *Report to the Congress, U.S. Participation in the World Health Organization, Department of State, Department of Health, Education, and Welfare, By the Comptroller General of the United States* (Washington, D.C.: U.S. Government Printing Office, 1969); Johan Kaufmann, *Conference Diplomacy* (Leyden, The Netherlands: A.W. Sythoff, 1968); Norbert Kohlhase, "Le rôle des missions permanentes dans le processus de décision budgetaire des Commanautés européenes, de l'OCDE et de l'OIT," in Dotation Carnegie Pour la Paix Internationale, *Les Missions Permanentes Aupres des Organisations Internationales,* vol. 2 (Brussels: Etablissements Emile Bruylant, 1973), pp. 11-189; Roger Gregoire, *Administrations Nationales et Organisations Internationales. Les problemes administratifs qui se posent aux nouveaux etats de fait de leur participation a L'Organisation des Nations Unies et aux Institutions Specialisees* (Paris: Organisation Des Nations Unies Pour L'Education La Science et La Culture, circa 1954); idem, *National Administration and International Organization: A Comparative Survey of Fourteen Countries* (Brussels: UNESCO and Institut International Des Sciences Administratives Bruxelles, 1951).

18. WHO, *Twenty-First World Health Assembly,* Official Records of WHO, no. 169 (1968), p. 15.

19. Ibid., p. 14.

20. For an overview of research on the executive head, see Mark W. Zacher,

"The Secretary-General: Some Comments on Recent Research," *International Organization* 23(1969):932-50.

21. *Yearbook of the United Nations, 1947-48* (New York: United Nations, 1949), p. 827; *Yearbook of the United Nations, 1970* (New York: United Nations, 1972), p. 891.

22. For general information on the role of the secretariat, see Walter R. Sharp, *Field Administration in the United Nations System* (New York: Frederick A. Praeger, 1961); Sydney D. Bailey, *The Secretariat of the United Nations* (New York: Carnegie Endowment for International Peace, 1962); Georges Langrod, *The International Civil Service: Its Nature, Its Evolution* (Leyden, The Netherlands: A.W. Sythoff, 1963); Leland M. Goodrich, "The Secretariat of the United Nations," in *UN Administration of Economic and Social Programs,* ed. Gerard J. Mangone (New York: Columbia University Press, 1966), pp. 1-36.

23. For an overview of the activities of the resident representative, see Gerard J. Mangone, "Field Administration: The United Nations Resident Representative," in Mangone, *UN Administration,* pp. 158-230.

24. *Yearbook of International Organizations,* 14th ed. (Brussels: Union of International Associations, 1972), p. 879.

25. For general information on inter-organizational relations and relations among IGOs specifically, see Harold Guetzkow, "Relations Among Organizations," in *Studies on Behavior in Organizations: A Research Symposium,* ed. Raymond V. Bowers (Athens: University of Georgia Press, 1966), pp. 13-44; Sharp, *Field Administration,* pp. 295-501; Martin Hill, "The Administrative Committee on Coordination," in *The Evolution of International Organizations,* ed. Evan Luard (London: Thames and Hudson, 1966), pp. 104-57; WHO, "Organizational Study: Coordination with the United Nations and the Specialized Agencies," *Executive Board, Twenty-Ninth Session,* Official Records of WHO, no. 115 (1962), pp. 122-42.

26. *Report of the Fourteenth Session of the Conference, 4-23 November 1967* (Rome: Food and Agriculture Organization of the United Nations, 1968), p. 360.

27. For general information on the role of NGOs, see Donald G. Blaisdell, "Relationship of Inter-Governmental to Non-Governmental Organization" (Paper presented at the Sixth World Congress of the International Political Science Association, Geneva, September 21-25, 1964); J.J. Lador-Lederer, *International Non-Governmental Organizations* (Brussels: Union of International Associations, 1957).

28. *Report of the Fourteenth Session,* p. 367.

29. WHO, *The Work of WHO, 1968,* Official Records of WHO, no. 172 (1969), p. 231.

30. Otto A. Davis, M.A.H. Dempster, and Aaron Wildavsky, "A Theory of the Budgetary Process," *American Political Science Review* 60(1966):534.

31. Oliver E. Williamson, "A Rational Theory of the Federal Budgeting Process," *Papers on Non-Market Decision-Making* 2(1967):71-89.

32. For a presentation of the elite and pluralist debate, see Dahl, *Who Governs?*; and Hunter, *Community Power Structure.* For a presentation of the incremental and comprehensive discussion, see Charles E. Lindblom, "The Science of Muddling Through," *Public Administration Review* 19(1959):79-88; idem, *The Intelligence of Democracy* (New York: The Free Press, 1965); Aaron Wildavsky and Arthur Hammann, "Comprehensive Versus Incremental Budgeting in the Department of Agriculture," *Administrative Science Quarterly* 10(1965):321-46. For clarification on the rational and bounded rational positions, see Herbert A. Simon, "A Behavioral Model of Rational Choice," *Quarterly Journal of Economics* 60(1955):99-118. For a discussion of the executive and legislative nature of decision-making, see Samuel P. Huntington, *The Common Defense* (New York: Columbia University Press, 1961). Regarding the individual and collective aspects of policy-making, see Mancur Olson, Jr., *The Logic of Collective Action* (New York: Schocken Books, 1968).

33. J[ohn] Johnston, *Econometric Methods* (New York: McGraw Hill Book Co., 1963), p. 232.

34. Ibid., pp. 4-9.

35. Williamson, "Rational Theory," pp. 71-89.

36. Davis, Dempster, and Wildavsky, "A Theory of the Budgetary Process"; idem, "On the Process of Budgeting: An Empirical Study of Congressional Appropriation," *Papers on Non-Market Decision-Making* 1(1966):63-132; John P. Crecine, "A Computer Simulation Model of Municipal Budgeting," *Management Science* 13(1967):786-815; idem, *Governmental Problem Solving: A Computer Simulation of Municipal Budgeting* (Chicago: Rand McNally and Co., 1969); Joseph Frankel, *The Making of Foreign Policy: An Analysis of Decision-Making* (New York: Oxford University Press, 1963), pp. 176-218; Leon N. Lindberg, "Political Integration as a Multidimensional Phenomenon Requiring Multivariate Measurement" in Lindberg and Scheingold, *Regional Integration*, pp. 64-7; J. David Singer, *Financing International Organizations: The United Nations Budget Process* (The Hague: Martinus Nijhoff, 1961), pp. 30-172.

37. *Report of the Director-General on the Activities of the Organization in 1965* (Paris: UNESCO, 1966), p. 117.

38. *Everyman's United Nations*, p. 503.

39. Lindberg and Scheingold, *Europe's Would-be Polity*, p. 83.

40. UNESCO, *Report of the Director-General, 1965*, p. 117.

41. *Everyman's United Nations*, pp. 14-16.

42. UNESCO, *Records of the General Conference, Fourteenth Session, Resolutions* (Paris: UNESCO, 1967), p. 79.

43. WHO, *Handbook of Resolutions*, vol. 1, p. 226.

44. International Labour Organisation, *Draft Budget*, p. 11.

45. For a discussion of recursive and block recursive systems, see Phoebus J. Dhrymes, *Econometrics, Statistical Foundations and Applications* (New York: Harper and Row, 1970), pp. 303-13.

Chapter 3

1. Scholarly literature on WHO includes Robert Berkov, *The World Health Organization: A Study of Decentralized Administration* (Paris: Libraries Minnd, 1957); Hilary Rose, "A Rejection of the WHO Research Centre: A Case Study of Decision-Making in International Scientific Collaboration," *Minerva* 5(1967):340-56; Frederick William Clements, "The WHO in Southern Asia and the Western Pacific," *Pacific Affairs* 25(1952):334-48; Howard B. Calderwood, "The World Health Organization and Its Regional Organizations," *Temple Law Quarterly* 37(1963):15-27; Frank Gutteridge, "The World Health Organization: Its Scope and Achievements," *Temple Law Quarterly* 23(1963):1-14; Charles E. Allen, "World Health and World Politics," *International Organization* 4(1950):27-43; Brock Chisolm "Barriers to World Health," *International Conciliation* 491(1953):260-6; Ascot Mudaliar, "World Health Problems," *International Conciliation* 491(1953):229-59; Charles S. Ascher, "Current Problems in the World Health Organization's Program,"*International Organization* 6(1952):27-50; Charles E. Winslow, "World Health Organization," *International Conciliation* 437(1948):109-52; Philip E. Jacob and Alexine L. Atherton, "Safeguarding the World's Health," in *The Dynamics of International Organization: The Making of World Order* (Homewood, Ill.: The Dorsey Press, 1965), pp. 493-522; R. Pethybridge, "The Influence of International Politics on the Activities of 'Non-Political' Specialized Agencies: A Case Study," *Political Studies* 13(1965):247-51; Albert Deutsch, *The World Health Organization: Its Global Battle Against Disease* (New York: Public Affairs Committee, Inc., 1958); Robert Weiner, "Patterns of Interaction in a Main Committee of the World Health Assembly," mimeographed (Boston: Boston State College, 1974).

2. For the best historical treatment of WHO, see WHO, *The First Ten Years of the World Health Organization* (Geneva: WHO, 1958); idem, *The Second Ten Years of the World Health Organization, 1958-1967* (Geneva: WHO, 1968).

3. For a detailed treatment of WHO's historical precedents, see WHO, *The First Ten Years*, pp. 3-34.

4. For a detailed treatment of the founding of WHO, see ibid., pp. 37-145.

5. WHO, *Basic Documents*, 19th ed. (Geneva: WHO, 1968), p. 2.

6. WHO, *Basic Documents*, 21st ed. (Geneva: WHO, 1970), pp. 1-18.

7. WHO, *First World Health Assembly*, Official Records of WHO, no. 13 (1948).

8. For a detailed treatment of WHO's activities during the late 1950s and 1960s, see WHO, *The Second Ten Years*.

9. *Yearbook of International Organizations*, 12th ed. (Brussels: Union of International Associations, 1969), p. 13.

10. In a technical sense, there are only thirteen specialized agencies. The International Atomic Energy Agency has been treated as a specialized agency because it is felt that by most criteria it must be considered so.

11. The factor analysis was done on the CDC 6600 computer at Wrubel Computing Center, Indiana University, Bloomington, Indiana. The SPSS factor analysis program PA1 was used. See Norman Nie, Dale H. Bent, and C. Hadlai Hull, *SPSS: Statistical Package for the Social Sciences* (New York: McGraw Hill Book Co., 1970), pp. 208-44. For an introduction to factor analysis, see R. J. Rummel, "Understanding Factor Analysis," *The Journal of Conflict Resolution* 11(December 1967):444-80.

Some noise may be introduced into the analysis because of considerable deviation from the normal distribution by certain of the arrays of data. I considered transforming the data, but in the final analysis decided not to do so. It is my feeling that the product moment correlation coefficient is robust and partially compensates for this problem. I chose to keep everything as simple as possible. The correlation matrix used in the factor analysis is given below. The variables are in the same order as in Table 1.

	1	2	3	4	5	6	7	8	9	10	11
1	1.00										
2	.53	1.00									
3	-.13	.33	1.00								
4	-.15	.24	.67	1.00							
5	-.26	-.74	-.46	-.11	1.00						
6	.17	.61	.24	.06	-.86	1.00					
7	-.81	-.16	.36	.35	.02	.10	1.00				
8	.75	.56	-.27	-.36	-.48	.31	-.69	1.00			
9	.01	-.49	-.65	-.55	.32	-.10	-.14	.03	1.00		
10	-.24	.37	.54	.30	-.67	.56	.36	.09	-.53	1.00	
11	-.09	.35	.89	.50	-.46	.25	.27	-.18	-.44	.31	1.00

12. The information presented in the table involved coding of formal resolutions of the World Health Assembly into five different categories. Identification of resolutions presented no problem since they are listed, and even numbered, in the Official Records of WHO. A second individual independently coded a randomly selected sample of 20 percent of the years covered in the table. There was complete agreement between the two coders on 93.5 percent of the resolutions.

13. For general information on the WHO budget cycle, see WHO, *Background Information Submitted by the World Health Organization to the United Nations Advisory Committee on Administrative and Budgetary Questions* (Geneva: WHO, 1969).

14. WHO, *Basic Documents,* 23rd ed. (Geneva: WHO, 1972), p. 115.

15. WHO, *Executive Board, Forty-Fifth Session,* Official Records of WHO, no. 182 (1970), pp. 2-11.

16. WHO, *Handbook of Resolutions and Decisions of the World Health Assembly and the Executive Board, 1948-1972,* vol. 1 (Geneva: WHO, 1973), pp. 193-240.

17. WHO, *Basic Documents,* 23rd ed., pp. 72-3.

18. WHO, *Handbook of Resolutions,* vol. 1, pp. 227-8.

19. WHO, *Official Records of WHO,* no. 182, pp. 8-11. It is interesting to note there is no attempt to balance the budget by matching expenses to anticipated income.

Chapter 4

1. For general information on the WHO budget cycle, see WHO, *Background Information Submitted by the World Health Organization to the United Nations Advisory Committee on Administrative and Budgetary Questions* (Geneva: WHO, 1969); WHO, *Executive Board, Forty-Third Session,* Official Records of WHO, no. 174 (1968). This chapter is based in large part on knowledge gained from reading documents, observing meetings, and interviewing policy-makers during a twelve-month stay at WHO headquarters in Geneva, 1968-69.

2. WHO, *Basic Documents,* 19th ed. (Geneva: WHO, 1968), p. 13.

3. WHO, *Official Records of WHO,* no. 174; idem, *Background Information,* pp. 6-45; idem, *WHO Manual, Budget, Section III* (Geneva: WHO, 1974), pp. III.1, 1-11; idem, "Organizational Study of the Executive Board: Methods of Planning and Execution of Projects," *Executive Board, Thirty-Fifth Session,* Official Records of WHO, no. 140 (1965), pp. 115-46; idem, "Long Term Planning in the Field of Health and Biennial Programming," *Executive Board, Forty-Third Session,* Official Records of WHO, no. 173 (1969), pp. 56-62; idem, "Proposals for Further Improvement and Strengthening of the Evaluation Process of the World Health Organization," *Executive Board, Forty-Third Session,* Official Records of WHO, no. 173 (1969), pp. 62-7; idem, "Continued Assistance to Newly Independent States," *Fifteenth World Health Assembly,* Official Records of WHO, no. 118 (1962), pp. 84-97; idem, "Continued Assistance to Newly Independent States, *Executive Board, Thirty-First Session,* Official Records of WHO, no. 124 (1963), pp. 75-82; idem, "Policy Governing Assistance to Developing Countries," *Twenty-First World Health Assembly,* Official Records of WHO, no. 168 (1968), pp. 47-50; idem, "Organizational Study on the Education and Training Programme," *Executive Board, Eleventh Session,* Official Records of WHO, no. 46 (1953), pp. 131-56; idem, "Organizational Study on Regionalization," *Executive Board, Eleventh Session,* Official Records of WHO, no. 46 (1953), pp. 157-84.

4. WHO, *Executive Board, Fifth Session,* Official Records of WHO, no. 25 (1950), pp. 30-5; idem, *Executive Board, Fifteenth Session,* Official Records of WHO, no. 60 (1955), pp. 67-73; idem, *Thirteenth World Health Assembly,* Official Records of WHO, no. 102 (1960), pp. 54-9; idem, *Eighteenth World Health Assembly,* Official Records of WHO, no. 143 (1965), pp. 64-8. For an overview of the development of the "General Programme of Work Covering a Specific Period," see idem, *Handbook of Resolutions and Decisions of the World Health Assembly and the Executive Board, 1948-1972,* vol. 1 (Geneva: WHO, 1973), pp. 1-5. For allocation of resources between regions, see idem,

Executive Board, Thirteenth Session, Official Records of WHO, no. 52 (1954), pp. 61-73.

5. WHO, *Background Information,* p. 12.

6. Ibid.

7. Cf. WHO, *Proposed Regular Programme and Budget Estimates for the Financial Year 1 January-31 December 1968,* Official Records of WHO, no. 154 (1966).

8. WHO, *Basic Documents,* 19th ed., p. 13.

9. Ibid, p. 8.

10. Ibid.

11. WHO, *Sixth World Health Assembly,* Official Records of WHO, no. 48 (1953), pp. 172-3.

12. WHO, *Basic Documents,* 19th ed., p. 6; see also idem, "Procedure for Discussing in the World Health Assembly Matters Relating to the Programme and Budget of the Organization," *Executive Board, Thirty-Ninth Session,* Official Records of WHO, no. 157 (1967), pp. 52-61.

13. See the financial regulations of WHO: WHO,*Basic Documents,* 19th ed., p. 72.

14. WHO, "Plan of Operation for a Public Health Nutrition Project," *Executive Board, Forty-First Session,* Official Records of WHO, no. 166 (1968), pp. 91-4.

15. WHO, *WHO Manual, Finance and Accounts, Section IV* (Geneva: WHO, 1974).

16. WHO, *Basic Documents,* 19th ed., pp. 71-9, 82-7.

17. Ibid., pp. 80-1.

18. WHO, *The Work of WHO, 1968,* Official Records of WHO, no. 172 (1969); idem, *Financial Report, 1 January-31 December 1968,* Official Records of WHO, no. 175 (1969).

19. WHO, *Proposed Programme and Budget Estimates for the Financial Year 1 January-31 December 1973,* Official Records of WHO, no. 196 (1971); idem, *Handbook of Resolutions,* no. 1, pp. 199-240; Francis W. Hoole, "Decision-Making in the World Health Organization: The Budgetary Process," (Ph.D. diss., Northwestern University, 1971), pp. 237-64.

20. John Wanat, "Bases of Budgetary Incrementalism," *American Political Science Review* 68(1974):1221-8.

21. John P. Crecine, "Defense budgeting: organizational adaptation to environmental constraints," in *Studies in Budgeting,* ed. R.F. Byrne, et al. (Amsterdam: North-Holland Publishing Co., 1971), pp. 210-61.

22. For a detailed study of the role of the United States government in the WHO budget process, see United States General Accounting Office, *Report to the Congress, U.S. Participation in the World Health Organization, Department of State, Department of Health, Education and Welfare, By the Comptroller General of the United States* (Washington, D.C.: U.S. Government Printing Office, 1969).

23. The WHO had two Directors-General during the period covered in this study. Dr. Brock Chisholm, of Canada, headed the secretariat of the Interim Commission from 1946 to 1948 and served as the first Director-General from 1948 to 1953. Dr. Marcolino Candau, of Brazil, served as Director-General from 1953 to 1973. As Assistant Director-General, Milton P. Siegel was especially influential on budgetary matters during the years of this study. Siegel served as Assistant Director-General for Administration and Finance from 1948 until 1971.

24. For general information, see WHO, *Basic Documents*, 19th ed., pp. 38-66; idem, "Organizational Study: Coordination with the United Nations and the Specialized Agencies," *Executive Board, Twenty-Ninth Session*, Official Records of WHO, no. 115 (1962), pp. 112-42.

25. WHO, *Basic Documents*, 19th ed., pp. 67-70; idem, "Report of the Standing Committee on Non-governmental Organizations," *Executive Board, Forty-Third Session*, Official Records of WHO, no. 173, pp. 35-7.

26. WHO, *Basic Documents*, 19th ed., pp. 88-96.

Chapter 5

1. The behavior during the first two years of the organization's history (1949-50) will not be used in the analysis of policy-making rules because of its non-typical pattern. The first two years were devoted to founding the organization and making it function.

The data for 1951-69 used in estimating the parameters and checking the fit for the policy-making rules in both this and the next chapter were collected from the Official Records of the World Health Organization, nos. 34, pp. 10-11; 41, pp. 8-9; 47, pp. 8-9; 54, pp. 8-9; 62, pp. 10-11; 70, pp. 10-11; 78, pp. 12-13; 85, pp. 12-13; 93, pp. 12-13; 101, pp. 12-13; 109, pp. 12-13; 117, pp. 12-13; 126, pp. 12-13; 134, pp. 12-13; 142, pp. 12-13; 150, pp. 12-13; 159, pp. 12-13; 167, pp. 10-11; 175, pp. 10-11; 183, pp. 12-13; 18, pp. 26-7; 26, pp. 6, 17, 33; 40, pp. 15, 41; 46, pp. 33, 43; 53, pp. 14, 23; 60, p. 30; 61, pp. 73-4; 68, pp. 9-10; 69, pp. 10-12; 76, p. 29; 77, p. 16; 84, pp. 15, 63; 92, pp. 17, 85; 100, p. 69; 107, p. 62; 116, p. 75; 125, pp. 87-8; 132, p. 14; 141, p. 65; 149, pp. 90-1; 158, p. 84; 166, pp. 11, 87; 18, pp. 20-2; 23, pp. 11-19. For the dependent variable data used in this chapter, see Appendix E.

2. For a detailed chronological history of actions taken at the proposal development step between 1949 and 1968, see Francis W. Hoole, "Decision-Making in the World Health Organization: The Budgetary Process" (Ph.D. diss., Northwestern University, 1971), pp. 238-45.

3. For a detailed chronological history of actions taken at the executive body step between 1949 and 1968, see ibid, pp. 245-9.

4. For a detailed chronological history of actions taken at the assembly step between 1949 and 1968, see ibid., pp. 249-56.

5. For a detailed chronological history of actions taken at the supplementary change step between 1949 and 1968, see ibid., pp. 256-62.

6. This is actually not a very plausible rule for WHO. Nevertheless, because one version of this rule is the familiar simple cell model and a slightly different version the familiar Markov process, the rule was examined.

7. For a detailed treatment of actions taken at the implementation step between 1949 and 1968, see Hoole, "Decision-Making," pp. 262-4.

8. See note 6.

9. See Carl F. Christ, *Econometric Models and Methods* (New York: John Wiley and Sons, 1966), pp. 226-33.

10. See Mordecai Ezekiel and Karl A. Fox, *Methods of Correlation and Regression Analysis*, 3rd ed. (New York: John Wiley and Sons, 1967), pp. 55-68.

11. Ibid., pp. 69-117.

12. See Hoole, "Decision-Making," pp. 238-64.

13. For an excellent discussion of the general linear regression model, see J[ohn] Johnston, *Econometric Methods* (New York: McGraw Hill Book Co., 1963), pp. 9-29, 106-35. For a discussion of constrained least squares, see Christ, *Econometric Models*, pp. 358-60, 384-7.

14. See Christ, *Econometric Models*, pp. 358-60, 384-7; and Wrubel Computing Center, "Update of McGraw-Hill SPSS Manual," Indiana University, Bloomington, Ind., 1973, p. 220.1.

15. For a discussion of the error terms and assumptions regarding them, see Johnston, *Econometric Methods*, pp. 3-9.

16. Ibid., p. 179.

17. Ibid., p. 192.

18. See J. Durbin, "Testing for Serial Correlation in Least Squares Regression When Some of the Regressors are Lagged Dependent Variables," *Econometrica* 38(1970):410-21.

19. See Hamid Habibagahi and John L. Pratschke, "A Comparison of the Power of the Von Neumann Ratio, Durbin-Watson and Geary Tests," *Review of Economics and Statistics* 54(1972):179-85.

20. H. Theil and A.G. Nagar, "Testing the Independence of Regression Disturbances," *Journal of the American Statistical Association* 56(1961):793-806; Habibagahi and Pratschke, "A Comparison of the Power of . . .," p. 180.

21. Johnston, *Econometric Methods*, pp. 179-92.

22. Ibid., pp. 264-6. However, it should be noted that the estimates cannot be considered to be unbiased because the predetermined variables are nonstationary.

23. Phoebus J. Dhrymes, *Econometrics, Statistical Foundations and Applications* (New York: Harper and Row, 1970), pp. 303-13.

24. Ezekiel and Fox, *Methods of Correlation*, pp. 499-503.

25. See Johnston, *Econometric Methods*, pp. 115-35. For an argument that distribution free criteria should be used in these circumstances, see Otto A. Davis, M.A.H. Dempster, and Aaron Wildavsky, "On the Process of

Budgeting: An Empirical Study of Congressional Appropriations," *Papers on Non-Market Decision Making* 1(1966):73.

26. G.C. Chow, "Tests of Equality Between Sets of Coefficients in Two Linear Regressions," *Econometrica* 28(1960):591-605.

27. F.N. David, *Tables of the Ordinates and Probability Integral of the Distribution of the Correlation Coefficient in Small Samples* (Cambridge: Cambridge University Press, 1954).

28. Henri Theil, *Principles of Econometrics* (New York: John Wiley and Sons, 1971), pp. 178-9.

29. I would like to thank Professor Jeffery Green of the Department of Economics, Indiana University, for bringing this to my attention.

30. See John L. Stromberg, *The Internal Mechanisms of the Defense Budget Process—Fiscal 1953-68* Memorandum RM-6243 (Santa Monica, Calif.: Rand Corporation, 1970), pp. 21-4.

31. See L.R. Klein, *An Essay on the Theory of Economic Prediction* (Chicago: Markham Publishing Co., 1971), p. 39.

32. Calculations of regression coefficients, standard errors of the regression coefficients, and the Durbin-Watson statistic were done on the CDC 6600 Computer at Indiana University's Wrubel Computing Center. The SPSS regression program was used. A special program was written to handle the generalized least squares transformation and the SPSS regression program was again utilized to obtain estimates. Correlations between estimated error terms were calculated on the Wang 700 calculating machine using the statistical package. Calculations for Chow's F test and the adjustments to the r^2 were done on the Wang 360 calculating machine.

33. There is almost no limit to the alternatives in curvilinear analysis. Given the data used in this study, however, it seemed reasonable to go fishing with the polynomial. Some other technique might also have been appropriate. Cf. Ezekiel and Fox, *Methods of Correlation,* pp. 69-117. The analysis was done on the CDC 6600 computer at Indiana University's Wrubel Computing Center. The BMD05R polynomial regression program was used.

The choice of the value of k was somewhat limited by the n of 19 and the effect of the adjustment for degrees of freedom. The fifth degree polynomial was chosen because it transforms the original data four times, a number which equals the number of events checked for step changes in the linear equations. It would have been possible to use some other degree polynomial; but, given this data, it is doubtful that the results would have been significantly different.

34. The variance explained by the polynomial was adjusted in the same manner as the variance for the linear rules.

Chapter 6

1. The possibility exists for using mathematics to obtain analytical solutions.

However, I feel more comfortable with numerical solutions and the computer model. The same answers for WHO are obtained either way.

2. J[ohn] Johnston, *Econometric Methods* (New York: McGraw Hill Book Co., 1963), pp. 3-9.

3. Phoebus J. Dhrymes, *Econometrics, Statistical Foundations and Applications* (New York: Harper and Row, 1970), pp. 303-13.

4. Thomas H. Naylor, *Computer Simulation Experiments with Models of Economic Systems* (New York: John Wiley and Sons, 1971), pp. 396-7.

5. Ibid., pp. 397-9.

6. Since this process of breaking the budget total into organizational, external, and leadership factors is crucial for the development of the model and the sensitivity analysis in the next two chapters, some clarification of the coding process may be helpful. In studying documentation on the WHO budget process, it is easy to see how changes from the prior step in the process are presented and justified. The portion of the change which is presented and justified in regard to organizational factors was coded into the organizational category; the external and leadership categories were handled in the same manner. The fact that a second coder, working with a sample of 20 percent of the years, obtained identical results suggests the straightforward nature of the enterprise.

7. See "Statistical Considerations" in Chapter 5.

8. See footnote 32 of Chapter 5 for the details on programs used in the parameter estimation procedures.

9. For an examination of different approaches to validating a simulation, see Charles Hermann, "Validation Problems in Games and Simulations with Special Reference to Models of International Politics," *Behavioral Science* 12(1967):216-31; Naylor, *Computer Simulation Experiments*, pp. 153-64.

10. See Carl F. Christ, *Econometric Models and Methods* (New York: John Wiley and Sons, 1966), pp. 546-9.

11. See Linton C. Freeman, *Elementary Applied Statistics: For Students in Behavioral Science* (New York: John Wiley and Sons, 1965), p. 62.

12. Given a normal distribution, it can be expected that 99.7 percent of the cases fall within three standard deviations of the mean.

13. For a discussion of the use of naive alternative models, see Christ, *Econometric Models*, pp. 571-5.

14. This familiar model appears to be the most realistic alternative growth model. For an excellent discussion of growth models, see William H. Starbuck, "Organizational Growth and Development," in *Handbook of Organizations*, ed. James G. March (Chicago: Rand McNally and Co., 1965), pp. 451-533.

15. The parameters were estimated through use of the SPSS regression program on the CDC 6600 computer at Indiana University's Wrubel Computing Center.

16. While this book was in press, I discovered that the number of member-

states in WHO from the prior year quite accurately predicted the WHO expenditure total for each year from 1951 to 1969. This simple alternative model can be stated in the following way: $Y_t = a + bZ_{t-1} + u_t$, where Y_t is the WHO expenditure total for a year; Z_{t-1} is the number of member-states in WHO for the prior year; a is an intercept; b is a constant multiplier term; and u_t is a stochastic disturbance. Using regression estimates of a and b (which were generated using 1951-69 data and the ordinary least squares technique) and WHO membership data for 1969-73, the following predicted expenditure totals were generated: 1970, \$68,126,000 (off by 1.4 percent); 1971, \$73,629,000 (off by -2.1 percent); 1972, \$81,726,000 (off by -4.1 percent); 1973, \$92,204,000 (off by -3.5 percent); and, 1974, \$103,171,000 (off by -4.8 percent). Thus, even though this model starts each year's prediction process with actual data, instead of running forward for several years like the computer model, it still does not provide as good a fit to the actual WHO expenditure data as does the computer model.

Chapter 7

1. The term "counterfactual" was borrowed from Hayward R. Alker, Jr. and William J. Greenberg, "The UN Charter: Alternate Pasts and Alternate Futures," in *The United Nations: Problems and Prospects*, ed. Edwin H. Fedder (St. Louis: Center for International Studies, University of Missouri-St. Louis, 1971), p. 132.

2. For a discussion of experimentation with a computer simulation, see Thomas H. Naylor, *Computer Simulation Experiments with Models of Economic Systems* (New York: John Wiley and Sons, 1971), pp. 165-319.

3. Cf. Donald T. Campbell and Julian C. Stanley, *Experimental and Quasi-Experimental Designs for Research* (Chicago: Rand McNally and Co., 1966), pp. 7-12.

4. Ibid.

5. Ibid., pp. 25-7.

6. For a discussion of this test, see William L. Hays, *Statistics for Psychologists* (New York: Holt, Rinehart and Winston, 1963), pp. 301-35. All statistical analysis reported in this chapter was done on the CDC 6600 computer at Indiana University's Wrubel Computing Center. The SPSS program was used.

Chapter 8

1. An earlier, but significantly different, version of this chapter appeared as Francis W. Hoole, "The Simulation of Alternative Budgetary Futures for the World Health Organization," in *The United Nations: Problems and*

Prospects, ed. Edwin H. Fedder (St. Louis: Center for International Studies, University of Missouri-St. Louis, 1971), pp. 143-64.

2. See Lester B. Pearson, et al., *Partners in Development* (New York: Frederick A. Praeger, 1969), pp. 136-52; and *International Development Strategy* (New York: United Nations, 1970), p. 9.

3. No step change was found in the WHO policy-making rules which were developed from 1951-69 data. For additional information see "Empirical Findings" in Chapter 5.

4. Francis W. Hoole, "Decision-Making in the World Health Organization: The Budgetary Process" (Ph.D. diss., Northwestern University, 1971), pp. 67-8.

5. WHO, *Handbook of Resolutions and Decisions of the World Health Assembly and the Executive Board, 1948-1972,* vol. 1 (Geneva: WHO, 1973), pp. 228-39.

6. WHO, *Twentieth World Health Assembly,* Official Records of WHO, no. 160 (1967), p. 32.

7. See William L. Hays, *Statistics for Psychologists* (New York: Holt, Rinehart and Winston, 1963), pp. 356-412.

8. Ibid., pp. 380-1.

9. This analysis was done on the CDC 6600 computer at Indiana University's Wrubel Computing Center. The BMD02V program for analysis of variance for factorial design was used. Unfortunately, the program can handle only 999 cases; I had 1000 cases. It is not worth the effort involved to rewrite the computer program for such a small discrepancy, so the last case was simply eliminated and the analysis done with 999 cases.

10. This analysis was done on the CDC 6600 computer at Indiana University's Wrubel Computing Center. The SPSS program was used.

11. The data reported here were collected from the Official Records of the World Health Organization, nos. 171, p. xxv; 174, p. 90; 176, p. 7; 179, p. xxv; 182, pp. 22, 105; 190, pp. 17, 92; 191, pp. 16-17; 193, p. 5; 199, pp. 14-15, 77; 200, pp. 16-17; 201, pp. 2-4, 23-4; 204, pp. xx; 207, pp. 2-4, 54; 208, pp. 30-1; 214, pp. 4-5; 217, pp. 2-3; 222, pp. 4-5.

Chapter 9

1. Otto A. Davis, "Empirical Evidence of 'Political' Influences Upon the Expenditure and Taxation Policies of Public Schools," in *The Public Economy of Urban Communities,* ed. Julius Margolis (Washington, D.C.: Resources for the Future, 1965), pp. 92-111.

2. See the study directed by Robert Jackson: *A Study of the Capacity of the United Nations Development System,* vols. 1 and 2 (Geneva: United Nations, 1969). See also Lester B. Pearson, et al., *Partners in Development* (New York: Frederick A. Praeger, 1969); *Final Report of the President's Commission on*

the Observance of the Twenty-Fifth Anniversary of the United Nations (Washington, D.C.: Department of State, 1971); *U.S. Foreign Assistance in the 1970s: A New Approach* (Washington, D.C.: U.S. Government Printing Office, 1970); *Deficiencies in the Management and Delivery of UN Technical and Pre-Investment Assistance* (Washington, D.C.: U.S. Government Printing Office, 1971); *The United Nations in the 1970s* (New York: United Nations Association, 1971).

3. Peter B. Natchez and Irvin C. Bupp, "Policy and Priority in the Budgetary Process," *American Political Science Review* 67(1973):951-63.

4. Lewis F. Richardson, *Arms and Insecurity* (Pittsburgh, Pa.: The Boxwood Press, 1960), pp. 12-36; Nazli Choucri and Robert C. North, "Dynamics of International Conflict: Some Policy Implications of Population, Resources, and Technology," *World Politics* 24(Supplement 1972):115-22; William Caspary, "Richardson's Model of Arms Races: Description, Critique and an Alternative Model," *International Studies Quarterly* 11(1967):63-88; Paul Smoker, "Fear in the Arms Race: A Mathematical Study," in *International Politics and Foreign Policy*, ed. James N. Rosenau, rev. ed. (New York: The Free Press, 1969), pp. 573-82.

5. Marilyn Manser, Thomas H. Naylor, and Kenneth Wertz, "Effects of Alternative Policies for Allocating Federal Aid for Education to the States," in Thomas H. Naylor, *Computer Simulation Experiments with Models of Economic Systems* (New York: John Wiley and Sons, 1971), pp. 338-52.

6. Mancur Olson, Jr., *The Logic of Collective Action* (New York: Schocken Books, 1968); Mancur Olson, Jr. and Richard Zeckhauser, "An Economic Theory of Alliances," *Review of Economics and Statistics* 48(1966):266-79; Bruce M. Russett, *What Price Vigilance?* (New Haven, Conn.: Yale University Press, 1970); Bruce M. Russett and John D. Sullivan, "Collective Goods and International Organization," in *The United Nations: Problems and Prospects*, ed. Edwin H. Fedder (St. Louis: Center for International Studies, University of Missouri-St. Louis, 1971), pp. 91-112; John Gerard Ruggie, "Collective Goods and Future International Collaboration," *American Political Science Review* 66(1972):874-93; William Loehr, "Collective Goods and International Cooperation: Comments," *International Organization* 27(1973):421-30.

7. Robert O. Keohane and Joseph S. Nye, "Transnational Relations and World Politics: An Introduction," *International Organization* 25(1971): 329-49.

Bibliography

Books

Alker, Hayward R. Jr., and Russett, Bruce M. *World Politics in the General Assembly*. New Haven, Conn.: Yale University Press, 1965.

Allison, Graham T. *Essence of Decision*. Boston: Little, Brown and Co., 1971.

Almond, Gabriel A. *The American People and Foreign Policy*. New York: Frederick A. Praeger, 1960.

Anton, Thomas. *The Politics of State Expenditure in Illinois*. Urbana: University of Illinois Press, 1966.

Bailey, Sydney D. *The Secretariat of the United Nations*. New York: Carnegie Endowment for International Peace, 1962.

——————. *The United Nations: A Short Political Guide*. New York: Carnegie Endowment for International Peace, 1962.

Beer, Francis A., ed. *Alliances: Latent War Communities in the Contemporary World*. New York: Holt, Rinehart and Winston, 1970.

Berkov, Robert. *The World Health Organization: A Study in Decentralized Administration*. Paris: Libraire Minnd, 1957.

Biddle, Bruce J., and Thomas, Edwin J., eds. *Role Theory: Concepts and Research*. New York: John Wiley and Sons, 1966.

Blaisdell, Donald C. *International Organization*. New York: Ronald Press Co., 1966.

Braybrooke, David, and Lindblom, Charles E. *A Strategy of Decision*. New York: The Free Press, 1963.

Brunner, Ronald D., and Brewer, Garry D. *Organized Complexity: Empirical Theories of Political Development*. New York: The Free Press, 1971.

Buchan, Alastair, ed. *Europe's Futures, Europe's Choices*. New York: Columbia University Press, 1969.

Buehrig, Edward H. *The UN and the Palestinian Refugees: A Study in Nonterritorial Administration*. Bloomington: Indiana University Press, 1971.

Caiden, Naomi, and Wildavsky, Aaron. *Planning and Budgeting in Poor Countries*. New York: John Wiley and Sons, 1974.

Campbell, Donald T., and Stanley, Julian C. *Experimental and Quasi-Experimental Designs for Research*. Chicago: Rand McNally and Co., 1963.

Cherryholmes, Cleo H., and Shapiro, Michael J. *Representatives and Roll*

Calls: A Computer Simulation of Voting in the Eighty-eighth Congress.
Indianapolis: The Bobbs-Merrill Co., 1969.

Christ, Carl F. *Econometric Models and Methods.* New York: John Wiley and Sons, 1966.

Claude, Inis L. Jr. *Swords into Plowshares: The Problems and Progress of International Organization.* 3d ed. New York: Random House, 1964.

——————. *The Changing United Nations.* New York: Random House, 1967.

Codding, George Arthur. *The International Telecommunication Union: An Experiment in International Organization.* Leyden, The Netherlands: B.J. Brill, 1952.

Coplin, William. *The Functions of International Law.* Chicago: Rand McNally and Co., 1966.

Cox, Robert W., and Jacobson, Harold K. *The Anatomy of Influence: Decision-Making in International Organization.* New Haven, Conn.: Yale University Press, 1973.

Crecine, John P. *Defense Budgeting: Organizational Adaptation to External Constraints.* Memorandum RM-6121-PR. Santa Monica, Calif.: Rand Corporation, 1970.

——————. *Governmental Problem Solving: A Computer Simulation of Municipal Budgeting.* Chicago: Rand McNally and Co., 1969.

Curtis, Michael. *Western European Integration.* New York: Harper and Row, 1965.

Cyert, Richard M., and March, James G., eds. *A Behavioral Theory of the Firm.* Englewood Cliffs, N.J.: Prentice-Hall, 1963.

Dahl, Robert A. *Who Governs?* New Haven, Conn.: Yale University Press, 1967.

David, F.N. *Tables of the Ordinates and Probability Integral of the Distribution of the Correlation Coefficient in Small Samples.* Cambridge: Cambridge University Press, 1954.

Deutsch, Albert. *The World Health Organization—Its Global Battle Against Disease.* New York: Public Affairs Committee, Inc., 1958.

Deutsch, Karl W., et al. *Political Community and the North Atlantic Area.* Princeton, N.J.: Princeton University Press, 1957.

Dhrymes, Phoebus J. *Econometrics: Statistical Foundations and Applications.* New York: Harper and Row, 1970.

Easton, David. *A Framework for Political Analysis.* Englewood Cliffs, N.J.: Prentice-Hall, 1965.

——————. *A Systems Analysis of Political Life.* New York: John Wiley and Sons, 1965.

——————. *The Political System: An Inquiry Into the State of Political Science.* New York: Alfred A. Knopf, 1953.

Etzioni, Amitai. *Political Unification: A Comparative Study of Leaders and Forces.* New York: Holt, Rinehart and Winston, 1965.

Everyman's United Nations. 8th ed. New York: United Nations, 1968.

Ezekiel, Mordecai, and Fox, Karl A. *Methods of Correlation and Regression Analysis.* 3d ed. New York: John Wiley and Sons, 1967.

Fenno, Richard F. Jr. *The Power of the Purse: Appropriations Politics in Congress.* Boston: Little, Brown and Co. 1966.

Frankel, Joseph. *The Making of Foreign Policy: An Analysis of Decision-Making.* New York: Oxford University Press, 1963.

Freeman, Linton C. *Elementary Applied Statistics: For Students in Behavioral Science.* New York: John Wiley and Sons, 1965.

Gerwin, Donald A. *Budgeting Public Funds: The Decision Process in an Urban School District.* Madison: University of Wisconsin Press, 1969.

Guetzkow, Harold; Alger, Chadwick F.; Brody, Richard A.; Noel, Robert C.; and Snyder, Richard C. *Simulation in International Relations.* Englewood Cliffs, N.J.: Prentice-Hall, 1963.

Haas, Ernst B. *Beyond the Nation State: Functionalism and International Organization.* Stanford, Calif.: Stanford University Press, 1964.

_____. *The Uniting of Europe: Political, Social, and Economic Forces, 1950-1957.* Stanford, Calif.: Stanford University Press, 1958.

Hadwen, John G., and Kaufmann, Johan. *How United Nations Decisions Are Made.* Leyden, The Netherlands: A.W. Sijthoff, 1960.

Hays, William L. *Statistics for Psychologists.* New York: Holt, Rinehart and Winston, 1963.

Hilsman, Roger. *To Move a Nation: The Politics of Foreign Policy in the Administration of John F. Kennedy.* New York: Dell Publishing Co., 1964.

Hoffman, Stanley, ed. *Contemporary Theory in International Relations.* Englewood Cliffs, N.J.: Prentice-Hall, 1960.

Hovet, Thomas. *Africa in the United Nations.* Evanston, Ill.: Northwestern University Press, 1963.

_____ . *Bloc Politics in the United Nations.* Cambridge, Mass.: Harvard University Press, 1960.

Hunter, Floyd. *Community Power Structure: A Study of Decision Makers.* Garden City, N.Y.: Anchor Books, 1963.

Huntington, Samuel P. *The Common Defense: Strategic Programs in National Politics.* London: Columbia University Press, 1966.

Hyman, Herbert H. *Political Socialization.* Glencoe, Ill.: The Free Press, 1959.

Ikle, Fred C. *How Nations Negotiate.* New York: Frederick A. Praeger, 1967.

International Political Communities. Garden City, N.Y.: Doubleday Books, 1966.

Jacob, Philip E.; Atherton, Alexine L.; and Wallenstein, Arthur M. *The Dynamics of International Organization.* Rev. ed. Homewood, Ill.: The Dorsey Press, 1972.

Jensen, Finn B., and Walter, Ingo. *The Common Market: Economic Integration in Europe.* Philadelphia: J.B. Lippincott Co., 1965.

Johnston, J[ohn]. *Econometric Methods.* New York: McGraw Hill Book Co., 1963.

Jones, Susan D., and Singer, J. David. *Beyond Conjecture in International Politics: Abstracts of Data-Based Research.* Ithaca, N.Y.: F.E. Peacock Publishers, 1972.

Jordan, Robert S., ed. *International Administration: Its Evolution and Contemporary Applications.* New York: Oxford University Press, 1971.

_____ , ed. *Multinational Cooperation: Economic, Social, and Scientific Development.* New York: Oxford University Press, 1972.

Kaplan, Abraham. *The Conduct of Inquiry.* San Francisco: Chandler Publishing Co., 1964.

Katz, Daniel, and Kahn, Robert L. *The Social Psychology of Organizations.* New York: John Wiley and Sons, 1966.

Kaufmann, Johan. *Conference Diplomacy.* Leyden, The Netherlands: A.W. Sijthoff, 1968.

Kelman, Herbert C., ed. *International Behavior: A Social-Psychological Analysis.* New York: Holt, Rinehart and Winston, 1966.

Keohane, Robert O., and Nye, Joseph S., eds. *Transnational Relations and World Politics.* Cambridge, Mass.: Harvard University Press, 1972.

Kerlinger, Fred N. *Foundations of Behavioral Research: Educational and Psychological Inquiry.* New York: Holt, Rinehart and Winston, 1966.

Klein, L.R. *An Essay on the Theory of Economic Prediction.* Chicago: Markham Publishing Co., 1971.

Knorr, Klaus, and Rosenau, James N., eds. *Contending Approaches to International Politics.* Princeton, N.J.: Princeton University Press, 1969.

Lador-Lederer, J.J. *International Non-Governmental Organizations.* Brussels: Union of International Associations, 1957.

Lall, Arthur. *How Communist China Negotiates.* New York: Columbia University Press, 1968.

Langrod, Georges. *The International Civil Service: Its Origins, Its Nature, Its Evolution.* Leyden, The Netherlands: A.W. Sijthoff, 1963.

Lasswell, Harold D. *Psychopathology and Politics.* New York: The Viking Press, 1966.

Laves, Walter H.C., and Thomson, Charles A. *UNESCO: Purpose, Progress, Prospects.* Bloomington: Indiana University Press, 1957.

Lindberg, Leon N. *Dynamics of European Economic Integration.* Stanford, Calif.: Stanford University Press, 1963.

Lindberg, Leon N., and Scheingold, Stuart A. *Europe's Would-be Polity: Patterns of Change in the European Community.* Englewood Cliffs, N.J.: Prentice-Hall, 1970.

_____ , eds. *Regional Integration: Theory and Research.* Cambridge, Mass.: Harvard University Press, 1971.

Lindblom, Charles E. *The Intelligence of Democracy*. New York: The Free Press, 1965.

Lyden, Fremont J., and Miller, Ernest G., eds. *Planning, Programming, Budgeting: A Systems Approach to Management*. Chicago: Markham Publishing Co., 1967.

McGowan, Patrick J., and Shapiro, Howard B. *The Comparative Study of Foreign Policy: A Survey of Scientific Findings*. Beverly Hills, Calif.: Sage Publications, 1973.

Mangone, Gerard J., ed. *Administration of Economic and Social Programs*. New York: Columbia University Press, 1966.

March, James G., and Simon, Herbert A. *Organizations*. New York: John Wiley and Sons, 1958.

Mitrany, David. *A Working Peace System*. Chicago: Quadrangle Books, 1966.

Modelski, George. *A Theory of Foreign Policy*. New York: Frederick A. Praeger, 1962.

Naylor, Thomas H., ed. *Computer Simulation Experiments with Models of Economic Systems*. New York: John Wiley and Sons, 1971.

Naylor, Thomas H.; Balintfy, Joseph L.; Burdick, Donald S.; and Chu, Kong. *Computer Simulation Techniques*. New York: John Wiley and Sons, 1966.

Nicholas, H.G. *The United Nations as a Political Institution*. 3d ed. New York: Oxford University Press, 1968.

Nie, Norman; Bent, Dale H.; and Hull, C. Hadlai. *SPSS: Statistical Package for the Social Sciences*. New York: McGraw Hill Book Co., 1970.

Nye, Joseph S., ed. *International Regionalism: Readings*. Boston: Little, Brown and Co., 1968.

——————— . *Peace in Parts: Integration and Conflict in Regional Organization*. Boston: Little, Brown and Co., 1971.

Olson, Mancur Jr. *The Logic of Collective Action*. New York: Schocken Books, 1968.

Paige, Glenn D. *The Korean Decision*. New York: The Free Press, 1968.

Pearson, Lester B., et al. *Partners in Development*. New York: Frederick A. Praeger, 1969.

Plano, Jack C., and Riggs, Robert E. *Forging World Order: The Politics of International Organization*. London: The Macmillan Co., 1971.

Pool, Ithiel de Sola; Abelson, Robert P.; and Popkin, Samuel L. *Candidates, Issues, and Strategies*. Cambridge, Mass.: M.I.T. Press, 1964.

Raser, John R. *Personal Characteristics of Political Decision-Makers: A Literature Review*. La Jolla, Calif.: Western Behavioral Sciences Institute, 1965.

Richardson, Lewis F. *Arms and Insecurity*. Pittsburgh, Pa.: The Boxwood Press, 1960.

Riker, William H. *The Theory of Political Coalitions*. New Haven, Conn.:

Yale University Press, 1962.

Riker, William H., and Ordeshook, Peter C. *An Introduction to Positive Political Theory*. Englewood Cliffs, N.J.: Prentice-Hall, 1973.

Rosenau, James N., ed. *International Politics and Foreign Policy*. Rev. ed. New York: The Free Press, 1969.

——————— , ed. *Linkage Politics: Essays on the Convergence of National and International Systems*. New York: The Free Press, 1969.

——————— . *Public Opinion and Foreign Policy*. New York: Random House, 1961.

——————— . *The Scientific Study of Foreign Policy*. New York: The Free Press, 1971.

Rudner, Richard S. *Philosophy of Social Science*. Englewood Cliffs, N.J.: Prentice-Hall, 1966.

Russett, Bruce M. *What Price Vigilance?* New Haven, Conn.: Yale University Press, 1970.

Salmon, Wesley C. *Logic*. Englewood Cliffs, N.J.: Prentice-Hall, 1963.

Schelling, Thomas. *The Strategy of Conflict*. New York: Oxford University Press, 1963.

Sharp, Walter R. *Field Administration in the United Nations System*. New York: Frederick A. Praeger, 1961.

Simon, Herbert A. *Administrative Behavior: A Study of Decision-Making Processes in Administrative Organization*. 2d ed. New York: The Free Press, 1966.

Singer, J. David. *Financing International Organizations: The United Nations Budget Process*. The Hague: Martinus Nijhoff, 1961.

——————— , ed. *Quantitative International Politics: Insights and Evidence*. New York: The Free Press, 1968.

Snyder, Richard C.; Bruck, H.W.; and Sapin, Burton. *Decision-Making as an Approach to the Study of International Politics*. Foreign Policy Analysis Series, no. 3. Princeton University, Organizational Behavior Section, 1954.

——————— , eds. *Foreign Policy Decision-Making: An Approach to the Study of International Politics*. New York: The Free Press, 1962.

Snyder, Richard C., and Robinson, James A. *National and International Decision-Making*. New York: Institute for International Order, 1961.

Sterling, Theodor D., and Pollack, Seymour V. *Introduction to Statistical Data Processing*. Englewood Cliffs, N.J.: Prentice-Hall, 1968.

Stoessinger, John G., et al. *Financing the United Nations System*. Washington, D.C.: Brookings Institution, 1964.

Stromberg, John L. *The Internal Mechanisms of Defense Budget Processes—Fiscal 1953-1968*. Memorandum RM-6243. Santa Monica, Calif.: Rand Corporation, 1970.

Theil, Henri. *Principles of Econometrics*. New York: John Wiley and Sons, 1971.

Thompson, James D. *Organizations in Action*. New York: McGraw Hill Book Co., 1967.

Wasserman, Paul. *Decision-Making: An Annotated Bibliography, Supplement 1958-1963*. Ithaca, N.Y.: Cornell University Press, 1965.

Wildavsky, Aaron. *The Politics of the Budgetary Process*. Boston: Little, Brown and Co., 1964.

Wolfers, Arnold. *Discord and Collaboration*. Baltimore, Md.: Johns Hopkins University Press, 1962.

Wood, Robert S., ed. *The Process of International Organization*. New York: Random House, 1971.

World Health Organization. *The First Ten Years of the World Health Organization*. Geneva: World Health Organization, 1958.

_____ . *The Second Ten Years of the World Health Organization, 1958-1967*. Geneva: World Health Organization, 1968.

Yearbook of International Organizations. 11th ed. Brussels: Union of International Associations, 1966.

Yearbook of International Organizations. 12th ed. Brussels: Union of International Associations, 1968.

Yearbook of the United Nations. New York: United Nations, 1947-70.

Periodicals

Alger, Chadwick F. "Interaction and Negotiation in a Committee of the United Nations General Assembly." *Peace Research Society (International) Papers* 5(1966):141-60.

_____ . "Research on Research: A Decade of Quantitative and Field Research on International Organization." *International Organization* 24(1970):414-50.

_____ . "United Nations Participation as a Learning Experience." *Public Opinion Quarterly* 27(1963):411-26.

Alker, Hayward R. Jr. "Dimensions of Conflict in the General Assembly." *American Political Science Review* 58(1964):642-57.

Allen, Charles E. "World Health and World Politics." *International Organization* 4(1950):27-43.

Allison, Graham T. "Conceptual Models and the Cuban Missile Crisis." *American Political Science Review* 63(1969):689-718.

Allison, Graham T., and Halperin, Morton H. "Bureaucratic Politics: A Paradigm and Some Policy Implications." *World Politics* 24(1972): 40-79.

Angell, Robert C. "An Analysis of Trends in International Organizations." *Peace Research Society (International) Papers* 3(1965): 185-95.

Ascher, Charles S. "Current Problems in the World Health Organization's Program." *International Organization* 6(1952):27-50.

Bowman, Gary W.; Davis, Otto A.; Gailliot, Henry J.; and Hess, Alan C. "A Note on Supplementary Appropriations in the Federal Budgeting Process." *Papers on Non-Market Decision Making* 2(1967):91-101.

Browning, Rufus P. "Computer Programs as Theories of Political Processes." *Journal of Politics* 24(1962):562-82.

Calderwood, Howard B. "The World Health Organization and Its Regional Organizations." *Temple Law Quarterly* 37(1963):15-27.

Caspary, William. "Richardson's Model of Arms Races: Description, Critique and an Alternative Model." *International Studies Quarterly* 2(1967):63-88.

Chisholm, Brock. "Barriers to World Health." *International Conciliation* 491(1953):260-6.

Choucri, Nazli, and North, Robert C. "Dynamics of International Conflict: Some Policy Implications of Population, Resources, and Technology." *World Politics* 24(1972):80-122.

Chow, G.C., "Tests of Equality between Sets of Coefficients in Two Linear Regressions." *Econometrica* 28(1960):591-605.

Clarkson, Geoffrey P.E., and Simon, Herbert A. "Simulation of Individual and Group Behavior." *American Economic Review* 50(1960): 920-32.

Claude, Inis L. Jr. "The Political Framework of the United Nations' Financial Problems." *International Organization* 17(1963):831-59.

Clements, Frederick William. "The WHO in Southern Asia and the Western Pacific." *Pacific Affairs* 25(1952):334-48.

Colliard, Claude-Albert. "La Procedure Budgetaire des Organisations Internationales." *Revue de Science Financiere* 2(1958):237-60.

—————— . "La Procedure Budgetaire des Organisations Internationales." *Revue de Science Financiere* 3(1958):437-60.

Cox, Robert W. "The Executive Head: An Essay on Leadership in International Organization." *International Organization* 23(1969):205-30.

Crecine, John P. "A Computer Simulation Model of Municipal Budgeting." *Management Science* 13(1967):786-815.

Davis, Otto A.; Dempster, M.A.H.; and Wildavsky, Aaron. "A Theory of the Budgetary Process." *American Political Science Review* 60(1966): 529-47.

—————— . "On the Process of Budgeting: An Empirical Study of Congressional Appropriation." *Papers in Non-Market Decision-Making* 1(1966):63-132.

Durbin, J., "Testing for Serial Correlation in Least Squares Regression

When Some of the Regressors Are Lagged Dependent Variables." *Econometrica* 38(1970):410-21.

Easton, David, "An Approach to the Analysis of Political Systems." *World Politics* 9(1957):383-400.

Edinger, Lewis J., and Searing, Donald D. "Social Background in Elite Analysis: A Methodological Inquiry." *American Political Science Review* 61(1967):428-45.

Edwards, Ward. "Behavioral Decision Theory." *Annual Review of Psychology* 12(1961):473-98.

––––––––––– . "The Theory of Decision-Making." *Psychological Bulletin* 51(1954):380-417.

Goodrich, L.M. "The Political Role of the Secretary General." *International Organization* 16(1962):720-35.

Gore, William J., and Silander, Fred S. "A Bibliographical Essay on Decision-Making." *Administrative Science Quarterly* 4(1959):97-121.

Greenstein, Fred I. "The Impact of Personality on Politics: An Attempt to Clean Away Underbrush." *American Political Science Review* 61 (1967):629-41.

Guetzkow, Harold. "A Use of Simulation in the Study of Inter-National Relations." *Behavioral Science* 4(1959):183-91.

Gutteridge, Frank. "The World Health Organization: Its Scope and Achievement." *Temple Law Quarterly* 37(1963):1-14.

Haas, Ernst B., and Schmitter, Philippe C. "Economics and Differential Patterns of Political Integration: Projections about Unity in Latin America." *International Organization* 18(1964):705-37.

Habibagahi, Hamid, and Pratschke, John L. "A Comparison of the Power of the Von Neumann Ratio, Durbin-Watson and Geary Tests." *Review of Economics and Statistics* 54(1972):179-85.

Hansen, Roger D. "Regional Integration: Reflections on a Decade of Theoretical Efforts." *World Politics* 21(1969):242-71.

Hermann, Charles. "Validation Problems in Games and Simulations with Special Reference to Models of International Politics." *Behavioral Science* 12(1967):216-31.

Higgins, Terence. "The Politics of United Nations Finance." *The World Today* 19(1963):380-9.

Hill, Norman. "The Allocation of Expenses in International Organizations." *American Political Science Review* 21(1927):128-37.

Hilsman, Roger. "The Foreign-Policy Consensus: An Interim Research Report." *Journal of Conflict Resolution* 3(1959):361-82.

Hoffman, Stanley. "International Relations: The Long Road to Theory." *World Politics* 11(1959):346-77.

Jackson, Elmore. "The Developing Role of the Secretary-General." *International Organization* 11(1957):431-45.

Jackson, John E. "Politics and the Budgetary Process." *Social Science Research* 1(1972):35-60.

Kalleberg, Arthur L. "The Logic of Comparison: A Methodological Note on the Comparative Study of Political Systems." *World Politics* 19 (1966):69-82.

Kanter, Arnold. "Congress and the Defense Budget: 1960-1970." *American Political Science Review* 66(1972):129-43.

Keohane, Robert O. "The Study of Political Influence in the General Assembly." *International Organization* 21(1967):221-37.

Keohane, Robert O., and Nye, Joseph S. "Transnational Relations and World Politics: An Introduction." *International Organization* 25 (1973):329-49.

Key, V.O. Jr. "The Lack of a Budgeting Theory." *American Political Science Review* 34(1940):1137-44.

Latham, Earl. "The Group Basis of Politics: Notes for a Theory." *American Political Science Review* 46(1952):376-97.

Lijphart, Arend. "The Analysis of Bloc Voting in the General Assembly: A Critique and a Proposal." *American Political Science Review* 57 (1963):902-17.

Lindberg, Leon N. "Decision Making and Integration in the European Community." *International Organization* 19(1965):56-80.

Lindblom, Charles E. "The Science of Muddling Through." *Public Administration Review* 19(1959):79-88.

Loehr, William. "Collective Goods and International Cooperation: Comments." *International Organization* 27(1973):421-30.

Mangone, Gerald J., and Srivastava, Anand K. "Budgeting for the United Nations." *International Organization* 12(1958):473-85.

Miles, Edward. "Organizations and Integration in International Systems." *International Studies Quarterly* 12(1968):196-224.

Mudalair, Ascot. "World Health Problems." *International Conciliation* 491(1953):229-59.

Murdock, George P. "Anthropology as a Comparative Science." *Behavioral Science* 2(1957):249-54.

Natchez, Peter B., and Bupp, Irvin C. "Policy and Priority in the Budgetary Process." *American Political Science Review* 67(1973):951-63.

Olson, Mancur Jr., and Zeckhauser, Richard. "An Economic Theory of Alliances." *The Review of Economics and Statistics* 48(1966):266-79.

Pethybridge, R. "The Influence of International Politics on the Activities of 'Non-Political' Specialized Agencies: A Case Study." *Political Studies* 13(1965):247-51.

Pratt, Richard, and Rummel, R.J. "Issue Dimensions in the 1963 United Nations General Assembly." *Multivariate Behavioral Research* 6 (1971):251-86.

Rieselbach, Leroy N., "Quantitative Techniques for Studying Voting Behavior in the UN General Assembly." *International Organization* 14(1960):291-306.

Riggs, Robert E., et al. "Behavioralism in the Study of the United Nations." *World Politics* 22(1970):197-236.

Rose, Hilary. "A Rejection of the WHO Research Centre: A Case Study of Decision-Making in International Scientific Collaboration." *Minerva* 5(1967):340-56.

Ruggie, John Gerard. "Collective Goods and Future International Collaboration." *American Political Science Review* 66(1972):874-93.

Russett, Bruce M. "Discovering Voting Groups in the United Nations." *American Political Science Review* 60(1966):327-39.

Shapiro, Michael J. "The House and the Federal Role: A Computer Simulation of Roll-Call Voting." *American Political Science Review* 62 (1968):494-517.

Sharkansky, Ira. "Agency Requests, Gubernatorial Support and Budget Success in State Legislatures." *American Political Science Review* 62(1968):1220-31.

──────── . "Economic and Political Correlates of State Government Expenditures: General Tendencies and Deviant Cases." *Midwest Journal of Political Science* 2(1967):173-92.

Simon, Herbert A. "A Behavioral Model of Rational Choice." *Quarterly Journal of Economics* 60(1955):99-118.

──────── . "Theories of Decision-Making in Economics and Behavioral Science." *American Economic Review* 69(1959):253-83.

Sjoberg, Gideon. "The Comparative Method in the Social Sciences." *Philosophy of Science* 22(1955):106-17.

Snyder, Richard C., and Paige, Glenn D. "The United States Decision to Resist Aggression in Korea: The Application of an Analytical Scheme." *Administrative Science Quarterly* 3(1958):341-78.

Theil, H., and Nagar, A.L. "Testing the Independence of Regression Disturbances." *Journal of the American Statistical Association* 56 (1961):793-806.

Vincent, Jack E. "The Convergence of Voting and Attitude Patterns at the United Nations." *The Journal of Politics* 31(1969):952-98.

──────── . "National Attributes as Predictors of Delegate Attitudes at the United Nations." *American Political Science Review* 62 (1968):916-31.

Wallace, Michael, and Singer, J. David. "Intergovernmental Organization in the Global System, 1815-1964: A Quantitative Description." *International Organization* 24(1970):239-87.

Wanat, John. "Bases of Budgetary Incrementalism." *American Political Science Review* 68(1974):1221-8.

Wildavsky, Aaron B. "The Analysis of Issue-Contexts in the Study of Decision-Making." *Journal of Politics* 24(1962):717-32.

Wildavsky, Aaron B., and Hammann, Arthur. "Comprehensive Versus Incremental Budgeting in the Department of Agriculture." *Administrative Science Quarterly* 10(1965):321-46.

Williamson, Oliver E. "A Rational Theory of the Federal Budgeting Process." *Papers on Non-Market Decision-Making* 2(1967):71-89.

Winslow, Charles E. "World Health Organization." *International Conciliation* 437(1948):109-52.

Yalem, Ronald J. "The Study of International Organization, 1920-1965: A Survey of the Literature." *Background* 10(1966):1-56.

Zacher, Mark W. "The Secretary-General: Some Comments on Recent Research." *International Organization* 23(1969):932-50.

Essays in Collections

Abelson, Robert. "The Simulation of Social Behavior." In *The Handbook of Social Psychology.* Edited by G. Lindzey and E. Aronson. Reading, Pa.: Addison-Wesley, 1968.

Alger, Chadwick F. "Decisions to Undertake New Activities in Assemblies and Councils of the UN System." In *The United Nations: Problems and Prospects.* Edited by Edwin H. Fedder. St. Louis: Center for International Studies, University of Missouri-St. Louis, 1971.

_____ . "Interaction in a Committee of the United Nations General Assembly." In *Quantitative International Politics: Insights and Evidence.* Edited by J. David Singer. New York: The Free Press, 1968.

_____ . "Personal Contact in Intergovernmental Organizations." In *International Behavior: A Social-Psychological Analysis.* Edited by Herbert C. Kelman. New York: Holt, Rinehart and Winston, 1966.

Alker, Hayward R. Jr., and Christensen, Cheryl. "From Causal Modelling to Artificial Intelligence: The Evolution of a UN Peace Making Simulation." In *Experimentation and Simulation in Political Science.* Edited by J. LaPonce and P. Smoker. Toronto: University of Toronto Press, 1972.

Alker, Hayward R. Jr., and Greenberg, William J. "The UN Charter: Alternate Pasts and Alternate Futures." In *The United Nations: Problems and Prospects.* Edited by Edwin H. Fedder. St. Louis: Center for International Studies, University of Missouri-St. Louis, 1971.

Benson, Oliver. "A Simple Diplomatic Game." In *International Politics and Foreign Policy.* Edited by James N. Rosenau. New York: The Free Press, 1961.

Cartwright, Dorwin. "Influence, Leadership, Control." In *Handbook of Organizations.* Edited by James G. March. Chicago: Rand McNally and Co., 1965.

Cohen, Kalman J., and Cyert, Richard M. "Simulation of Organization Behavior." In *Handbook of Organizations*. Edited by James G. March. Chicago: Rand McNally and Co., 1965.

Coleman, James S. "Mathematical Models and Computer Simulation." In *Handbook of Modern Sociology*. Edited by R.E.L. Faris. Skokie, Ill.: Rand McNally and Co., 1964.

Crecine, John P. "Defense Budgeting: Organizational Adaption to Environmental Constraints." In *Studies in Budgeting*. Edited by R.F. Byrne, et al. Amsterdam: North-Holland Publishing Company, 1971.

——————— . "A Simulation of Municipal Budgeting: The Impact of Problem Environment." In *Simulation in the Study of Politics*. Edited by William D. Coplin. Chicago: Markham Publishing Co., 1968.

Davis, Otto A. "Empirical Evidence of 'Political' Influences Upon the Expenditure and Taxation Policies of Public Schools." In *The Public Economy of Urban Communities*. Edited by Julius Margolis. Washington, D.C.: Resources for the Future, 1965.

Feldman, Julian, and Kanter, Hershel E. "Organizational Decision-Making." In *Handbook of Organizations*. Edited by James G. March. Chicago: Rand McNally and Co., 1965.

Gerwin, Donald A. "Towards a Theory of Public Budgetary Decision Making." In *Studies in Budgeting*. Edited by R.F. Byrne, et al. Amsterdam: North-Holland Publishing Co., 1971.

Goodrich, Leland M. "The Secretariat of the United Nations." In *UN Administration of Economic and Social Programs*. Edited by Gerard J. Mangone. New York: Columbia University Press, 1966.

Guetzkow, Harold. "Relations Among Organizations." In *Studies on Behavior in Organizations: A Research Symposium*. Edited by Raymond V. Bowers. Athens: University of Georgia Press, 1966.

——————— . "Simulation in International Relations." In *Proceedings of the IBM Scientific Computing Symposium on Simulation Models and Gaming*. Yorktown Heights, N.Y.: IBM, 1964.

——————— . "Some Correspondences between Simulations and 'Realities' in International Relations." In *New Approaches to International Relations*. Edited by Morton Kaplan. New York: St. Martins Press, 1968.

Hagan, Charles. "The Group in a Political Science." In *Approaches to the Study of Politics*. Edited by Roland Young. Evanston, Ill.: Northwestern University Press, 1958.

Hill, Martin. "The Administrative Committee on Coordination." In *The Evolution of International Organizations*. Edited by Evan Luard. London: Thames and Hudson, 1966.

Hoole, Francis W. "The Simulation of Alternative Budgetary Futures for the World Health Organization." In *The United Nations: Problems and Prospects*. Edited by Edwin H. Fedder. St. Louis: Center for International Studies, University of Missouri-St. Louis, 1971.

Kohlhase, Norbert. "Le rôle des missions permanentes dans le processus de decision budgetaire des Commanautés européenes, de l'OCDE et de l'OIT." In *Les Missions Permanentes Aupres des Organizations Internationales.* Comp. Dotation Carnegie Pour la Paix Internationale. Vol. 2 Brussels: Etablissements Emile Bruylant, 1973.

Lasswell, Harold D. "The Decision Process: Seven Categories of Functional Analysis." In *Politics and Social Life: An Introduction to Political Behavior.* Edited by Nelson W. Polsby, Robert A. Dentler, and Paul A. Smith. Boston: Houghton Mifflin Co., 1963.

Mangone, Gerard J. "Field Administration: The United Nations Resident Representative." In *UN Administration of Economic and Social Programs.* Edited by Gerard J. Mangone. New York: Columbia University Press, 1966.

Manser, Marilyn; Naylor, Thomas H.; and Wertz, Kenneth. "Effects of Alternative Policies for Allocating Federal Aid for Education to the States." In *Computer Simulation Experiments with Models of Economic Systems.* Edited by Thomas H. Naylor. New York: John Wiley and Sons, 1971.

McClosky, Herbert. "Concerning Strategies for a Science of International Politics." In *Foreign Policy Decision-Making: An Approach to the Study of International Politics.* Edited by Richard C. Snyder, H.W. Bruck, and Burton Sapin. New York: The Free Press, 1962.

Robinson, James A., and Majak, R. Roger. "The Theory of Decision-Making." In *Contemporary Political Analysis.* Edited by James C. Charlesworth. New York: The Free Press, 1967.

Robinson, James A., and Snyder, Richard C. "Decision-Making in International Politics." In *International Behavior: A Social-Psychological Analysis.* Edited by Herbert C. Kelman. New York: Holt, Rinehart and Winston, 1965.

Rosenau, James N. "Pre-Theories and Theories of Foreign Policy." In *Approaches to Comparative and International Politics.* Edited by R. Barry Farrell. Evanston, Ill.: Northwestern University Press, 1966.

_____ . "The Premises and Promises of Decision-Making Analysis." In *Contemporary Political Analysis.* Edited by James C. Charlesworth. New York: The Free Press, 1967.

Rummel, Rudolph J. "The Relationship Between National Attributes and Foreign Conflict Behavior." In *Quantitative International Politics: Insights and Evidence.* Edited by J. David Singer. New York: The Free Press, 1968.

Russett, Bruce M., and Sullivan, John D. "Collective Goods and International Organization." In *The United Nations: Problems and Prospects.* Edited by Edwin H. Fedder. St. Louis: Center for International Studies, University of Missouri-St. Louis, 1971.

Sawyer, Jack, and Guetzkow, Harold. "Bargaining and Negotiation in International Relations." In *International Behavior: A Social-Psychologi-*

cal Analysis. Edited by Herbert C. Kelman. New York: Holt, Rinehart and Winston, 1965.

Schilling, Warner R. "The Politics of National Defense: Fiscal 1950." In *Strategy, Politics, and Defense Budgets.* Edited by Warner R. Schilling, Paul Y. Hammond, and Glenn H. Snyder. New York: Columbia University Press, 1962.

Schmitter, Philippe C. "A Revised Theory of Regional Integration." In *Regional Integration, Theory and Research.* Edited by Leon N. Lindberg and Stuart A. Scheingold. Cambridge, Mass.: Harvard University Press, 1971.

Simon, Herbert A. "Political Research: The Decision-Making Framework." In *Varieties of Political Theories.* Edited by David Easton. Englewood Cliffs, N.J.: Prentice-Hall, 1966.

Simon, Herbert A., and Newell, Allen. "Models: Their Use and Limitations." In *The State of the Social Sciences.* Edited by Leonard D. White. Chicago: University of Chicago Press, 1956.

Smoker, Paul. "Fear in the Arms Race: A Mathematical Study." In *International Politics and Foreign Policy.* Edited by James N. Rosenau. Rev. ed. New York: The Free Press, 1969.

Snyder, Richard C. "A Decision-Making Approach to the Study of Political Phenomena." In *Approaches to the Study of Politics.* Edited by Roland Young. Evanston, Ill.: Northwestern University Press, 1958.

Starbuck, William H. "Organizational Growth and Development." In *Handbook of Organizations.* Edited by James G. March. Chicago: Rand McNally and Co., 1965.

Stinchcombe, Arthur L. "Social Structure and Organizations." In *Handbook of Organizations.* Edited by James G. March. Chicago: Rand McNally and Co., 1965.

Tanter, Raymond. "International War and Domestic Turmoil: Some Contemporary Evidence." In *Violence in America: Historical and Comparative Perspectives.* Edited by Hugh D. Graham and Ted R. Gurr. New York: Signet Books, 1969.

Taylor, Donald W. "Decision Making and Problem Solving." In *Handbook of Organizations.* Edited by James G. March. Chicago: Rand McNally and Co., 1965.

Documents

A Study of the Capacity of the United Nations Development System. Vols. 1 and 2. Geneva: United Nations, 1969.

Annual Report of the World Meteorological Organization, 1966. Geneva: Secretariat of the World Meteorological Organization, 1967.

Bertrand, Maurice. *Draft Report on Programming and Budgets in the United Nations Family of Organizations.* Geneva: Joint Inspection

Unit, 1969.

Conference Internationale Du Travail, Cinquantieme Session, Geneve, 1966, Compte Rendu Des Travaux. Geneva: Bureau Internationale du Travail, 1967.

Deficiencies in the Management and Delivery of U.N. Technical and Pre-Investment Assistance: Report of a Staff Survey Team to the Committee on Foreign Affairs, U.S. House of Representatives. Washington, D.C.: U.S. Government Printing Office, 1971.

Final Report of the President's Commission on the Observance of the 25th Anniversary of the United Nations. Washington, D.C.: Department of State, 1971.

Food and Agriculture Organization. *Fifteenth Session, Rome, October 1968, Regular Program, Financial Report and Statements, 1966/1967.* Vol. 1. Rome: Food and Agriculture Organization of the United Nations, 1968.

_____ . *Report of the Fourteenth Session of the Conference, 4-23 November, 1967.* Rome: Food and Agriculture Organization of the United Nations, 1968.

_____ . *Report of the 13th Session of the Conference, 20 November-9 December 1965.* Rome: Food and Agriculture Organization of the United Nations, 1966.

_____ . *The Work of FAO, 1966-1967.* Rome: Food and Agriculture Organization of the United Nations, 1967.

Gregoire, Roger. *Administrations Nationales et Organisations Internationales: Les problemes administratifs qui se posent aux nouveaux etats de fait de leur participation a L'Organisation des Nations Unies et aux Institutions Specialisees.* Paris: Organisation des Nations Unies Pour L'Education La Science et La Culture, circa 1954.

International Atomic Energy Agency. *Annual Report to the Economic and Social Council of the United Nations.* Vienna: International Atomic Energy Agency, 1967.

International Bank for Reconstruction and Development, International Development Association. *Annual Report, 1968.* Washington, D.C.: International Bank for Reconstruction and Development, International Development Association, 1968.

_____ . *1963-1964 Annual Report.* Washington, D.C.: International Bank for Reconstruction and Development, International Development Association, 1964.

_____ . *1965-1966 Annual Report.* Washington, D.C.: International Bank for Reconstruction and Development, International Development Association, 1966.

International Civil Aviation Organization. *Annual Report of the Council to the Assembly for 1966.* Montreal: International Civil Aviation Organization, 1967.

International Development Strategy. New York: United Nations, 1970.

International Finance Corporation. *Annual Report, 1965-1966.* Washington, D.C.: International Finance Corporation, 1966.

International Labour Organisation. *Draft Budget, Programme and Budget Proposals, 1967, and Other Financial Questions.* Geneva: International Labour Office, 1966.

International Telecommunication Union. *Report on the Activities of the International Telecommunication Union in 1963.* Geneva: International Telecommunication Union, 1964.

National Administration and International Organization: A Comparative Survey of Fourteen Countries. Brussels: United Nations Educational, Scientific and Cultural Organization (UNESCO) and Institute International Des Sciences Administratives Bruxelles, 1951.

Organisation des Nations Unies. *Missions Permanentes Aupres Des Nations Unies a Geneve.* No. 16. Geneva: Organisation des Nations Unies, 1968.

United Nations Economic and Social Council. *Expenditures of the United Nations System in Relation to Programmes.* Document E/4209. New York: United Nations Economic and Social Council, 16 May 1966.

United Nations Educational, Scientific and Cultural Organization. *Records of the General Conference, Fourteenth Session, Proceedings.* Paris: UNESCO, 1966.

——————— . *Records of the General Conference, Fourteenth Session, Resolutions.* Paris: UNESCO, 1967.

——————— . *Report of the Director-General on the Activities of the Organization in 1965.* Paris: UNESCO, 1966.

——————— . *Report of the Director-General on the Activities of the Organization in 1966.* Paris: UNESCO, 1967.

United Nations General Assembly. *Audit reports for the year ended 31 December 1966 relating to expenditure by participating and executing agencies of funds allocated from the Special Fund Account of the United Nations Development Programme.* Official Records, Document A/6902. New York: UN General Assembly, 1967.

——————— . *Audit Reports for the year ended 31 December 1966 relating to expenditure by participating and executing agencies of funds earmarked from the Technical Assistance Account of the United Nations Development Programme.* Official Records, Document A/6901. New York: UN General Assembly, 1967.

——————— . *Implementation of the Recommendations made by the Ad Hoc Committee of Experts to Examine the Finances of the United Nations and the Specialized Agencies, Report of the Secretary-General.* Official Records, Document A/7124. New York: UN General Assembly, 1968.

United States General Accounting Office. *Report to the Congress, U.S.*

Participation in the World Health Organization, Department of State, Department of Health, Education and Welfare, by the Comptroller General of the United States. Washington, D.C.: U.S. Government Printing Office, 1969.

Universal Postal Union. *Report on the Work of the Union, 1967.* Bern: International Bureau of the Universal Postal Union, 1968.

U.S. Foreign Assistance in the 1970s: A New Approach. Washington, D.C.: U.S. Government Printing Office, 1970.

World Health Organization. *Background Information Submitted by the World Health Organization to the United Nations Advisory Committee on Administrative and Budgetary Questions.* Geneva: World Health Organization, 1969.

——————— . *Basic Documents.* 19th ed. Geneva: World Health Organization, 1968.

——————— . *Basic Documents.* 21st ed. Geneva: World Health Organization, 1970.

——————— . *Basic Documents.* 23rd ed. Geneva: World Health Organization, 1972.

——————— . *Handbook of Resolutions and Decisions of the World Health Assembly and the Executive Board.* 10th ed. Geneva: World Health Organization, 1969.

——————— . *Handbook of Resolutions and Decisions of the World Health Assembly and the Executive Board.* 12th ed. Geneva: World Health Organization, 1973.

——————— . *WHO Manual: Budget.* Section 3. Geneva: World Health Organization, 1969.

——————— . *WHO Manual: Finance and Accounts.* Section 4. Geneva: World Health Organization, 1969.

——————— . *Official Records of the World Health Organization.* English edition. Geneva: World Health Organization.

The Work of WHO—Annual Report of the Director-General to the World Health Assembly and to the United Nations.

Year	Official Record Number (ORN)	Printing Date	Year	Official Record Number (ORN)	Printing Date
1948	16	1949	1956	75	1957
1949	24	1950	1957	82	1958
1950	30	1951	1958	90	1959
1951	38	1952	1959	98	1960
1952	45	1953	1960	105	1961
1953	51	1954	1961	114	1962
1954	59	1955	1962	123	1963
1955	67	1956	1963	131	1964

Year	ORN	Printing Date	Year	ORN	Printing Date
1964	139	1965	1970	188	1971
1965	147	1966	1971	197	1972
1966	156	1967	1972	205	1973
1967	164	1968	1973	213	1974
1968	172	1969	1974	221	1975
1969	180	1970			

Financial Report, 1 January-31 December (Supplement to the Annual Report of the Director-General) and Report of the External Auditor to the World Health Assembly.

Year	ORN	Printing Date	Year	ORN	Printing Date
1948	20	1949	1962	126	1963
1949	27	1950	1963	134	1964
1950	34	1951	1964	142	1965
1951	41	1952	1965	150	1966
1952	47	1953	1966	159	1967
1953	54	1954	1967	167	1968
1954	62	1955	1968	175	1969
1955	70	1956	1969	183	1970
1956	78	1957	1970	191	1971
1957	85	1958	1971	200	1972
1958	93	1959	1972	208	1973
1959	101	1960	1973	214	1974
1960	109	1961	1974	222	1975
1961	117	1962			

Proceedings of the World Health Assembly: Resolutions and Decisions, Verbatim Records of the Plenary Meetings, Summary Records and Reports of the Committees, Annexes.

Year	ORN	Assembly	Printing Date	Year	ORN	Assembly	Printing Date
1948	13	1st	1948	1960	102	13th	1960
1949	21	2d	1949	1960	103	13th	1960
1950	28	3d	1950	1961	110	14th	1961
1951	35	4th	1952	1961	111	14th	1961
1952	42	5th	1952	1962	118	15th	1962
1953	48	6th	1953	1962	119	15th	1962
1954	55	7th	1954	1963	127	16th	1963
1955	63	8th	1955	1963	128	16th	1963
1956	71	9th	1956	1964	135	17th	1964
1957	79	10th	1957	1964	136	17th	1964
1958	86	10th Anniversary	1958	1965	143	18th	1965
1958	87	11th	1958	1965	144	18th	1965
1959	95	12th	1959	1966	151	19th	1966

Year	ORN	Assembly	Printing Date	Year	ORN	Assembly	Printing Date
1966	152	19th	1966	1971	193	24th	1971
1967	160	20th	1967	1971	194	24th	1971
1967	161	20th	1967	1972	201	25th	1972
1968	168	21st	1968	1972	202	25th	1972
1968	169	21st	1968	1973	209	26th	1973
1969	176	22d	1969	1973	210	26th	1973
1969	177	22d	1969	1974	217	27th	1974
1970	184	23d	1970	1974	218	27th	1974
1970	185	23d	1970				

Reports of the Executive Board.

Year	ORN	Session	Printing Date	Year	ORN	Session	Printing Date
1948	14	1st & 2d	1948	1961	112	28th	1961
1949	17	3d	1949	1962	115	29th	1962
1949	22	4th	1949	1962	116	29th	1962
1950	25	5th	1950	1962	120	30th	1962
1950	26	5th	1950	1963	124	31st	1963
1950	29	6th	1950	1963	125	31st	1963
1951	32	7th	1951	1963	129	32d	1963
1951	33	7th	1951	1964	132	33d	1964
1951	36	8th	1951	1964	133	33d	1964
1952	40	9th	1952	1964	137	34th	1964
1952	43	10th	1952	1965	140	35th	1965
1953	46	11th	1953	1965	141	35th	1965
1953	49	12th	1953	1965	145	36th	1965
1954	52	13th	1954	1966	148	37th	1966
1954	53	13th	1954	1966	149	37th	1966
1954	57	14th	1954	1966	153	38th	1966
1955	60	15th	1955	1967	157	39th	1967
1955	61	15th	1955	1967	158	39th	1967
1955	65	16th	1955	1967	162	40th	1967
1956	68	17th	1956	1968	165	41st	1968
1956	69	17th	1956	1968	166	41st	1968
1956	73	18th	1956	1968	170	42d	1968
1957	76	19th	1957	1969	173	43d	1969
1957	77	19th	1957	1969	174	43d	1969
1957	80	20th	1957	1969	178	44th	1969
1958	83	21st	1958	1970	181	45th	1970
1958	84	21st	1958	1970	182	45th	1970
1958	88	22d	1958	1970	186	46th	1970
1959	91	23d	1959	1971	189	47th	1971
1959	92	23d	1959	1971	190	47th	1971
1959	96	24th	1959	1971	195	48th	1971
1960	99	25th	1960	1972	198	49th	1972
1960	100	25th	1960	1972	199	49th	1972
1960	106	26th	1960	1972	203	50th	1972
1960	107	26th	1960	1973	206	51st	1973
1961	108	27th	1961	1973	207	51st	1973

Year	ORN	Session	Printing Date	Year	ORN	Session	Printing Date
1973	211	52d	1973	1974	219	54th	1974
1974	215	53d	1974	1975	223	55th	1975
1974	216	53d	1974	1975	224	55th	1975

Proposed Programme and Budget Estimates (Containing details of the proposed programme and estimated obligations for the relevant financial year, under the regular budget and other sources of funds).

Year	ORN	Printing Date	Year	ORN	Printing Date
1950	18	1949	1964	121	1962
1951	23	1950	1965	130	1963
1952	31	1951	1966	138	1964
1953	39	1952	1967	146	1965
1954	44	1952	1968	154	1966
1955	50	1953	1969	163	1967
1956	58	1954	1970	171	1968
1957	66	1955	1971	179	1969
1958	74	1956	1972	187	1970
1959	81	1957	1973	196	1971
1960	89	1958	1974	204	1972
1961	97	1959	1975	212	1973
1962	104	1960	1976-77	220	1974
1963	113	1961			

Interim Commission: Minutes, Reports, and Documents.

Year	ORN	Session	Printing Date	Year	ORN	Session	Printing Date
1946	3	1st	1947	1948	7	5th	1948
1946	4	2d	1947	1948	9		1948
1947	5	3d	1947	1948	10		1948
1947	6	4th	1948	1948	12		1948

Wrubel Computing Center. "Update of McGraw-Hill SPSS Manual." Bloomington: Indiana University, 1973.

Unpublished Materials

Alger, Chadwick F. "A Partial Inventory of Data on International Organizations." Paper prepared for Workshop on International Organizations Data, International Studies Association Annual Convention, March 17-20, 1971, at San Juan, Puerto Rico.

——————— . "Methodological Innovation in Research on International Organizations." Paper presented at the Specialist Meeting on Theory and Method in International Relations, Seventh World Congress, International Political Science Association, September 18-23, 1967, at Brussels, Belgium.

_____ . "Negotiation, Regional Groups, Interaction, and Public Debate in the Development of Consensus in the United Nations General Assembly." Paper presented at the Sixth World Congress of Sociology, International Sociology Association, September 1966, at Evian, France.

_____ . "Research on Research: A Decade of Quantitative and Field Research on International Organizations." Paper presented at the Annual Meeting of the American Political Science Association, September 2-6, 1969, at New York City.

_____ . Unpublished working papers, Northwestern University, 1968.

Blaisdell, Donald C. "Relationship of Intergovernmental to Non-Governmental Organization." Paper presented at the Sixth World Congress of the International Political Science Association, September 21-25, 1964, at Geneva.

Chung, Hoon. "Decision-Making in IBRD and ILO: A Comparative Analysis." Paper presented at the Annual Convention of the International Studies Association, April 2-4, 1970, at Pittsburgh, Pa.

Cox, R.W., and Jacobson, H.K. "Decision-Making in International Organizations: An Interim Report." Paper presented at the Annual Meeting of the American Political Science Association, September 2-6, 1969, at New York City.

Crecine, John P. "A Computer Simulation Model of Municipal Resources Allocation." Ph.D. dissertation, Carnegie Institute of Technology, 1966.

Davis, Otto A.; Dempster, M.A.H.; and Wildavsky, Aaron. "Towards a Predictive Theory of Government Expenditure: U.S. Domestic Appropriations." Paper presented at the Annual Meeting of the American Political Science Association, September 4-8, 1973, at New Orleans, La.

Gerwin, Donald A. "A Process Model of Budgeting in a Public Organization." Unpublished paper, University of Wisconsin, Milwaukee, 1967.

Guetzkow, Harold. "Man-Computer Simulation as a Heuristic in the Comparative Study of International Organizations." Paper presented at the Sixth World Congress of the International Political Science Association, September 21-25, 1964, at Geneva.

Hoole, Francis W. "Decision-Making in the World Health Organization: The Budgetary Process." Ph.D. dissertation, Northwestern University, 1971.

Rosenau, James N. "The Politics of National Adaptation." Paper presented at the Annual Meeting of the American Political Science Association, September 2-6, 1969, at New York City.

Weiner, Robert. "Patterns of Interaction in a Main Committee of the World Health Assembly." Unpublished manuscript. Boston State College, Boston, Mass., 1974.

Index

Actions: concept of, 16-7; types of, 17-9. *See also* Administrative actions; Budget-finance actions; Election-appointment actions; Procedural actions; Program actions

Administrative actions: defined, 18; in WHO, 41-3

Alger, Chadwick F. 11, 18, 112

Alker, Hayward R. Jr., 11, 13, 18, 133, 136-7

Allison, Graham T., 5-7, 131, 137

Alternative futures, 112-5, 115-21, 121-2, 122-6, 126-9

Anton, Thomas, 8

Asha, Rafik, 23

Assembly step: concept of, 28-9; in WHO budget process, 54; history of behavior in WHO, 63, 65; plausible policy-making rules in WHO, 69-70; best fitting rule in WHO, 79-82; in computer model, 85-95; counterfactual analysis of, 104-7

Behavioral budgetary theory, 6-9, 131-2, 135-6

Bruck, H.W., 4, 16, 131

Budget-finance actions: defined, 19; in WHO, 41-8, 63-6

Bupp, Irvin C., 8, 135

Campbell, Donald T., 103

Carreri, Louis, 23

Choucri, Nazli, 136

Chow, G.C., 74, 77, 80-1

Christ, Carl F., 72

Clarkson, G.P.E., 83

Claude, Inis L. Jr., 13

Colliard, Claude-Albert, 13

Computer model: logic of, 83-5; details of specification, 85-95;

estimation of parameters for, 95-8; validity of, 98-100; counterfactual analysis of, 102-11; simulation of alternative futures for WHO, 112-29; contribution to literature, 130-3

Conseil sanitaire de Tanger, 33

Conseil Sanitaire de Teheran, 33

Conseil sanitaire maritime et quarantenaire de Egypt, 33

Conseil superior de Sante de Constantinople, 33

Coplin, William, 18

Counterfactual analysis, 102-11 passim

Cox, Robert W., 12, 18

Crecine, John P., 7, 8, 26, 57, 132, 136-7

Cyert, Richard M., 10, 13, 133, 137

David, F.N., 75, 98

Davis, Otto A., 7-8, 24, 26, 48, 63, 131-2

Dempster, M.A.H., 7-8, 24, 48, 63, 131-2

Deutsch, Karl W., 5, 19, 131, 137

Durbin, J., 73, 98

Easton, David, 1, 5, 19

Election-appointment actions: defined, 18; in WHO, 41-3

Executive body step: concept of, 28; in WHO budget process, 52-4; history of behavior in WHO, 63-5; plausible policy-making rules in WHO, 69-70; best fitting rule in WHO, 78, 80-2; in computer model, 85-95; counterfactual analysis of, 104-7

Executive head: defined, 22; role in WHO budget process, 47, 49-52, 55-6, 60-1, 63-6; possible future

223